MUSIC
WORD SEARCH
& CROSSWORD
PUZZLES

Thunder Bay Press
An imprint of Printers Row Publishing Group
9717 Pacific Heights Blvd, San Diego, CA 92121
www.thunderbaybooks.com • mail@thunderbaybooks.com

Correspondence regarding the content of this book should be sent to Thunder Bay Press, Editorial Department, at the above address. Author and rights inquiries should be addressed to Pyramid, an imprint of Octopus Publishing Group Ltd., Carmelite House, 50 Victoria Embankment, London, EC4Y 0DZ
www.octopusbooks.co.uk

Thunder Bay Press
Publisher: Peter Norton • Associate Publisher: Ana Parker
Editor: Dan Mansfield
Acquisitions Editor: Kathryn Chipinka Dalby

Produced by Pyramid
Publisher: Lucy Pessell
Editor: Sarah Kennedy • Designer: Hannah Coughlin
Editorial Assistant: Emily Martin

ISBN: 978-1-64517-916-0

Printed in China

25 24 23 22 21   1 2 3 4 5

MUSIC
WORD SEARCH
& CROSSWORD
PUZZLES

THUNDER BAY
P·R·E·S·S

San Diego, California

INTRODUCTION

If you've picked up this book, then there's a pretty good chance that you love music, or know someone else who does . . . but then who doesn't love music? The question invariably becomes "What type?" There are so many different genres of music, and one person's passion is another person's poison.

Luckily, this is a puzzle book, which means there's no competition (except perhaps with your own ego's desire to see all the squares in the crosswords filled in correctly—and there's nothing wrong with that!). We have, however, made sure to cater to all musical tastes and levels of knowledge, with themes that will be familiar to all, and others that are slightly more niche or only hovering vaguely on the periphery of your consciousness.

The wonderful thing about music is how evocative it can be. The mad screaming of an electric guitar may not be your preferred listening today, but it can take you back to the first time you heard it or a key moment in your life . . . perhaps a first kiss, a sun-drenched beach resort vacation, a road trip, or sitting in your bedroom with the radio blaring. And no one can ignore the resonance of the key figures in popular music history—those pioneers and headline-makers, such as Elvis Presley, Jim Morrison, the Beatles, the Stones, Bob Marley, Aretha Franklin, Miles Davis, Johnny Cash, Alice Cooper, the Who, Talking Heads, Debbie Harry, Eminem, Prince, U2, Coldplay, Kurt Cobain, Amy Winehouse . . . the list is endless.

Compiling this puzzle book was no easy task. First, we had to take into account the endless number of artists, bands, and genres—not forgetting alter egos, backing bands, and the more obscure sounds. Then there were other things to think of, such as the greatest gigs of all time, famous clubs and concert venues, decade-defining anthems and albums . . . the list is never-ending. And while you may be able to think of several other entries that aren't included in the following puzzles, hopefully you will learn and discover something new about your favorite (or least favorite!) music to listen to—because whatever you think you know about music, this book is guaranteed to test your knowledge.

A little note on how the book is organized. It is split into two chapters—crosswords and word searches (which follow the same themes as the crosswords)—with all of the answers at the back of the book (only to be used in an absolute emergency, of course!). As with all questions, the crosswords are only easy if you know the answers, but some are worth a guess or some investigation using the power of the internet. By the end of this book, your musical knowledge will have expanded tenfold. You may still love the same music, but perhaps have added to your ultimate playlist.

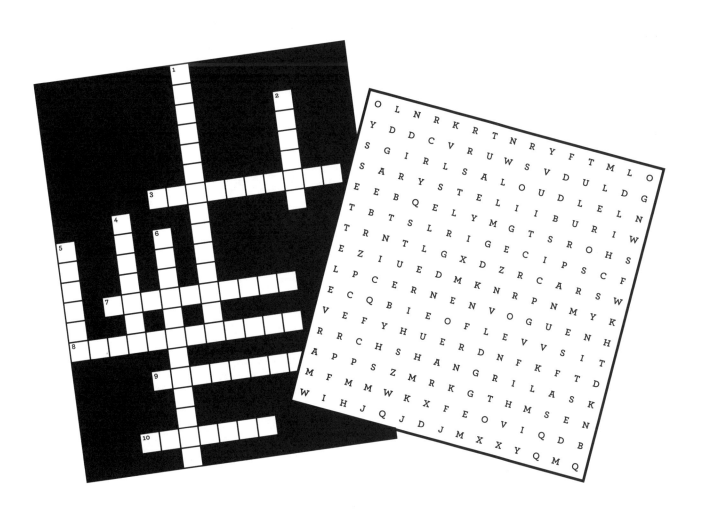

MUSIC
CROSSWORD
PUZZLES

Think you're an expert on all things music? The following crosswords will put your knowledge to the test. Featuring best-loved singers and bands, genres, famous concerts, and more—these puzzles will have even the biggest of music nerds scratching their heads.

1. FRONTMEN/WOMEN

A vital focal point providing passion, excitement, and a real sense of contact with the audience, or just an inflated ego whose delusions of grandeur get in the way of the lead guitarist and block a decent view of the drummer? Whatever your opinion, the role of a frontperson really can't be overstated.

ACROSS

2. Debbie _____. Blondie singer—impossible to ignore; the look, the voice, she had it all ... and she's still got it.

4. He has created a role and a style of his own that flies in the face of the classic rock stereotype. Pioneer, singer with Pulp, _____ Cocker.

5. Fela ___ has to be the Godfather of Afrobeat. Multi-instrumentalist, singer, and a captivating showman.

7. Stage-diver, artist, and natural performer, _____ _____ was singer with the Stooges.

9. Jim _____. A poetic voice and spiritual figurehead of the 1960s West Coast countercultural scene. The Doors frontman always took audiences on a rip-roaring journey.

DOWN

1. Roger _____. One quarter of the Who; one quarter of the High Numbers; his attitude and powerful vocals make him one of the best to ever do it.

3. Supposedly, the Stones' frontman has "forgotten more about stagecraft than most singers will ever know." Evergreen into his 70s, however, it doesn't appear as if _____ _____ has forgotten much.

4. It's one thing to have the audience in the palm of your hand, but your band as well! The Godfather of Soul, _____ _____, was as much a conductor as a frontman, in control of performance *and* reaction.

6. Look no further than his 1985 Live Aid performance. Legendary vocalist and master of theater on the biggest stage. Freddie _____.

8. Janis _____. Her amazing voice and electrifying performances were unforgettable, though her life was cruelly cut short at the age of 27.

2. KEYBOARD WIZARDS

Layering melody, texture, and color to incomplete song sketches, the best keyboard players are like accomplished painters. Quite how the analogy extends to the treatment some of the more excitable in the puzzle mete out to their instrument of choice is unclear, but the musicians here hit all the right notes and, crucially, in the right order.

ACROSS

2.   Ray _____. The organist for the Doors pulled more than his fair weight and generated many of the group's most memorable hooks.

3.   Billy _____. One of only two musicians outside of the Fab Four to be credited on a Beatles release. His signature soulful, gospel-infused style is at the front of many hit records.

5.   _____ _ Jones. A child prodigy, then a session player, then a bandleader with the MG's. Their driving success "Green Onions" is a song that many will know, perhaps without being familiar with all of this man's work.

6.   Rick _____. Prog Rock supergroup Yes keyboardist, who, true to form, overawes audiences with his talent and exuberance.

7.   Cornerstone of the boundary-busting phenomenon that was Parliament Funkadelic. _____ Worrell's legacy is a long and lasting one.

8.   Lonnie _____-_____. Jazz pianist who played with Miles Davis, but his own band, the Cosmic Echoes, made strides with their fusion masterpieces.

DOWN

1.   Progressive rock composer and superstar, Keith _____. His staggering virtuosity and creative talent came to the forefront in the ELP supergroup.

4.   If there is one reason he's here … it's the neck-snapping grooves that _____ Wonder created on the massive TONTO synthesizer over the course of *Innervisions* and *Talking Book*. The rest, as they say, is history.

6.   Richard _____. Perhaps something of an unsung hero in Pink Floyd, his textured, luxurious playing holds together many of the band's beloved soundscape masterpieces.

8.   Jon _____. Keys for Deep Purple, his repertoire was impressive, and it is him we owe for some of their most memorable hooks, such as that of "Hush."

3. LESSER-KNOWN GUITAR GREATS

Diddley, Clapton, Hendrix . . . any list of the guitar greats inevitably ends up following a well-worn path. So, what about the lesser-known visionaries? People who invented a whole new sound or whose playing possesses unmistakable personality? The overlooked guitar heroes. This puzzle celebrates the fretboard less traveled.

ACROSS

4. Randy _____. Played with a very young Jimi Hendrix and then went on to form the band Spirit. Led Zep's Jimmy Page has been accused of borrowing heavily from his song "Taurus."

6. Al _____. The Earth, Wind and Fire guitarist has a sense of rhythm and feel beyond compare.

8. Dinosaur Jr. frontman who teases melody from chaos. Achingly effortless tone, J _____.

9. Finding room to shine between Sly Stone's psychedelic organ and Larry Graham's booming bass is a tall order. _____ Stone managed it with his choppy, scratchy style and influenced a whole generation of guitarists.

10. Joey _____. His playing was as much a defining part of the Pixies' tour de force as Frank Black's songwriting.

DOWN

1. To invent a new sound is one thing, but to make white noise sound so appealing is quite another. _____ Shields bulldozed down the wall of sound with his band My Bloody Valentine.

2. Roy _____. Achieved previously unheard, spine-tingling sounds using just his intuition and, on occasion, a razor blade.

3. Funk, soul, pop icon who created countless great albums, always outdoing himself in the realm of theatrics. Not a bad guitarist either. The Purple One, Minneapolis's own, _____.

5. Johnny _____. If he'd retired after the release of Radiohead's "Creep," he'd still make the list. As it is, we have the rest of his mesmerizing body of work over three decades with the British band.

7. Steve _____ manages to make a guitar sound like sheet metal. Many have tried to ape the Big Black and Shellac man's sound; none have come close.

4. DRUMMERS

The drummer is victim to a host of stereotypes. To some, they're little more than a sentient metronome—one that speeds up toward the end of songs and gets uncontrollably drunk after gigs. In most cases this isn't true—the best not only keep heads nodding, but they also possess a talent for the unpredictable that can cause jaws to drop.

ACROSS

4. Not many drummers could contain Page and Plant. John _____ made sure they never strayed too far from that undeniable blues groove.

6. The Foo Fighters frontman, Dave _____, was the pummeling force behind Nirvana. Technically brilliant with a hard-hitting style.

7. Terry ___, Pentangle's drummer, whose subtle shifts and deceptively unshowy style are on display in such songs as "Rain and Snow," "Travelling Song" and "I Saw an Angel."

8. Can's drummer, Jaki _____, was able to meld the intellectual concerns of the German band's musical manifesto with a phenomenal funk sensibility.

9. Notoriously difficult to get along with, yes, but perhaps the most influential drummer of his generation. One third of Cream, a jazz specialist on the London Rock 'n' roll scene, and a part of the Afrobeat explosion in 1970s West Africa. _____ Baker.

10. Despite no formal training, ____ Rich, the jazz virtuoso, had it all—speed, technique, intelligence, and power.

DOWN

1. Max _____. One of the most influential jazz drummers ever. The greats—Charlie Parker, Dizzy Gillespie, Miles Davis—they came and went, and they all played with this extraordinary percussionist.

2. Clyde _____. The break on James Brown's "Funky Drummer" is one of the most sampled pieces of music ever.

3. Tony _____. The Africa '70 sticksman without whom there would be no Afrobeat.

5. Keith ___ played like he lived—flamboyant, chaotic, exhilarating. The Who's drummer is staggering on tracks like "The Real Me" from *Quadrophenia*.

5. BASS PLAYERS

"My spine is the bassline," sang post-punk pioneers Shriekback, and while it may sound like nonsense, they've actually got a point. The bassist provides the framework around which everything else sits, and rein in the worst excesses of their bandmates with good grace and quiet authority, lest they be forced to use the two most feared words in the English language . . . bass solo.

ACROSS

2. Once part of James Brown's backing band, _____ Collins's personality and talent were truly realized in Funkadelic.

4. John Paul _____ was a well-regarded session bass player before stepping onto a stage with Led Zeppelin. He was the band's backbone and, along with Bonham, part of arguably the best rock rhythm section ever.

5. Bernard _____. Chic's bassman laid down the fluid, irresistible disco-funk lines that stand out so irresistibly from "Le Freak" and "Good Times."

9. Robbie _____. With reggae's deep register, the bass takes on an added importance—particularly when you can feel it in your chest. He's best known as part of Sly and Robbie.

10. Rich, famous, and beloved for his songwriting, it's hard to believe Paul _____ only took up the bass following Stuart Sutcliffe's departure.

DOWN

1. The bassist's bassist, he is probably best known for his work as part of jazz-fusion group Weather Report. Jaco _____ reinvented the electric bass as a lead instrument and died before his time.

3. Known as "the Ox" and "Thunderfingers," John _____, the Who's bassist, managed to produce a truly enormous sound and provide a much-needed tether for Keith Moon.

6. Bass-player of choice for legendary Stax label. Part of Booker T and the MGs. Donald "Duck" _____.

7. The Red Hot Chili Peppers bassist, _____, has developed a sound uniquely his own, melding perfectly rock power and bouncing funk slap with the attitude of punk.

8. Jack _____. His innovative lead style and innate musicality was the perfect match for Cream.

6. RAPPERS

Rap was forged in the 1970s by African Americans and Latino Americans, growing out of increasingly popular New York City block parties. Taking just the percussion elements of funk, soul and disco songs, MCs began to lyricize to DJs' percussive breaks, and a new genre of music was born. This puzzle celebrates the lyrical dexterity and rhythmic mastery of the very best.

ACROSS

3. One-time member of Organized Konfusion, Pharoahe _____ showed a more aggressive and hard-hitting style with 1999's solo debut "Simon Says."

4. _____ ____'s laid-back, melodic drawl and incredible ability to weave narrative have made him one of the most beloved musicians alive.

8. ___ debuted with the 1994 tour de force *Illmatic,* and has continued to stay on top with his assured and literate approach, using some of the best producers available.

9. The masked man's lyrical flow is truly astounding. _._. ____ is prolific, but best known for the albums *Madvillainy* and *Operation: Doomsday.*

10. One half of Public Enemy. An unapologetically political and confrontational voice of a generation, who also historically crossed genres to collaborate with Aerosmith. _____ _.

DOWN

1. Sadly, Biggie Smalls is remembered by most for his very public spat with Tupac Shakur and his early death, reflecting the violence he talked about in his music. The _____ B.I.G. was a masterful wordsmith and clear contender for best rapper of all time.

2. _._. ___ _. is one of the originals whose forthright, powerful delivery on tracks like "Rock the Bells" and "Mama Said Knock You Out" that have stood the test of time.

5. _____ Killah. A member of the revolutionary hip-hop crew Wu-Tang Clan with a husky, guttural delivery.

6. _____ is regarded as one of the most skillful M.C.s of all time. He also dropped four breakthrough albums paired with D.J. Eric B.

7. A deeply politicized lyricist whose fierce intellect is clear to anyone lucky enough to have heard the album *By All Means Necessary.* K.R.S. ___.

7. COUNTRY FUNK

Take one part melancholic melodies and two parts beat-heavy back line. Add a dash of laconic bass work and sprinkle liberally with feeling. Explaining what makes a country funk classic is nigh-on impossible, but you know it when you hear it—suddenly your head's moving and there's a smile on your face.

ACROSS

2. _____ Reed. While the lyrics to "Oh What a Woman" belong to a time long gone, the combination of stuttering, scratchy guitar, lazy, rolling drums, and lolloping bass will never grow old.

6. Don _____ is a criminally underrated artist. The interplay between the shuffling drums, bass, and his vocals in "Bless the Children" is typical.

7. "Fire and _____." As the title suggests, this is a big song, off the legendary guitarist's 1971 album, and although not well-received at the time, has since been covered by the Neville Brothers and Nick Cave.

8. _____ Gentry. While "Ode to Billie Joe" may be more well known, it lacks the percussive persuasiveness and killer horn stabs "Fancy" boasts.

10. Jim ____'s "I'm Going to Make Her Love Me" has a simple but effective backbeat that sets the tone before the melody of the refrain comes in.

DOWN

1. Tony Joe White's voice sounds like a drunk Elvis, while his guitar playing manages to sound bright, sharp, and relaxed in "Soul _____."

3. "New Horizon" was recorded when ____ Whitren was just 19 years old. The guitar, banjo, and voice are all hers, but a mention also has to go to drummer Gerry Conway.

4. Dolly Parton's "_____." Perhaps technically not funky, but there's a groove to this song that is undeniable and rare for such a popular hit.

5. From the 1975 LP *Mother Trucker*, "Piledriver" begins almost like an out-and-out funk tune with the heavy beat and mellow Hammond sound, then _____ the Fox's voice comes in sounding utterly perfect.

9. "Fido" is a perfectly pleasant tale of a stray dog until drummer Gene Parsons interrupts proceedings with exactly the sort of muscular funk you might expect from the _____.

8. FOLK ROCK

As the 1960s rolled on and boundaries blurred between genres, new ones emerged. Of these, folk rock was one of the broadest, including as it did rock acts who took their influences from the folk scene as well as folk musicians who plugged in, turned on, and tuned up.

ACROSS

2.   _____. Forget the dreamy wash of "Harry's Game" for a moment as it's the Irish folk band's earlier stuff that catches the ear on this list.

4.   When Bob _____ picked up an electric guitar at the Newport Folk Festival, it was seen as an act of betrayal. Where he led, however, others would follow.

5.   The albums *The Garden of Jane Delawney* and *On the Shore* have retrospectively become classics of the genre for _____.

6.   When Fairport's Ashley Hutchings wanted a more traditional sound, he left to form this band, Steeleye ____. Although best known for "All Around My Hat," it's their first two albums that stand up best today.

7.   _____ Springfield led the way for both folk rock and country rock in the U.S. The light acoustic of songs like "For What It's Worth" had huge impact.

9.   The _____. Combining folk music with the 1960s pop sound might not seem like a big deal now, but when they took an Old Testament passage set to music by Pete Seeger and came up with "Turn, Turn, Turn," it was visionary.

10.   Greg Weeks's band, _____, hold their own in such illustrious company— their intense 2003 self-titled debut set the bar high with melancholic melody and psychedelic flourishes.

DOWN

1.   Mellow _____'s only album, *Swaddling Songs*, is a beautiful collection, made all the more extraordinary by how young they were at the time of its 1972 release.

3.   Something of a folk supergroup, _____ consisted of guitarists Bert Jansch and John Renbourn, drummer Terry Cox, bassist Danny Thompson, and the then-unknown singer Jacquie McShee.

8.   _____ Convention reached a pinnacle with their *Liege and Lief* album, where they combined traditional English folk and electric instruments.

9. FUSION FLINGS

To many, fusion represents the very worst excesses of rock and jazz conveniently put together in one place, so it's easier to ignore. They're missing out, however, on some inspiring and incredibly rewarding music. Once you get past the tricky time signatures and extended solos, there's beauty in the albums.

ACROSS

3. Herbie _____ took influences from far and wide to create "Mwandishi"—a record of odd grooves and exciting tension.

4. Soft _____ had several marked shifts in their style during their career. *Third* is, arguably, the starkest of these. Each side is a song.

6. Weather _____. While *Heavy Weather* may have been the commercial high point for the band, *Black Market*, the first album to feature bass player Jaco Pastorius, is perhaps even more interesting.

7. *Spectrum* is an absolute classic of the genre from the drummer _____ Cobham. The album boasts fabulous guest players, including Jan Hammer.

8. *Good _____*. This beauty came after his work with the Gary Burton Quartet. The distorted rock sound of the vibraphone and the loose, almost unhinged feel on tracks like "Vibrafinger" mark this out as an essential album.

9. Proving that fusion can be fun is the irreverent wit of _____ Zappa. The *Hot Rats* album is largely instrumental, but tracks like "Peaches En Regalia" and "Willie the Pimp" manage to be both complex and immediate.

DOWN

1. Having left the Rendell-Carr Quartet, Ian Carr went on to form Nucleus. *Elastic _____* was their first album, with *1916 The Battle of Boogaloo* a particular favorite.

2. Almost like an ambient album in parts, *In a Silent Way* is a recording of understated beauty and subtle musicality by Miles _____.

4. The mercurial playing of John McLaughlin on the album *The Inner Mounting Flame* is intense and dynamic, but he's ably backed up by possibly the best band of its type. The _____ Orchestra.

5. Their self-titled LP is not what you would call a well-known album, sure, but it is an under-the-radar classic by the Czech band _____,

10. GIRL GROUPS

What makes a classic girl group? There's the songs, of course—you've got to have the hits, perfect pop but not too saccharine. And there's the image too . . . but there's something else, it's getting the mix right. Making sure that there's the perfect blend of voices and personality to keep the customer satisfied and the bands' egos in check.

ACROSS

3. Combining talent, power, and style without compromise, En _____ bagged hit singles and awards as if for fun. "My Lovin' (You're Never Gonna Get It)" and "Free Your Mind" made everyone raise their game.

4. Hit after hit kept Diana Ross, Mary Wilson, and Florence Ballard at the top during the mid-1960s. The _____.

6. Girls _____. Winners of *Popstars: The Rivals* in 2002, they confounded critics by releasing a string of clever, sophisticated pop hits and ruling the British charts for a decade.

7. Lisa "Left Eye" Lopez and company emerged on the scene in 1993; however, it wasn't until 1999 that ___ hit heights with the towering "No Scrubs."

9. Sporty, Scary, Baby, Ginger, and Posh became the biggest-selling girl group of all time. That the _____ Girls did so on the back of some genuinely brilliant pop songs is to their eternal credit.

DOWN

1. Schoolfriends discovered at a high-school talent show in 1957, their doo wop/pop cross gave them several hits, including the timeless classic "Will You Love Me Tomorrow." The _____.

2. It was a phone call from Estelle Bennet to Phil Spector that launched the _____, one of the greatest girl groups of the 1960s.

4. In an age of demure smiles and prom dresses, the _____-La's were like a slap in the face.

5. Their 1961 number-one, a rendition of "Please Mr. Postman" for the Tamla label, was the first Motown chart topper. Sadly, they ended up on the wrong side of a head-to-head career battle with the Supremes. The _____.

8. Sixty million albums sold. Reputation guaranteed. Destiny's _____ conquered the planet during the late 1990s and early 2000s.

11. BOY BANDS

The secret to a successful boy band is as difficult to pin down as the perfect soccer team formation. Obviously, you play your star striker up front, but what then? Whatever the game plan, nothing is more important than a team who complement each other in all the right ways. The following bands all got it spot-on.

ACROSS

5. After a hilariously ramshackle debut on Ireland's *Late Kate Show*, _____ went on to become one of the most successful boy bands in the UK, which made the untimely death of Stephen Gately all the sadder.

7. The original boy band, put together for a TV show, that eventually bargained for control against the record companies. Interestingly, Jimi Hendrix was at one time their warm-up act. The _____.

8. With great songs and wide grins, ____ That took the pop world by surprise. The devastation when they announced their split showed how important they had become, as did the response to their comeback.

10. ____ 17 weren't the band you could take home to meet your mother. It didn't hamper their appeal, or their sales, but may have distracted from the fact that Tony Mortimer is a gifted and smart songwriter.

DOWN

1. It seems strange to imagine in an age of internet connectedness, but the _____ 5 were everywhere when all they had was TV, radio, and papers.

2. The young pretenders in an all-time top ten. They're about as successful as it's possible to be, having worked tirelessly across America. One _____.

3. Boy-next-door charm coupled with ballads composed with laser-like efficiency and managed by Louis Walsh. _____.

4. It wasn't until their second album, *Hangin' Tough*, that things started to happen for New Kids on the _____. What ensued was full-blown mania.

6. "I Want It That Way," "Quit Playing Games," and many more. Theirs was not overnight success; the _____ Boys put in the hours getting there.

9. New _____. Forerunners to the modern U.S. boy band, their 1983 hit "Candy Girl" was as infectious as pop can be. The band launched Bobby Brown, Bel Biv Devoe, and the New Jack Swing sound.

12. POP PERFECTION

Music forces us all to be subjective. There are times when we grow to love a song—our judgments inevitably clouded by association and colored by memories. There are others, however, where a tune sounds so immediately perfect, so right, that it's like it's been there forever just waiting to be unearthed. Like these, for instance . . .

ACROSS

3. A huge hit and actually a Neil Diamond song—one he occasionally performs live. It's easy to see why: this version of "I'm a _____" by the Monkees is all wide-eyed wonder and sunny optimism.

4. The 1983 release "Let's Dance" came as something of a shock to many fans of _____ Bowie, particularly after the fairly downbeat *Scary Monsters*.

7. "Don't You Want Me" was probably the most hummed bassline in the whole of pop music, 1981's huge statement by what was left of _____ League.

8. "Be My ____" by the Ronettes is a phenomenal vocal performance—full of tension and resolution—and Phil Spector's "wall of sound" technique.

9. "_____ Jean." That *Thriller* producer Quincy Jones thought it a weak link is gobsmacking. Its minor-key melody and rolling bass are addictive.

DOWN

1. Britney _____. It was always going to be a toss-up between "Toxic" and "Baby One More Time," but the former wins for its mix of sophisticated melody, exotic strings, and echo-drenched guitar.

2. Had you grown up in a forest, with no electricity, company, or language, you'd still be singing along to "Dancing Queen" by ____ within 30 seconds.

5. "Good _____" is possibly the oddest pop song here, with the sudden shifts in tempo and tone, but it's so accessible and that's down to the genius of Brian Wilson.

6. Written by Felice and Boudleaux Bryant, "Bye Bye ____" by the Everly Brothers clearly struck a chord with the record-buying public of 1957—but then again, breakup numbers like this will always sell.

7. Andre 3000 is lauded as one of the greatest rappers of all time, but "___ Ya," the pop song by Outkast!, is timeless and catchy as chicken pox.

13. MUSICAL PERSONAE

"Can you see the real me?" sang Roger Daltrey. When it comes to these masters of disguise, the answer is a resounding "no." Popular music has always been about image, and performance through the ages has featured masks of all kinds. The most successful performers are acutely aware of this and have learned how to use it to stunning effect.

ACROSS

1. _____. The evil cartoon creations taken up by U.S. rock band–inspired fans and media alike. Marvel even jumped in with a comic before NBC released a feature-length cartoon.

5. Kevin Donovan left the Black Spades street gang and adopted his Zulu moniker, Afrika _____ (meaning "affectionate leader"), to unleash his pioneering electro on the world.

6. __ _____. Identifiable only by his metal mask, inspired by the Marvel character Dr. Doom.

7. Insane _____ Posse. The horrorcore hip-hop act's sheer dedication to their own mythology means it's almost impossible to know where the theater stops—they're also a professional wrestling tag team!

9. Alice _____. Vincent Furnier has been slapping on the makeup and reaching for the guillotine for more than half a century.

DOWN

2. David Bowie is a man of many parts, but none quite as remarkable as the lightning-flashed face persona of Ziggy _____.

3. When Eminem's crazed alter ego ___ Shady appeared, it enabled the rapper to lash out lyrically while also maintaining a degree of artistic distance from the words.

4. "Vogue," "Material Girl," "Like a Virgin." Stark shifts in style and a knack of hiring cutting-edge producers, _____ has led the way for decades.

8. Ozzy _____. One of the biggest rock stars ever, his onstage persona has, at times, been difficult to separate from his offstage behavior.

10. When a whole band creates another persona, it had better be good. This heralded one of the most important concept LPs of the 1960s—maybe even the greatest album ever. *Sgt. _____'s Lonely Hearts Club Band.*

14. MUSICAL FAMILIES

As the saying goes, "You can choose your friends, but not your family." So why would you decide to spend your working day in a cramped studio with your siblings? The following examples suggest that, for some at least, keeping it in the family could be a very good thing indeed . . .

ACROSS

1. The _____ Brothers. Five brothers have passed through the ranks of this band, from their gospel beginnings to the smooth funk of "Summer Breeze."

6. Brother and sister Richard and Karen were one of the best pop duos of all time, and before Karen's death at only age thirty-two, the _____ had amassed a slew of hits and proved themselves phenomenal musicians.

7. The _____. Perhaps it was creative tension that sparked some of their most enduring hits but, crucially, the warring between Ray Davies and younger brother Dave never managed to drown out the songs.

9. The _____ Boys. "I may not always love you," sang Carl Wilson in his brother Brian's song "God Only Knows" and there isn't a better examination of family ties—or band dynamics—in pop.

10. Scottish brothers Jim and William Reid created a tense, angry, and chaotic sound unlike anything that had gone before. The Jesus and ____ _____.

DOWN

2. _____ _____. The archetypal sibling act, not least due to the all-encompassing popularity of their 1979 hit "We Are Family."

3. ___ ____. The brothers Gibb formed a group where perfect harmony, particularly when set against a driving disco backbeat, was to gain them worldwide popularity.

4. Noel and Liam. No-shows and mid-gig walkouts illustrated sibling rivalry even when you're in one of the biggest bands on the planet: _____.

5. Considered a joke in some quarters, the TV favorites smuggled some real quality among the pop hits that gave the _____ worldwide adulation. Give "Traffic in My Mind" a listen and prepare for a shock.

8. The chemistry between this band of brothers made the _____ 5 one of pop's all-time greats, until Michael's solo star started to rise.

15. ROCK-STAR CHILDREN

It could be the genes, learned behavior, or just the luck of the draw, but there seems to be a lot of rock stars whose children end up following them into the business—whether they have the requisite talent or not. Having said that, often the good example set for them pays off . . .

ACROSS

3. Though his brother Seun performs with his father's old band, the Egypt 80, it is eldest son Femi ____ who has gained the international plaudits.

6. Bob's eldest son, Ziggy _____, has carried on the family tradition with big success. He even wrote the theme music to the children's show *Arthur*.

10. _____ _____. One of Ravi Shankar's two musician daughters, her soft, jazz-inflected style has won her nine Grammys and gave us the enormous 2002 hit album *Come Away with Me*.

DOWN

1. A career that produced the breathtaking album *Grace*. Sadly, his life was to mirror his father Tim's, in that he died in 1997 aged just thirty. Jeff _____.

2. _____ Cyrus. The daughter of country star Billy Ray Cyrus made the transition from child TV star to pop star seamlessly enough.

4. Charlotte _____. After a controversial start to her career, aged twelve, when she sang with her father, Serge, on the risqué "Lemon Incest," there was a twenty-year gap before "5:55."

5. Martha and Rufus _____. Both acclaimed singer-songwriters, both from musical royalty.

7. Both a singer and an actress, in keeping with the family tradition, _____ Sinatra is best known for the 1966 hit "These Boots Are Made for Walkin'."

8. Taking the surname of her stepfather, jazz musician Don, she first found fame in 1988 with singles including "Buffalo Stance" and "Manchild" and continues to produce outstanding work. Neneh _____.

9. Julian and Sean _____. Julian, from John's first marriage, to Cynthia, and Sean, with Yoko Ono, have never managed to achieve the fame of their father, but then who could?

16. GREAT GIGS

One of the most potentially controversial categories, as everyone has their favorite gig. The one where they met their partner, finally got to see a most-loved band . . . and that's exactly the point when compiling a puzzle like this—context becomes everything, and the word "best" is rendered redundant.

ACROSS

2. The _____ at Apple studios rooftop gig, 1969. Although they had stopped gigging in 1966, this gig was the Fab Four's last public performance.

4. When the Stone Roses pulled out of Glastonbury '95, Jarvis Cocker and co. stepped up. They won over a potentially difficult crowd and marked the arrival of their band, _____.

6. The Velvet _____ and Nico at the Exploding Plastic Inevitable, 1966—a series of "happenings" organized by pop artist Andy Warhol.

7. Last gig of the _____ _____ tour, 1973, at the Hammersmith Odeon Theatre, London, was when David Bowie announced the retirement of his alter ego. It was a huge shock to fans, the press, and most of his band, too.

10. _____ was a gig beset by problems both with sound and organization (not least the decision to hold it on a reclaimed toxic waste site). The Stone Roses' 1990 folly has nonetheless achieved near mythical status.

DOWN

1. ___ _____. On the Queen of England's Silver Jubilee, June 7, 1977, Johnny Rotten and co. set sail on the Thames to play their anti-monarchy anthem "God Save the Queen."

3. Not just a gig, more a worldwide phenomenon. The sheer scale of ____ ___, the culmination of Bob Geldoff's fund-raising project, was staggering.

5. _____ Folk Festival. The moment that broke folk fans' hearts. Bob Dylan's insistence on playing with an amplified band changed everything.

8. In three years, they had gone from playing a small room at London's School of Oriental and African Studies to headlining one of the biggest festivals in Britain. Nirvana's last gig in Britain: _____ 1992.

9. With delays and hitches, by the time _____ Hendrix stepped onstage to close the show at Woodstock, it was 9 a.m. on Monday morning, half the audience had left. Even so, it was a jaw-dropping performance.

17. LIVE RECORDINGS

The best live albums capture not just the songs but the whole atmosphere of a gig—the feeling in the room. When done well, they can transport the avid listener to a specific moment in time and bestow upon them all the thrills of a front-row seat, and with better toilet facilities to boot.

ACROSS

3. The main problem when talking about Aretha _____'s second live album, *Live at Fillmore West,* is finding new superlatives.

4. *Live at Leeds.* Having ordered the destruction of all live tapes from their 1969 tour, it's just as well that this recording survived and went on to earn ___ ___ universal praise. It includes a fourteen-minute "My Generation."

5. *Live 66: The "Royal Albert Hall" Concert* album was actually recorded in Manchester in 1966. An acoustic set before Bob _____ "went electric."

6. *Live at Pompeii* by ____ _____ is lacking only one thing . . . an audience! One of the most engrossing live performances of all time, witnessed by no one but a film crew.

8. MC5's Wayne Kramer has said that _____ _____'s *Live at the Apollo* was the inspiration for his own live album. The connection isn't obvious, but the urgency and energy from the Godfather of Soul's recording certainly is.

DOWN

1. *Smell of _____* was recorded at the Peppermint Lounge (purportedly the birthplace of go-go dancing), the perfect venue for the seductive sleaze of psychobilly legends the Cramps.

2. *At _____ Prison* is a landmark album for Johnny Cash, who was no stranger to performing in prisons and would do so again, in San Quentin.

4. In essence a soundtrack to a self-financed live film, *Stop Making Sense* by _____ _____ has a great sense of theater and phenomenal songs that jostle for position—a battle eventually won by David Byrne's big suit.

7. Releasing a live album as your debut either shows confidence in your ability, or that you can't afford studio fees. *Kick out the ____,* recorded by MC5 in 1968 at Detroit's Grand Ballroom, is an essential recording.

9. *Live ____* by Neil Young. Listening to this 1978 release, it feels like pure emotion has been transferred to magnetic tape.

18. GIG VENUES

Tickets to see your favorite band lose something of value if they're playing in a venue so big you can barely see them. Similarly, it's nice to know that the small details are taken care of, like basic sanitation and fire exits. Thankfully, the world is full of phenomenal venues—and not all of them obvious.

ACROSS

1. _____'s. *The* place to see the *enfants terrible* of the New York scene grow up in public. Talking Heads, the Ramones, and Blondie are among its alumni.

3. Paradiso, _____. A city that is well served by superb venues, also boasting the excellent Melkweg. Keith Richards said the 1995 gigs the Stones played at this nineteenth-century former church were their career best.

7. The London _____. This much-missed venue was modest in size but big on sound. It was the perfect choice to see successful bands and hugely important to the LGBT scene for its G-A-Y club nights.

9. ___ _____. This amphitheater carved out of the surrounding rock, near Denver, Colorado, is quite something to behold.

10. Effenaar, _____. Opened in 1971, this venue is steeped in political history and was intended as a forum for young people. It was rebuilt in 2005 and stands as a testament to architecture as well as music.

DOWN

2. Empress Ballroom, _____. A Grade-II listed Victorian building, complete with chandeliers. The White Stripes recorded a live DVD here.

4. _____, L.A. From Buffalo Springfield, the Byrds, Love, and Joni Mitchell through to comedians such as Steve Martin and George Carlin, this West Hollywood venue is a legend.

5. The _____. A former railway shed in Chalk Farm, North London, it was converted into a concert venue that is still going strong today.

6. The _____. The people of San Francisco who wore flowers in their hair were almost certainly doing so here—it was the premier place to see the psychedelic acts of the time.

8. La _____, Paris. Opened in the mid-nineteenth century, it is still hosting gigs today. It has seen acts as varied as the Clash, Edith Piaf, and the Manic Street Preachers cross the distinctive, Chinese-influenced threshold.

19. SONGS ABOUT SMOKING

The days of smoking in bars and clubs may be gone, but the image of watching musicians through a smoky haze endures. Despite knowing how bad it is for us, the cigarette holds an unmistakable allure, and the musician is just as susceptible. Probably more so, given they don't have to stand outside an office in the rain to light up . . .

ACROSS

4. "Don't Just Do Something" by _____. As Jason Pierce opines, "And life ain't good without cigarettes." From 2001's *Let It Come Down*, this bittersweet ballad builds to a blistering climax before fading to nothing.

5. In Patsy Cline's "Three Cigarettes in an _____," she tells the story of a woman resigned to losing her lover to another woman.

7. "Don't _____ That Joint" by Fraternity of Man. Featured on the *Easy Rider* soundtrack, the title of this silly, intentionally funny ditty says it all really. Note: the missing word means to hog something.

8. Otis Redding's "Cigarettes and _____." It's quarter to three, and Otis is still awake. He's watching his health, though, and abstaining from cream and sugar on the basis that his girlfriend's sweet enough. What a song!

9. "Cigarette Smoke" by the _____ _____. Alex Turner's trademark tale of gritty urban realism.

10. "When I Get Low I Get High." Ella _____ may not be talking about tobacco in this 1936 riff on jazz cigarettes.

DOWN

1. "Cigarettes and Alcohol" by _____. Has there ever been a better ode to all that is bad for us? Liam lets loose with his trademark sneer.

2. "Smokin'" by the Super Furry _____. The lines, "Gonna manage my time, Just like Johann Cruyff, If we do it together, We've got meaning of life," indicate that considerable research had been undertaken.

3. My Bloody Valentine's "_____ in Your Bed." To say there's some unsettling imagery going on here (under swathes of distortion) is putting it very mildly. It remains, however, a stunning piece of music.

6. Simon & _____'s "America." This tale of young lovers on a voyage of discovery contains the beautifully weighted words, "Toss me a cigarette, I think there's one in my raincoat/We smoked the last one an hour ago."

20. DRINKING SONGS

It's one of the biggest motifs in popular music and has been both muse and unkind mistress to many. Whether it's a celebration or drowning your sorrows, there's bound to be a song to fit the occasion, such is the musician's preoccupation with drinking. So, raise your glasses and be upstanding please . . . to the hard stuff!

ACROSS

5. "Brass Monkey." The brass monkey in question is actually a cocktail . . . although the recipe seems as tricky to pin down as this rap/rock phenomenon by the _____ _____.

9. "Born Slippy" by _____. After featuring on the soundtrack to *Trainspotting*, the song's refrain, "Shouting lager lager lager lager," was belted out by thousands of pubs at weekends.

10. Latin-influenced American band the Champs recorded "_____," a largely instrumental, two-minute drinking classic.

DOWN

1. "_____ in the Jar." A bombastic and definitive version of the traditional Irish song by Thin Lizzy, it's perfectly designed for singing along to.

2. "One _____." Using a neat sample from French jazz-funk outfit Cortex, MF Doom begins this track with a ramshackle rendition of Cole Porter's *I Get a Kick Out of You*, before launching into his rambling rap.

3. "Milk & Alcohol." Known, appropriately enough, as the UK's premier pub-rock act. This song tells the tale of the author Dr. _____'s comeuppance after one too many Kahluas at a John Lee Hooker gig.

4. The _____'s "Happy Hour" was the band from Hull's first big hit. Upbeat and delightfully goofy, but the lyrics served up something more sobering, with a caustic appraisal of corporate culture.

6. "One _____, One Scotch, One Beer." An example of both a great drinking song and great jump blues by John Lee Hooker.

7. "_____ Morning Coming Down." Johnny Cash popularized the song, but it's Kris Kristofferson's hangover.

8. "Gin & _____." After introducing himself on his first single, "What's My Name?" Snoop Dogg's second hit left us in no doubt what to get him at the bar.

21. BLUES ROOTS

A world with no blues is one with no popular music. Thought to have risen from a combination of West African storytelling, the work songs of African slaves, and early forms of folk music, over the years it developed into what we would identify as the Blues, with standards forming the basis for pretty much everything that has come since.

ACROSS

2. "Boom Boom" by John Lee _____. The point where blues edges into pop, this irresistible 1961 track was a massive hit at the time of its release.

3. "House of the Rising Sun" by _____. While everyone is familiar with the Animals' version of this traditional American bard's tale, this deft and definitive twelve-string version from the 1940s is completely different.

4. Ragtime and blues, singer and guitarist, Blind Willie McTell's legacy has proved to be lasting. This 1933 song, "Lord Send Me an _____," covered in 2000 by the White Stripes, is truly timeless.

6. "Didn't It Rain, Children." A true pioneer of what was to become rock 'n' roll, Sister _____ Thorpe enjoyed a resurgence of interest with the UK blues revival. The version recorded in Manchester, 1964, is astounding.

9. "Me and the Devil Blues." The life of _____ _____, the blues guitarist, is shrouded in mystery.

10. "Nine Below Zero" by Sonny Boy _____. The second musician to go by this name, the harmonica player and singer had considerable sway over the blues revival scene.

DOWN

1. Howlin' Wolf's "_____ Lightning" was released in 1956, but he had been performing this song for at least two decades beforehand.

5. Familiar due to Led Zeppelin's reworking of the song for their *Led Zeppelin IV* album. "When the _____ Breaks" is a true great by the blues duo Kansas Joe and Memphis Minnie, written about the great Mississippi flood of 1927.

7. B.B. King played guitar like he wasn't even trying, so effortless was his style. This 1969 release of the 1931 song "The _____ Is Gone" marked something of a change in direction for him at the time but remains a classic.

8. "Baby Please Don't Go." Big Bill _____'s influence as a guitar player is second to none.

22. BLUES AND BEYOND

With a new generation besotted by the blues, it was inevitable that they would bring to it a new approach. Add to this the established artists keen to push the form as far as it would go and others who wanted to progress the more dance-floor sound of R&B, the stage was set for some truly original sounds . . .

ACROSS

3. In 1970, blues maestro Alexis Korner formed CCS (the Collective Consciousness Society). It's "_____," the B-side to their 1971 single "Walkin'," that best conveys their blues feel and rock rhythms combo.

5. The brainchild of Al Kooper, the LP that the track "Season of the _____" is from features two of the best guitarists of the day.

6. "_____ Pot," the title track of the 1971 album by Booker T & the MG's, puts the "rhythm" in rhythm and blues.

7. The Graham ____ Organisation were an infamous British rhythm and blues group that included Ginger Baker and Jack Bruce. Their wonderful cut of "Harmonica" is from the goofy 1965 sci-fi film *Gonks Go Beat*.

8. The 1966 single "Inside Looking Out" by British band the _____ is about as hard-hitting a take on the blues as you're ever likely to hear.

9. "A Little Bit _____" by Blues Incorporated. Primarily a live act with a fluid lineup, this track off their 1965 album shows a much jazzier feel.

DOWN

1. A talented blues harmonica player, Paul Butterfield joined forces with the twin guitar attack of Mike Bloomfield and Elvin Bishop. This track, "Got My _____ Working," from their first LP, brings a rock feel to the blues.

2. From the 1970 LP *The Black Gladiator*, the track "_____ Man" by Bo Diddley takes the urgent energy of funk and a raw rock sound while retaining his blues stylings to create something altogether more psychedelic.

4. "All Your Love" from the 1966 album by John Mayall and the _____ with Eric Clapton combines a more traditional take on the blues, with the energy and distortion of rock and almost psychedelic vocals.

6. An absolute visionary, Muddy Waters first recorded "_____ Boy" in 1955. It's the sprawling 1968 version on the *Electric Mud* LP that lives on.

23. TRIPPY TROUBADOURS

While some musicians are content to carry on doing what they do best, others, when left to their own devices, have tried to forge a path that is all their own. Often choosing quite different routes, the singers and songwriters on this list all ended up at the same destination—waaay out there.

ACROSS

2. Singer-songwriter _____ Wilson pays no heed to current fads, veering from waltz-time fairground fancy to 4/4 space rock in "Dear Friend."

4. "Full ____." Was Eden Ahbez the first hippie? Born in 1908, he wore his hair long and lived close to nature. He had followers too—called Nature Boys after the song he wrote, made famous by Nat King Cole.

6. "Beautiful People (Maravillosa Gente)" is by a traveling hippie who ended up in Madrid in the early 1970s. A chance meeting led ____ _____ to record an album that boasts this gentle and optimistic folk gem.

7. Susan Christie was destined to languish in obscurity after this album was shelved in 1970. Thankfully, *Paint a* ____ was reissued by the Finders Keepers label so we can revel in her far-out folk.

8. Singer, multi-instrumentalist, and avant-garde composer, _____ Peacock was unafraid to experiment, which "Pony" demonstrates perfectly.

9. D.R. Hooker—a quasi-religious philosopher musician who privately pressed copies of his album. This isn't usually a guarantee of quality, but the out-there oddity "Forge Your Own _____" is an amazing exception.

DOWN

1. Well known for his time in Crosby, Stills, Nash & (occasionally) Young. From the solo album *If Only I Could Remember My Name*, "Orleans" is a dreamy masterpiece featuring just guitar and David _____'s voice.

3. _____ was a musician who often shifted styles, covering folk rock, soul, and psychedelia in his short career. In "Sweet Surrender," from *Greetings from L.A.*, he embraces his vocal range and creativity in arrangement.

5. _____ Havens found a worldwide audience after his appearance at Woodstock. He took "Back to My Roots" somewhere totally different.

6. To some, Donovan is the poor man's Dylan, but to anyone who's really listened, original tracks like "Get Thy _____" remain memorable.

24. EASY LISTENING

There are times when only a crushed-velvet lounge suit and a martini will do, and those times are best soundtracked by the greats of easy listening. It's true that occasional slips in sartorial style haven't helped the giants of this genre to be taken altogether seriously, but the bow ties and bell-bottoms disguise some wonderful arrangements and superb musicianship.

ACROSS

1. "2001: A Space _____" from the Ray McVay *Road Show* album is a belter that breaks all speed limits as it takes flight into the stratosphere.

3. "The Two Ronnies Theme." A much-maligned composer, history will surely remember Ronnie _____ very fondly.

4. Keith _____'s "Funky Fanfare" is an easy listening classic that's proved rich pickings for hip-hop producers (Dangermouse used it as the main refrain in "Old School" with MF Doom and Talib Kweli).

6. Boasting flute, scratchy wah-wah guitar, and funk-filled back line, "Birds 'n' _____" by Fritzy Baby is notable not just for the soaring singers but for how the guitarist makes his instrument sound *exactly* like a cat.

7. Geoff Love made a career of reinterpreting film and TV scores in a lounge-friendly style. The horizontal funk of his take on Dave Gruin's original theme, "Three Days of the _____," is the standout.

9. Seventies German Moog ace Klaus Wunderlich produced some startlingly good, futuristic music, such as the Gershwin groove of "_____."

10. _____'s prodigious output is full of hidden gems. "Se a Cabo" from the *Voodoo Party* LP is Latin-tinged groovy rock of the sort you might expect from Santana.

DOWN

2. The version of Stevie Wonder's classic "_____," by Button Down Brass featuring Ray Davies doesn't go head-to-head with the original, but instead offers a very alternate—and very successful—take.

5. "_____" by the Gunter Kallmann Choir was heavily sampled by the Beta Band and I Monster in the early 2000s, and it's easy to see why.

8. "Quiet _____." Exotica par excellence, Martin Denny's most famous moment is so evocative.

25. FOLK FINGERPICKERS

While their opposite numbers in the rock fraternity get all the plaudits for their showmanship and solos, the deft touch and amazing dexterity of the folk guitarist shouldn't go unrewarded. Often showcasing their skills in small clubs to few people, their talent, nonetheless, is huge. Here are ten of the best.

ACROSS

2. _____ Jones's second album is a classic in the folk canon, featuring his great versions of "Beggar Man" and "Keep Your Lamp Trimmed and Burning."

5. Davy _____ was just nineteen when he wrote the instrumental touchstone "Angi." His folk *Blues & Beyond* album is absolutely essential.

6. _____ C. Frank was a troubled soul who proved a huge influence on artists including Sandy Denny and Paul Simon (who produced his debut album). "Blues Run the Game" and "Milk and Honey" are enduring pieces.

7. A hugely talented performer, John _____'s drawling vocal style and use of tape delay made for an unmistakable sound in his 1970s heyday. He also recorded earlier albums with wife Beverley, including the *Stormbringer* LP.

8. Richard _____. While in the fledgling Fairport Convention, it was the sophistication of his playing—at the age of eighteen—that endeared them to producer Joe Boyd. His "952 Vincent Black Lightning" is a monster track.

9. First coming to prominence in the late 1950s, Sandy _____'s proficiency on several instruments including the oud, and his extended, modal jams stood way out from the crowd.

DOWN

1. With a gentle, hushed guitar style that belies its impact, just like his voice, _____ _____ was the author of "Pink Moon" and "River Man."

3. His rendition of "Angi," done in one take at producer Bill Leader's home, is a good indication of his style. Neil Young called _____ _____ "the Jimi Hendrix of the acoustic guitar."

4. A true American original, _____ Fahey's best recordings weave wonderful, intricate melodies onto beautiful, droning backdrops.

6. _____ _____ has a distinctive style all his own, taking influence from jazz, classical, and baroque music. A perfect foil for fellow guitarist Bert Jansch in Pentangle.

26. SESSION MUSICIANS

Very much the unsung heroes of rock and pop, the jobbing musician may not get the plaudits, the fame, or the royalties, but they do get a solid daily rate and are able to walk the streets without being mobbed by the paparazzi. These largely anonymous musicians are responsible for some of the most recognizable moments in popular music . . .

ACROSS

2.   Billy _____ gets a mention here for the sheer volume of artists who have sought out his talents. Little Richard, Eric Clapton, Sly Stone, and the Red Hot Chili Peppers, for instance.

5.   Bernard _____. As well as laying down the good grooves for the godfather of funk, he's played for artists as diverse as Aretha Franklin, Steely Dan, Tim Rose, and guitarist Sandy Bull.

6.   It was their style that gave Stax its identity, and there's a whole roster of artists who owe _____ _ & the MG's a great debt.

8.   _____ Shoals Rhythm section. Also known as the Swampers, this group of session players defined an entire sound. Artists including the Stones, Wilson Pickett, and the peerless Tony Joe White worked with them.

10. His versatility soon saw Big Jim _____ become one of the most sought-after guitarists around. Pioneered the use of the wah-wah and fuzz pedals.

DOWN

1.   Having played for Frank Sinatra and Ella Fitzgerald, Alan _____ later churned out hits for tartan-clad teen dreams the Bay City Rollers.

3.   The Funk _____ were Motown's go-to backing band, and another group with a fluid lineup. The quality was consistent though, and the sound utterly unmistakable.

4.   Herbie _____. The bassline in "Walk on the Wild Side"—that was him. "Space Oddity?" Yes, him too.

7.   The _____ Crew. Given their name by drummer Hal Blaine, the alumni include Glen Campbell and Dr. John. Though best known for their work creating Phil Spector's "wall of sound," they were the first choice of any producer worth their salt in 1960s America.

9.   Carol _____. Another bass player who came up with a line so distinctive it should have earned a writing credit on the Beach Boys' "Good Vibrations."

27. BRITISH JAZZ HEROES

Taking inspiration from the American originators, the British exponents found their own, distinctive voice over time, taking influence from far and wide. However, while history has ensured many of their peers in the U.S. are household names, little is known of these British originals. This seems as good a time as any to attempt to redress that balance . . .

ACROSS

4. Norma _____ started out singing jazz standards, but soon became interested in the avant garde and a wordless, improvisational approach.

7. _____ Pine. The saxophonist came to fame during the 1980s and his work has been notable for taking influence from contemporary popular music, including drum and bass.

9. Michael _____ is notable for being largely self-taught and for experimenting with combinations of jazz and poetry. Pianist for the Rendell-Carr quintet, his work has been rediscovered to great acclaim.

10. Graham _____. A pioneer in many ways with his ensemble, this bass player was at the forefront of the British jazz scene.

DOWN

1. _____ Kirchin's percussion-heavy compositions featured on film and TV and he built up a wealth of unreleased material that has, more recently, found an outlet through the consistently impressive Trunk records imprint.

2. Heralded for his skill as an arranger as well as a pianist, Mike _____'s band produced music including 1969's album *Marching Song Vol. 2*.

3. ___ _____. The prodigious, self-taught trumpet player was a true visionary, forming the Rendell-Carr quintet in 1963 and then, subsequently, the groundbreaking jazz-rock band Nucleus.

5. Phenomenal composer and incredibly gifted saxophone player John _____ and his wife, Cleo Laine, were totemic in the British jazz scene.

6. A multi-instrumentalist, best known for his work on the alto sax, Tubby _____ played with Kenny Baker's sextet at age sixteen. He raised the game in UK jazz, and his residency in New York gained him a fan in Miles Davis.

8. One of the most highly regarded British jazz players in the world. "While we have Kenny _____, who needs Louis?" said the musician's union of their ban on visiting U.S. musicians.

28. GRUNGE GREATS

After heavy metal was largely co-opted by backcombed boys in spandex as the 1980s progressed, it was inevitable that the tide would turn. Toward the end of the decade these bands, largely from the U.S. coastal port of Seattle and favoring a look that said "My day job is as a lumberjack," paved the way for a monumental shift in guitar music.

ACROSS

2.   The _____ were the first non-Seattle band to sign with the hugely important Sub Pop label. "Cold Outside" is from their album *Clear Black Paper*.

4.   "Sex God _____." Sharing more in common musically with Nirvana than most, Tad were the obvious choice for the 1989 double headline tour that saw both bands hit the UK.

8.   While the album *Nevermind* got all the plaudits, _____'s first LP, *Bleach*— on which "School" appeared—was already a classic among the converted.

9.   The 1990 track "Retarded" by Greg Dulli's Cincinatti-based band the Afghan _____ gives an idea of what would happen if J Masics ever joined forces with Nirvana.

10. "Touch Me I'm Sick" by _____. If it ain't broke, don't fix it. When the blueprint is as perfect as this grunge-punk blast, you don't need to.

DOWN

1.   _____ _____ were the forefathers of the scene, comprising future members of Mudhoney and Pearl Jam. When this band re-formed for live gigs in 2008, it could legitimately be called a supergroup.

3.   The _____. Evan Dando's distorted, melodic offerings were far removed from the fuzz and the filth of grunge, but "Li'l Seed" from the 1990 LP *Lovey* is a standout tune.

5.   The future rock gods _____'s early sound included "Flower." Though polished, it still has that sense of urgency and abandon that was so abundant in the Seattle grunge scene.

6.   While some might go for the lighter, jauntier rock of "I Nearly Lost You," "Black Sun Morning" is darker, noisier, and grungier. _____ Trees.

7.   The Melvins were certainly hugely important in its development. The slow, punishing sludge groove of "_____," from their third album, *Bullhead,* owes more than a nod to the heavy riffs of Black Sabbath.

29. MOD MOVERS

Trying to pin down what constitutes a mod classic is like trying to swallow a hedgehog—a difficult and prickly issue. Go to a big mod event and you'll find vintage R&B and ska classics in one room and, next door, obscure 1960s psych unearthed by dedicated diggers. With that in mind, this is a puzzle with some unashamedly broad strokes.

ACROSS

4. Despite being ostensibly a pop band, the _____'s 1965 track "Til the End of the Day" has razor-sharp beats that marry the fuzz guitar perfectly to on-point harmonies.

5. "Wade in the _____" by Little Sonny. Given the number of versions of this spiritual song around, the claim that this is the best is a strong one, but the raw harmonica-led stomp has an energy that few can possibly match.

6. "Making Time" by the _____. Of all their songs, this 1967 release edged it for two reasons: one, you can actually dance to it; and two, as far as debut singles go, this is a brave and bold opening statement.

7. Paul _____. You know the actor? *Hair*? *Just Good Friends*? And "Run Shaker Life" is something of an unexpected delight—the B-side of his "Freedom City" single is built for dancing.

9. In just four years, the _____ _____ went from the urgent rhythm and blues of their wonderful debut, "Watcha Gonna Do About It," to the ambitious psychedelic steam train of their *Odgen's Nut Gone Flake* concept LP.

DOWN

1. _____ _____ is another R&B monster to make the list. "Can Your Monkey Do the Dog" came after "The Dog," "Walking the Dog," "Somebody Stole My Dog." The question is, why is he so obsessed with dogs?

2. The _____ member and ska legend Jackie Mittoo released the joyous, horn-led "Dr. Ring Ding" on the Studio One label.

3. _____ Edwards's "Keep on Running" is the original and still the best!

8. The _____ __ ___ & Sharon Tandy. The South African singer teamed up with the best blue-eyed soul band in town to record the single "Hold On."

10. Don Fardon's "I'm _____" was a hit in Holland when recently reissued, which goes to show the timeless quality of this cover of the Tommy James & the Shondells' tune.

30. GOTH GROOVES

It seemed for a while that goths had died a death. That's not unusual for goths—probably the makeup. Thankfully, rumors of their demise had been exaggerated, as had the notion that they sat in darkened rooms drinking snakebite and black and reading Victorian horror. Goths can (g)rave it up with the best of them.

ACROSS

3. _____ Dax. Does she count as goth? Yes, she does. The shuffling groove-led drums, jangling guitar, and punctuated bass of "Ostrich," the brilliant precursor to indie dance, are more than enough to decide.

4. Mission Tower of _____ released "Bombay Mix (John Paul Jones)" two years later. This remix (produced by Zeppelin's John Paul Jones) has a rhythmic chug that made it an end-of-night classic in some quarters.

6. _____ Manson's "Tainted Love" is as far removed from Gloria Jones's original as possible, with synths set to "sandblast" and drums to "punish."

8. The stuttering electronic effects in _____'s "Bela Lugosi's Dead" work in perfect harmony with the building treble of the guitars to create what is largely considered to be the first ever goth rock single, released in 1979.

9. "Lucretia My Reflection" by the Sisters of _____ was an instant hit on its 1988 release.

DOWN

1. Technically post-punk rather than goth, but "Bloodsport" by _____ ____ crosses over perfectly. The nearest thing to an all-out dance-floor track on this list, and a guaranteed floor filler in any number of clubs.

2. Before Ian Astbury and company discovered America, they used to be masters at anthemic and melodic goth-rock, as "She Sells _____" demonstrates.

5. "Head Like a Hole" is the go-to track on ____ ____ _____'s album *Pretty Hate Machine*, and there's no denying the powerful mix of electronic elements, rock posture, and extreme anger. Trent Reznor is very, very cross.

6. Before Al Jourgenson's outfit went all industrial and shouty, _____ were a synth-pop outfit, albeit one with dark and brooding lyrics.

7. "Fascination Street (Extended Mix)" by ___ ____ is notable for its four-minute-long instrumental passage before Robert Smith so much as opens his lipstick-smeared mouth.

31. NEW ROMANTIC CLUB HITS

Following the filth and fury of punk, a generation of kids scrubbed up, stuck on a bit of makeup, and decided that there was nothing wrong with a bit of glamour. All over the UK, clubs vibrated to a new kind of sound as bands took their lead from Bowie and Roxy music as well as the avant-garde art world.

ACROSS

2. The ethereal, unnerving introduction of "Ghosts" by _____, off final album *Tin Drum*, shows the band embracing an experimental approach.

3. "Fade to Grey" by _____. Steve Strange and Rust Egan were the people behind London's infamous Blitz Club where the scene was born, so it's no surprise that they should be behind one of the biggest records of the genre.

5. "Memorabilia" by ____ ____. This 1982 track, while not their most immediate, is almost purpose-built for clubs.

6. "Love Is the Drug" by ____ Music. Their flamboyant fashion and art-house pop inspired, rather than came directly from, the New Romantic scene.

7. Early on, Simple _____ had the look and the electronic Germanic sound that fitted the New Romantic label, epitomized in "I Travel (Extended mix)."

8. "Chant No.1" by _____ _____. This band of Blitz Club kids introduced the funk to the scene with this single off their second album.

9. Produced by krautrock legend Conny Plank, "Slow Motion" is a world away from _____'s later hits. With a guitar tone straight out of Neu!, it shows a different side to the New Romantic sound.

DOWN

1. _____ _____ was one of the artists who inspired the scene, and "Heroes" was something of an anthem at the Blitz Club. In fact, he turned up and hand-picked Steve Strange to be in the *Ashes to Ashes* video!

4. Following the departure of founding members Martyn Ware and Ian Marsh, Human League changed direction and became associated with the New Romantic scene. "Love _____" is pop perfection from the album *Dare*.

5. The most glamorous thing to come out of Birmingham for some time, _____ _____ assaulted the charts and the pop consciousness with tenacity. "Planet Earth" was their spot-on debut single.

32. SHOEGAZE SWAYERS

As the 1980s became the 1990s, many young UK bands stopped looking to the past or the future for their inspiration and focused on their shoes instead. In truth, this onstage, heads-down habit (which led to the term "shoegaze") was probably down to shyness, but it became a handy adjective for a whole new sound—ethereal, dreamy, and epic.

ACROSS

3. You could be forgiven for thinking that _____ were just another band capitalizing on the Madchester bandwagon. However, "Falling Down" from 1991 soon morphs into something altogether more interesting.

5. Leeds band ____ _____ came to the attention of the indie world with their 1989 EP *Barging into the Presence of God*, of which "Sight of You" is best.

7. Slowdive's biggest hit, "Catch the _____," listening is like being allowed to lie down in the comfiest bed ever.

8. Released on the pioneering shoegaze label Sonic Cathedral, "What's Holding You?" from Lorelle Meets the _____'s third album, *Chambers*, is a thrilling and vital record.

9. "____" by My Bloody Valentine, from the album *Loveless*, has perhaps proved to be their most influential, not least due to the astonishing remix from Andrew Weatherall.

10. Ulrich _____'s 2001 track, "Wherever You Are," highlights the very best of the producer's unique tone and touch.

DOWN

1. Without doubt Ride is one of the most important bands of the shoegaze scene. Their first four EPs were absolutely essential. "_____ Trail," from the album *Nowhere,* takes a softer approach, but is no less impactful.

2. "_____" was re-recorded with the trademark chorus overdrive of Cocteau Twins' Robin Guthrie; it's the untreated version from Lush's debut mini LP, *Scar*, that holds the real treats.

4. East London band the _____ _____ manage to combine a krautrock influence with dreamy, textured guitars in "Fallen Star."

6. Released in 2011, the album *Perfect Life* added a dash of the Cure to create something new for _____, comprising U.S. duo Turk Dietrich and Michael.

33. CHILL-OUT TUNES

Whether on terrace bars, as the day's embers slowly fade, in rooms in which to escape the frantic pace of a club, or simply sound-tracking falling energy levels in a sitting room at dawn, there's always a place for chill-out tunes. This puzzle comprises a mixture of single tracks and albums because sometimes it's too much trouble to get off the sofa.

ACROSS

1. "Up With People (Zero 7 remix)" by _____. Production duo Zero 7 built layer upon beautiful layer around Kurt Wagner's voice to create something even better than the original.

5. At Britpop's height, Mark Pritchard and Tom Middleton, a.k.a. _____ Communication, released one hour, sixteen minutes, and fourteen seconds of blissful, shimmering joy in *76:14*.

7. The _____ ____ is a singular talent, and if the dates of *Selected Ambient Works 85-92* (LP) are accurate, it suggests that Richard D. James created some of its haunting masterpieces at the tender age of fourteen.

8. *Chill Out* (LP). When Bill Drummond and Jimmy Cauty from ___ ___ chill out, they really chill out.

9. Taking the Art of _____'s songs and stitching them together with sounds and spoken word was a stroke of genius and instantly made *The Ambient Collection* something much better than just a compilation album.

DOWN

2. It's difficult to know what to pick from Jason Swinscoe's project-turned-fully fledged band, the _____ Orchestra. However, "Channel 1 Suite," off their first album, *Motion*, wins for being the most like a big hug.

3. Featured on the *Super Discount* compilation, "_____ (EDC Remix)" manages to take a track by French duo Air and "calm it down a bit."

4. A sampled jazz drum loop, a simple piano line, some synth pads, and an upright bass are the main ingredients in "Existence," by Bugge _____.

6. The listener goes on a ride past planets and through space in the self-titled LP, an aural journey through the solar system by _____.

8. ___ ___'s classic of the genre, "Little Fluffy Clouds," isn't actually that chilled out. At 105 bpm, that it still manages to feel so relaxing is down to some wonderful production and the drawling tones of Rickie Lee Jones.

34. BRITPOP

In reaction to the plaid shirts of grunge, British bands pulled on a Fred Perry, rediscovered the Kinks songbook, and set about creating something far removed from the American carnation. Looking back—not in anger, of course—which ones have proved the most enduring tunes of the time?

ACROSS

2. Brett Anderson with Bernard Butler and _____ brought something new to the pop party with androgynous imagery, and the wonderful theatrics of their debut album, from which "Animal Nitrate" was the best track.

5. The Bluetones were no copyists. Theirs was a much more classic sound than many of their peers, yet "Slight _____" seemed to catch the zeitgeist.

6. "_____ (. . .And Me)" by the Boo Radleys. The ambition of their *Giant Steps* album is staggering, and this upbeat track is an understated gem.

7. "_____ __" by Elastica borrows heavily from the Stranglers' "No More Heroes" but does so with class and sharp intelligence.

9. Oxford band _____ had already turned heads with "Creep," but "Just," from their 1995 album *The Bends*, is the one that makes this list.

DOWN

1. "_____ Symphony," from the Verve's *Urban Hymns* album, has a Stones sample borrowed from Andrew Loog Oldham and a video homage to Massive Attack's "Unfinished Symphony."

3. "Caught by the Fuzz" by _____. The short fuzzy blast of singer Gaz Coombe's brush with the law is celebratory, fun, and energetic.

4. For many people, "_____ _____" by Pulp is the defining Britpop anthem. It manages to rhyme "thirst for knowledge" with "St. Martin's College"—a feat that should win a medal on its own.

6. Forget "Parklife." "Popscene," released in 1992, was where it all started for _____.

8. There's no shortage of sing-alongs in _____'s back catalog, but in "Live Forever," there's no simile, no subtlety, just a life-affirming classic with tears of joy in its eyes.

35. GREAT NIGHTS

The musician and—these days—the D.J. are habitually nocturnal creatures, coming into their own when nearly everything else is being tucked up in bed. Nighttime is when all the good stuff happens, but what are the best soundtracks for a night of wining and dining or dancing and prancing? We've given it some thought and come up with the following.

ACROSS

1. Not known for subtext in their lyrics, what __/__ are known for is good-time, blues-based rock 'n' roll, and "You Shook Me All Night Long"—the first to feature Brian Johnson—is no exception.

3. Far from being the band's finest moment, "_____ _____" by the Bee Gees is fun, frivolous, and familiar—perfect fodder for a night on the town.

5. "Give Me the Night" by George _____. If George wants the night, it seems a fair exchange for this smooth slice of disco funk.

7. Off the *Goodbye Yellow Brick Road* album, "Saturday Night's Alright (For Fighting)" was a big departure for _____ ____ at the time, and a much harder sound.

9. "Boogie nights are always the best in town!"_____ may well have a point with their 1982 classic "Boogie Nights." This up-tempo, pop disco hit is guaranteed to get people dancing.

10. In "Night _____," the disco-funk instrumental by Deodato, the feeling is one of driving home at the end of the night with the roof down, feeling warm air on your face.

DOWN

2. As the stuttering bass intro makes room for the backbeat and waka-waka guitar, you know that "Saturday night" is going to be all right courtesy of T-_____.

4. "Let's Spend the Night Together" by the _____ _____. While the Beatles wanted to "hold your hand," this plea to a young lady from Mick Jagger has all the subtlety of a house brick.

6. An ode to the disc jockey, the hit "Last Night a D.J. Saved My Life" by _____ presents the D.J. as an almost superhuman figure.

8. "All Night Long" by _____ Richie. There's no such thing as a guilty pleasure—either you like something or you don't!

36. CLUBS

What is it that makes a great club? Obviously, there's the music—the D.J.s—and the location . . . plus the crowd, you need a good audience. When all of these things come together, it can create something special and unique that's much greater than the sum of its parts. While not exhaustive—the world's just too big—here are ten of the best.

ACROSS

4.   Berlin has long been a destination for the discerning clubber and _____ is considered by many to be the best techno club in the world.

6.   _____ of Sound. While many are turned off by the big-business, mass-marketing sheen of the UK's best-known club, there's no doubting its influence and significance.

7.   The inspiration for the Chic song "Le Freak," after Nile Rogers and company fell foul of the N.Y.C. club's stringent door policy. Possibly the most famous nightclub of all time, celebrity is the common currency at _____ 54.

8.   Chicago club the _____ boasted Frankie Knuckles as its resident D.J. and musical director, who pioneered a style that became known as "house."

10. Sometimes a club just captures a moment in time perfectly. So it is with the 1980s and _____ in Ibiza. With D.J. Alfredo, the mix of European pop, funk, and disco was to launch Balearic Beat.

DOWN

1.   Pioneering a not-for-profit model in the 1970s that many modern clubs would do well to emulate, for David Mancuso the party was all at ___ ____.

2.   Unable to forget their experience in Ibiza, a group of British D.J.s came back to England where one of them, Danny Rampling, opened up _____ in 1987 on London's Southwark Street.

3.   Known by many as the home of Northern Soul, the huge club _____ Casino had legendary all-nighters.

5.   The nights—with the focus on Larry Levan's legendary D.J. sets—were dedicated to dancing and hedonism at _____ Garage.

9.   _____, the only club on the list with a catalog number, Factory Records' folly was one of the most important clubs in England when the burgeoning house scene was breaking.

37. FUNK FLOOR FILLERS

If ever there was a music so perfectly engineered for making people move, it's the funk. So insistent is its command that you dance, it's a bit like having a well-meaning but slightly pushy friend urging you ever nearer the dance floor where, before you know it, you're having the time of your life. Here are ten to get up to get down to . . .

ACROSS

2. Even if you don't know "Super Freak" by _____ _____, you do know it. It's instantly identifiable as the main hook from MC Hammer's 1990 hit "U Can't Touch This."

5. George Clinton's collective created a sound and a universe all their own in _____'s "Standing on the Verge of Getting It On."

6. His falsetto and inimitable, pioneering style are enough to set him apart from the pack, but writing songs as consistently good as "Super Fly" elevates _____ Mayfield to another level entirely.

7. "Kool Is Back" is a 1971 cover of "Kool's Back Again," but this version manages to be rawer, tighter, and bigger. Bobby Watley's ____ ___ found the funk and proceeded to keep it on a very tight leash.

9. In "I Need More Time," just as the bass notes tail off, the _____ resolve the tension with a funk groove so deep, it's virtually molten.

10. "Are you ready? Yeah!"—the introduction to _____ ___'s loose-yet-tight funk jam "Hook and Sling Parts 1 & 2" could not be more perfect. It's based around a simple refrain and played with expertise and style.

DOWN

1. Sly Stone and his band embraced rock without sacrificing the funk. The gritty, gnarly edges that they left unpolished in "_____ ___ (Falettinme Be Mice Elf Agin)" make for thrilling listening.

3. While in the studio with Tonto's Expanding Headband, Stevie Wonder expanded his mind to produce the best work of his career in "_____."

4. Of the Godfather's many genre-defining classics, "Hot _____," an ode to the female wardrobe, is the one that features.

8. Recorded after the _____ Brothers had left the tight grip of Berry Gordy's Motown label, "It's Your Thing" was a response to their former boss. A slick and a multi-layered sound full of raw power and energy.

38. DISCO DANCE-FLOOR BOMBS

The "Disco Sucks" campaign waged by D.J. Steve Dahl in 1979 successfully whipped up enough prejudice to ensure that thousands of records were destroyed—including a mass burning at a Chicago White Sox baseball game. Now, this most joyous of genres is seen as the genuine antecedent of modern dance music and is spoken about with hushed reverence.

ACROSS

5. Abandoning his trademark lush, orchestrated sound, French drummer and composer Cerrone used electronics to give him the futuristic sound in "_____," a track about mutant creatures rising up against mankind.

8. _____ L's "Go Bang (Francois K mix)" is a forward-looking spaced-out disco classic. The remix from Francois Kervorkian saw it become a crowd favorite at the Paradise Garage.

10. A Brit-jazz funk anthem, the underground track "Dancing in Outer Space" by _____ is as powerful today as ever.

DOWN

1. There aren't a huge number of "message songs" in the disco canon, but this gem, "There but for the Grace of God" from Jay Stovall's disco funk outfit, _____ is a stern cautionary tale about the dangers of leaving the city.

2. Loleatta_____'s 1980's hit "Love Sensation" is disco gold, and is instantly recognizable for the "because you're right on time" line taken by cloth-eared Italian house merchants Black Box for their single "Ride on Time."

3. Composer and cellist Arthur Russell was a unique and awe-inspiring talent. On "Is It All Over My Face? (Male Version)" by _____ _____, legend has it, he chose to record during a full moon to get "the energy levels right."

4. "_ ____ ____" by Donna Summer. Over Giorgio Moroder's synth backing, Donna sang her way into disco history with this visionary track.

6. Which song to choose by ____? "Le Freak" has the better story, true, but "Good Times" wins out on account of that immortal bassline.

7. Vincent Montana Jr.'s _____ orchestra got the balance just right in "You're Just the Right Size."

9. Canadian producer Gino Soccio scored a huge hit on U.S. dance charts when "_____" was released in 1979. The big sound was the result of just one man, lots of synths, and editing techniques on a limited budget.

39. JAZZ FINDS THE FUNK

Jazz-funk—basically fusion dressed up to the nines and on the lookout for a good party—is what happens when jazz musicians lock into a groove. Giving the 1970s a great big smile on its face, there's a joy to these songs that sees even those people who claim to hate jazz nodding their head and shuffling their shoes.

ACROSS

2. Precise funk is neatly joined to a smoother groove by a bridge of drums and bass to give the listener fifteen minutes of bliss in "_____," from Herbie Hancock's *Head Hunters* album.

3. Taken from the landmark *What's Going On,* Marvin Gaye managed to soundtrack desolation and despair with a plangent beauty in "_____ ____ Blues." He also managed to sneak in an understated bassline.

4. With the Mizell brothers, Larry and Fonce, on playing and production duties, _____ ____ was off to a good start. There's a string-led, cinematic feel to "Fallin' Like Dominoes," full of soaring ambition . . . and trumpets.

6. ___ Ayers has written more than his fair share of tunes that just have it, and "Running Away" is a 1979 example straight from the top drawer.

8. Given the uncanny similarity with Jamiroquoi's "Emergency on Planet Earth" to "Los Conquistadores Chocolates," Johnny _____ must be feeling very flattered indeed.

10. Has a triangle ever played a more significant part in a song? The unmistakable opening of "_____" by Lonnie Liston Smith sets the tone before the bass, drums, or keys have even had a chance to shine.

DOWN

1. Listening to the beginning of the track "Temse" by Marc Moulin and _____, it feels as if you've wandered into the middle of something, with a backing of unrelenting, unresolved tension.

5. The Ramsey Lewis Trio's version of the War song "Slippin' into _____" takes the tight funk of the original and proceeds to spread out the chords.

7. In "Sookie Sookie" from the Blue Note album *Alive!,* the jazz guitarist Grant _____'s funk offering is instantly recognizable.

9. "Yegelle Tezeta" by _____. It's jazz, it's funky, and it's sublime. The Egyptian maestro's recent work with the Heliocentrics is well worth hunting down.

40. THE PHILLY SOUND

Born and raised in Philidelphia . . . and that's thankfully where the similarities to *The Fresh Prince of Bel-Air* end. The lush, orchestrated funk and extended arrangements of Philly soul were really disco by another name, and the Philadelphia International label, set up by Kenneth Gamble and Leon Huff to showcase this sound, deserves to be as well known as Motown or Stax.

ACROSS

4. The 1975 single "Do It Any Way You Wanna" was an enormous hit for _____ _____—with bass, piano, synth, and at least two guitars playing the same part, it almost instantly locks onto a forceful groove.

5. "Heavy Vibes" by _____ Sextet. By taking the best bit of MSFB's "Love Is the Message" and spreading it out for more than five minutes, Vincent Montana Jr. created something that was more than the sum of its parts.

6. The title track from the *Going East* album, "____," finds Billy Paul in a contemplative, almost philosophical mood.

8. After leaving Motown, the _____ decided to take refuge under the welcoming wing of Philadelphia International. The understated number "Show You the Way to Go" was one of the good things to come of it.

10. "____ _____," a cautionary tale about trusting your fellow man, was the title track of the O'Jays' 1972 album and exhibits a slower, more plaintive sound than usual.

DOWN

1. Apparently a slight dig at the heavy guiding hands of Gamble and Huff, "Ain't No Stopping Us Now" by McFadden & _____ is classic Philly.

2. "The ____ I Lost" by Harold Melvin & the Bluenotes. The rich emotion of Harold Melvin's voice covers this track like tears on a cheek.

3. The backing band of choice for stars including Loleatte Holloway and Curtis Mayfield, _____ ____ could do it on their own too. "Got My Mind Made Up" boasts a majestic remix from Larry Levan.

7. "TSOP (The Sound of Philadelphia)" by ____, featuring the voices of the Three Degrees, was the theme to the TV show *Soul Train*.

9. "I Love Music" by The _'____. The band sings this with the sort of conviction that make you think it's a political manifesto rather than a song.

41. LESSER-KNOWN MOTOWN MOMENTS

With an output as great as Motown's, there are bound to be a few tunes that slip under most people's radar. In fact, there are hundreds. While the public, quite rightly, were dancing to the beat of Stevie Wonder, Diana Ross, the Temptations, and the Four Tops, records were still being released at an industrial rate. Here are ten lesser-known gems.

ACROSS

1. The Morse code piano intro in "S.O.S. (Stop Her on Sight)" by _____ _____ gives way to a Motown dancer that screams "Northern Soul."

3. "Finders Keepers, Losers Weepers" by the _____ is a beautifully crafted pop stomper recorded in 1964 but, criminally, didn't get a release until 1980 with Kim Weston's "Do Like I Do" on the flip.

6. Motown does rock 'n' roll? The B-side to the _____'s song "Greetings (This Is Uncle Sam)," the song "Number One in Your Heart" had everything it needed to be a hit. If only they'd stuck it on the A-side.

7. Smokey Robinson's song "Beat Me to the _____" is better known than some here, mainly due to it earning Mary Wells a Grammy nomination.

9. _____'s "Brick House"—recorded in 1977—sounds about as much like classic Motown as it does death metal.

DOWN

2. Far from sinking without trace on its release, "Heaven Must Have Sent You" by ___ _____ is a sweet and naive love song in the best tradition and has more than a little in common with "Baby Love."

4. With the unmistakable Motown production, it's tempting to wonder why "I Got a Feeling" wasn't a hit—particularly when Barbara _____ was considered big enough by the label to share the stage with Marvin Gaye.

5. The B-side to Terry _____'s single "Whatcha Gonna Do" on Gordy records, "Suzie" has a melody that's not unlike Franki Valli's best moments.

7. Notable as the only Supremes single on which Florence Ballard took lead duties, "Buttered _____" was beset by problems after its release—not least the shock discovery of a double entendre in the song's title.

8. The Velvelettes' "Let Love ____ (A Little Bit Longer)" was a track destined for Motown's V.I.P. label that didn't quite make it.

42. NORTHERN SOUL

Controversial? Perhaps. Difficult? Just a bit. To come up with a list for a musical genre that is obsessed with rarity, quality, and musical archaeology is a daunting task and one to be greatly sweated over. Thankfully, towels and talc were in plentiful supply to combat the perspiration while compiling the following puzzle.

ACROSS

4. In "__. ____," Bobby Sheen has an answer for broken hearts everywhere with his "Ph.D. in Loveology."

6. "Music to My Heart" by _____ _____. The Motown sound is stamped all over this 1968 B-side slice of pop perfection (released on the ABC label).

8. That Jimmy Radcliffe's voice manages to be heard over the clatter and drums of "_____" by the Steve Karmen Big Band is a feat in itself.

9. _____ ____'s "Out on the Floor" was a hit almost ten years after it was recorded, and even the most cursory of listens is enough to tell you why this was a hit in the clubs of Northern England.

10. Although Soft Cell made this their own, the original of "_____ ____" by Gloria Jones remains supreme.

DOWN

1. Notorious for its rarity—there are thought to be only two copies of this Motown single left in existence, worth nearly $36,000 each—it's best to forget the price and concentrate on the music when listening to Frank _____'s "Do I Love You (Indeed I Do)!"

2. "The _____" is exactly the sort of song that Tom Jones would have massively oversung, but Al Wilson focuses on storytelling and emotion.

3. "Twinkle Little Star" is a world away from the delicate shimmer that the title might suggest. This tune by the _____ gives a slap around the face in its bid to remind you how utterly, immediately affecting and all-consuming music can be.

5. Far from being a forceful shift of earth, "Landslide" by Tony _____ is all about persuasion, and within two and a half minutes the argument is won.

7. "___ _____" by Frankie Valli. Along with "Beggin'," this has to be Frankie's best moment ever committed to vinyl.

43. ELECTRONIC PIONEERS

There are always those in music whose inquisitive nature goes beyond writing a great tune and, instead, takes a step back to consider before taking a closer look at what's going on. The following people weren't content to simply harness the potential of technology—they wanted to test its breaking point and see what was beyond.

ACROSS

3.   Giorgio _____'s arpeggiated synth lines became the defining sound of disco, yet when he first recorded them, it was almost unthinkable that a popular dance tune should be made entirely using machines.

7.   After growing out of the burgeoning krautrock scene, Edgar Froese's band, _____ Dream, became forerunners in electronic music development.

9.   Although recorded fifty years ago, _____ Subotnick's "Silver Apples of the Moon" is seen as a precursor of modern techno and remains light-years ahead of its time.

10. One of the founders of the B.B.C. Radiophonic Workshop, _____ Oram's vision wasn't content with simply producing music, she built the "Oramics" machine, which, in the mid-1960s, could convert drawn symbols into music.

DOWN

1.   After a beginning based in free-form rock, the strict, sparse, and more disciplined _____ sound that was to become their trademark saw the band abandon traditional instruments in 1974 with "Autobahn."

2.   A musician, composer, and producer who puts theory over practice. _____'s series of groundbreaking ambient albums (such as "Before and After Science") have proved an inspiration.

4.   Jean-Michelle _____ scored a hit with "Oxygene (Part IV)," a tune recorded in a home studio—far removed from the big gigs that he ended up playing.

5.   In his short life, _____ _____ recorded some of the most innovative dance music ever produced—albums like 1981's *Megatron Man*.

6.   Best known for putting the musical flesh onto Ron Grainer's score for *Doctor Who*, Delia _____ was also one third of White Noise.

8.   Italian jazz keyboardist Alexander _____, a.k.a. Maurizio Dami, is a legend for fans of analog synth music everywhere.

44. ELECTRO

As the disco beat faded into the background, several new forms of funk-infused music came to the fore as producers looked for new inspiration. Like the techno scene that was to follow, many of these music makers latched onto sounds coming from Europe and created something heavier, weirder, and not unlike a disco populated and staffed entirely by robots.

ACROSS

2.   "We Are the _____ _____." Relying on the live playing of synthesizers rather than the programmed approach favored by many of their peers, there was a looser, more human feel to much of the band's *Lost in Space* album.

7.   The instrumental track "The Smurf" was _____ Brunson's only one to make an impact, with its percussion, which has been sampled to death.

8.   It's difficult to imagine electro without Kraftwerk. "The _____," off their *Man Machine* LP, is like the perfect distillation of all the requisite elements.

9.   "Rock It" was one of the first tracks to feature recorded scratching courtesy of Grand Mixer DXT. It was a brave and inspiring move for jazz musician _____ _____.

10.   The strings in _____'s 1983 masterpiece "Al Naafiysh (The Soul)" sounds uncannily similar to Duran Duran's "New Religion" recorded a year earlier.

DOWN

1.   "Moskow Disco" by ____. Marc Moulin's electronic outfit were another influential electro act. The computerized voices, train-like percussion, and cold synth lines picked up passengers around the world.

3.   The brainchild of Juan Atkins and Richard Davis, "Clear" by _____ is seen as a clear forerunner to the later, techno sound.

4.   Taking its core melody from Kraftwerk's "Trans-Europe Express," while a synth plays an Ennio Morricone refrain over a Roland TR-808 beat, _____ ____ by Afrika Bambaataa & the Soul Sonic Force is revolutionary.

5.   Reference to the 1982 classic "Hip Hop Be Bop Don't Stop" in the black comedy horror *Shaun of the Dead* left audiences in no doubt that this ___ _____ track is not hip-hop but electro.

6.   While West Street MOB's use of the Incredible Bongo Band's Apache gifts the single "_____ _____—Electric Boogie" a traditional hip-hop feel, a robot barking instructions on how to break-dance puts it firmly in electro territory.

45. HIP-HOP'S DEF JAMS

Hip-hop is all about reputation, and they don't come much bigger than Def Jam's. Formed by producer Rick Rubin and Russell Simmons (brother of Run DMC's Rev Run), the record label was one of the first to successfully stamp its size-nine shoe all over popular culture and has since gained near-mythical status. This puzzle aims to show why.

ACROSS

5. *The Great Adventures of* _____ ____ (LP). Having set the pace on "La Di Da Di," the B-side to Doug E. Fresh's "The Show," this 1988 debut shows why _____ ____ is one of the most influential M.C.s of all time.

6. Having signed to Def Jam for their third LP, the New York duo _._._._. lost none of their trademark funk or sample soundscapes and the album opener, "Brothers on My Jock," is no exception.

7. During the 1990s, the label continued the quality control with releases like "Bring the Pain" from the Wu-Tang Clan man, _____ ___. The track's haunting backdrop is courtesy of an inspired sample from Jerry Butler's "I'm Your Mechanical Man."

8. To parents, teachers, and owners of Volkswagens, the Beastie Boys were an affront to common decency. To their fans, they were the best thing to happen to music in years, as in "No Sleep til _____."

10. The album *Fishscale* was heralded as a return to form for Ghostface Killah, and "The _____" had heads nodding in agreement.

DOWN

1. It's hard to think of a hip-hop act with a bigger musical impact than _____ _____. "Rebel Without a Pause," the first single from their *It Takes a Nation of Millions to Hold Us Back* album, could reanimate the dead.

2. Funny, intelligent, and possessed of an almost superhuman talent for creating grooves, 3rd ____ were the perfect fit for Def Jam in the late 1980s.

3. "___ ___ Is Dead" by Nas. Disproving his own declaration from the off, Nas is lyrically inventive.

4. Part song, part crazed instruction manual, "How to Roll a Blunt" by _____ is funny, irreverent, and funky as hell.

9. Def Jam scored a hit with _._. _____ _.'s debut album and pioneered a new sound in hip-hop, which is perhaps best realized on "Rock the Bells."

46. FOUNDATIONS OF GOOD HOUSE

Built upon a solid layer of disco, electro funk, Italo, and electronic pop, house music's pulsing 4/4 beat has proved a more lasting structure than many might have expected and has influenced the musical landscape in a profound way. This puzzle looks at some of the architects of that sound with a couple of personal favorites thrown in for good measure.

ACROSS

2. "Muzik Xpress" by _____ 2. British producers came up with their own take on house, including Rocky, Diesel, and Ashley Beadle's 1992 release.

4. Feeling down? Don't worry, as this collaborative effort by _____ ____ and Paris Brightledge never tires of telling us, "It's All Right."

6. More like second-generation house, Pepe Bradock's 1999 release "____ _____" is a warm, enveloping cuddle of a track.

7. "Your Love" by Jamie _____. Often credited to Frankie Knuckles, the collaboration between the producer and the musician was to lead to other great tracks, including "Baby Wants to Ride."

8. A sublime bassline perfectly wrapped in sweeping sheets of synthesizer, with a spoken word history of house make "Can U Feel It?" by Larry Heard, a.k.a. __. _____ a lesson in more ways than one.

9. Though acid house originated in the U.S., you won't find many better examples of the form than "Northern Lights (Prime Kutz mix)," from British producer Crispin J. _____.

10. 1984 saw the release of "__ ___ __," what many believe to be the world's first house record. Using a loop from Mach's disco re-edit, Jesse Saunders created something that proved pivotal in the building of a whole new genre.

DOWN

1. Purported to be the first use of piano on a house record, "Move Your Body" by _____ Jefferson sounds so current it's amazing it came out in 1986.

3. To some, "Acid Tracks" sounded like a computer game gone into spasm, to others, it remains a welcome revolution. _____ played the Roland 303 like it was being punished.

5. Such is the sheer melodic force of the bassline, it's as if Glenn _____ took all the notes in existence and put them into the single "Sound Struck."

47. THE SYNTH-POP REVOLUTION

A bloodless coup, the march of the machines into the British charts during the 1980s was not without controversy. Accused by some embittered souls of lacking in creativity, ability, and emotion, it not only stood its ground, but set about annexing great swathes of Chartland and influencing pretty much everything that came after. That's a victory in anyone's book.

ACROSS

3. Forget "Vienna," _____'s earlier releases are phenomenal examples of what happens when you take a new wave band with ambition and flair and put them in a room with one of the best krautrock producers in the world.

4. A string of phenomenal pop singles would be enough to secure _____'s position on this list, but it's to songs like "The Game Above My Head" we must turn for a glimpse of their true genius.

7. Who'd have thought that _____ Mode, a bunch of boys from Essex, UK, could create perfect pop to capture the imagination of a generation?

9. As part of Tubeway Army, ____ _____ was one of the first to achieve success with the synth-pop sound. Something he capitalized on later with "Cars."

10. ____ ____'s first album, *Non-Stop Erotic Cabaret*, could not have been better titled. Marc Almond was always an accomplished cabaret singer.

DOWN

1. After the death of singer Ian Curtis, it would have been understandable for the rest of Joy Division to call it a day. Instead, they formed ___ ____, and became one of the most innovative bands in the world.

2. After the original band split, singer Phil Oakey hired singers Anne Sulley and Joanne Catherill and then turned to veteran producer Martin Rushent to create the _____ _____.

5. Behind the hits, there are breathtaking examples of experimental synth-pop genius from Annie Lennox and Dave Stewart as _____.

6. The ___ ____ Boys' debut, "West End Girls," fused pop songwriting sass with synth savvy.

8. Formed after Martyn Ware and Ian Marsh left Phil Oakey's band, _____17 responded to their former band's chart success by producing a contender for the best album of the 1980s in *Penthouse and Pavement*.

48. TOWERING TECHNO

Detroit's starker, more futuristic take on dance music took its cue in equal measure from the science-fiction funk of Funkadelic, European bands like Kraftwerk, and the city's automobile industry. The resulting metal machine music has proved just as lasting as its Chicago-based, disco-dipped cousin and every bit as influential.

ACROSS

3. Conceived by Mike Banks of Underground Resistance, the 1993 release "Journey of the _____" by Galaxy 2 Galaxy, has an altogether different feel to much of what had gone before.

6. _____ may be famous for the shouty stomp of "Born Slippy," but the disorientating shifting vocals of "Cowgirl" is far more interesting.

7. "_____ of Life" by Rhythim Is Rhythim is claimed as a classic by both the techno and house camps.

9. In _-_____'s "Banjo (Funk D'Void mix)," Kevin Saunderson gets a makeover courtesy of Funk D'Void, a.k.a. Lars Sandberg, in this belter.

10. "The Climax" by _____ _____. Carl Craig is an anomaly: people just aren't supposed to be as consistent—or make it sound as effortless as in the raw disco finish of this anthem.

DOWN

1. Unable to license "Jaguar" from Underground Resistance man the ____ _____, Sony tried to release a tone-by-tone copy onto the market, and started a fight they couldn't win.

2. "No _._._.'s," Juan Atkins's first single under the Model 500 moniker, was a calling card that was stark, uncompromising, and full of surprises.

4. The 1981 release "_____ of Your Mind" from Juan Atkins and Richard Davis's Cybotron proves that the line separating electro from techno is as thin as the one differentiating soup from stew.

5. "_____" by A Number of Names has the kick drum, the trembling, mesmerizing bass, a tough snare shackled to reverbed handclaps!

8. In ___ _____'s "Altered States," there's no buildup, no easy in, just bam! Pounding drums softened slightly by faint bells with the pendulum swing of the main melodic motif.

49. POST-PUNK

After the angry assault of punk's stripped-down, back-to-basics approach, post-punk started layering sounds back onto the palette. The ambition in doing so was huge and wide-ranging, but the most welcome development was the renewed interest in making music that you could dance to, leading us to ask, "Who were the most successful movers on the scene?"

ACROSS

3. Asked by his mother, on her deathbed, to write a disco song for her funeral, John Lydon of Public Image Ltd. came up with the song "_____ _____."

6. Given his fascination with Afrobeat, it's fair to assume it was producer Brian Eno who helped bring the African influence to the Talking Heads party in tracks like "Born Under _____."

8. There's not a trace of electronics in "Damaged Goods," or funk—just drums, voice, scratchy guitar, and a hyperactive bassline. Yet this post-punk delight from Leeds band _____ ___ _____ demands that you move to it.

9. Quite what Swiss musicians Boris Blank and Carlos Peron saw in billionaire Dieter Meier when looking for a singer is unclear, but the mix was perfect, as is the single "I Love You" off _____'s third album.

10. Recently rediscovered, remixed, and re-released, the 1979 original "High _____ Days" from the U.S. synth-punks the Units is still the best.

DOWN

1. The breathtaking cover of Sly and the Family Stone's "Thank You (Falettinme Be Mice Elf Agin)" by _____ goes into almost cinematic territory.

2. "My Spine Is the Bassline" by _____. When XTC's Barry Andrews got together with former Gang of Four member Dave Allen, they soon found themselves with a serious post-punk band.

4. Boasting an impressive arsenal of styles, from free jazz improvisation to odd electro and off-kilter krautrock, Glaxo Babies were hard to pin down, and "Shake the _____" is a good example.

5. "Dead Eyes Opened" saw the Australian band _____ _____ marry industrial beats, pulsating bass, and floating strings with a spoken word narrative detailing the 1924 murder of a pregnant woman.

7. The Sheffield band Cabaret _____'s conscious decision to write hits resulted in the sensational single "Sensoria," from the album *Micro-Phonies*.

50. INDIE DANCE

The broad appeal and cultural shift that acid house brought with it soon trickled down and permeated other areas of music too. Not content to stand in the corner any longer, a generation of shy, retiring, guitar-loving indie kids suddenly found themselves in bell-bottoms and gaudy hoodies and dancing to the beat of a different drum. Indie dance was born.

ACROSS

2. Spacemen 3 are associated more with passing out than dancing, yet drone-rock was married to an undulating acid line to great effect on "___ ____."

6. Before the Doc Martens and dustups with Oasis, ____ had a baggier beat to their drum, as on their second single, "There's No Other Way."

7. After Creation Records spent all their money on recording _._._.'s second album, it must have been some solace that *Loveless* contained "Soon."

9. Petrol Emotion's "_____ (Boys Own Mix)" saw Andrew Weatherall on remix duties, joined by Terry Farley for a radical rework.

10. With a bassline inspired by Flea's contribution to Young MC's "Know How," the single "_____ ____" abandoned the 1960s shimmer of the the Stone Roses' debut LP and got kids with fringes everywhere dancing.

DOWN

1. Most of _____ _____'s Mercury prize-winning LP *Screamedelica* could have made this list, but it's Andrew Weatherall's "Loaded" to which we turn.

3. The _____'s 1990 single "The Only One I Know" had the Hammond swirls and loose, groove-inflected drums that came to typify indie dance.

4. _____ _____ are one of the best indie dance bands ever to pick up a guitar and stumble onstage, and the 1989 track "WFL (Vince Clark remix)" had more authority than any before or since.

5. To many, Flowered Up were to London what the Happy Mondays were to Manchester, best captured on the 13-minute-long epic "_____," which also boasted an epoch-defining video.

8. In "Big (Baka)," D.J. and producer John Dasliva stuck Manchester band New Fast Automatic _____'s vocal line over the top of an acid house tune—resulting in musical alchemy.

51. ROCK COMES TO THE DISCO

Despite concern from some quarters, rock wasn't impervious to the dance-floor influence—it was, after all, a huge and very profitable market. Inevitably, when the disco rainbow was mixed with the primary colors of rock, a new hue was created, one that, at certain times, proved to be positively luminous. Here are ten that shine like stars.

ACROSS

3. Supertramp's "_____" has a simple piano refrain, and a beat and bassline so tight they sound like they're handcuffed together.

7. Having been through as many styles as most bands have outfits, the Bee Gees took to dance with characteristic aplomb, as is superbly demonstrated by "____ _____."

8. "_____ _____" was used as the sample source for Kenny Gonzalez's 1995 house smash "The Bomb," the truly surprising thing is how little he had to do to this 1979 single by U.S. rock stalwarts Chicago.

9. Early demos of "_____ __ _____" listed it as "The Disco Song"—something of an oddity for Blondie—at the forefront of New York's new wave scene.

10. Apparently, "____ ___" is the result of a jam session with session player and right-hand man Billy Preston. The Rolling Stones struck gold when they turned their hand to disco on the album *Some Girls*.

DOWN

1. "Another _____ __ ___ ____ (Part II)" by Pink Floyd. With attention generally focusing on the double negative of the uneducated children's choir, the band sneaked a perfectly formed disco delight under the radar.

2. "The Sharif don't like it," sang the Clash on their biggest hit, "Rock the _____." We can only assume then, that the Sharif wouldn't appreciate the sublime boogie of this punk-funk classic if it came with a name badge.

4. Lennon was carrying a tape of "Walking on ____ ___" on the fateful day he was shot. It shows a radical, exciting change of direction for Yoko Ono.

5. From psych-rock to delirious disco, the career of French band Martin Circus was wide-ranging. The disco track "Disco _____" from 1979 is a must.

6. Unsurprisingly, given the prominence of the bassline, "Another One _____ ___ ____" by Queen was written by John Deacon.

52. SOUND SYSTEMS

On the island of Jamaica in the 1950s, a musical movement was to send shock waves around the world—and not just because of the bass levels. The rise of the sound system was a social revolution, as D.J.s and selectors loaded up vans with turntables and speakers big enough to have their own gravitational field and took the party to the people.

ACROSS

2.   One of "the big three," King Edwards the _____ was formed after a trip to America in 1954, when his brother Vincent brought back some 45s.

5.   Running his roots sound system since the 1970s in South East London, ___ _____, a.k.a Zulu Warrior, is a musician, composer, and record label owner.

7.   Clement Seymour Dodd was nicknamed Sir Coxsone _____ after the Yorkshire cricketer Alex Coxon. The name stuck for his sound system.

8.   Duke Reid's the _____. Named after the trucks they used to transport the system to dance halls around Jamaica, this 1950s system comprised large speakers, a record-playing deck, and a powerful amplifier.

9.   Lewisham, London, might not seem like the obvious birthplace of an internationally renowned sound system, but in 1976 that's exactly what happened with _____ Studio Sound System.

DOWN

1.   Formed in 1958, Tubby's _____ Hi-Fi was one of the greatest sound systems in Jamaica.

2.   The first big sound system in Jamaica, Tom the _____ _____ was formed by Tom Wong.

3.   Throwing parties since the age of eleven, Afrika _____ started small, progressing from what was basically a home stereo system to louder equipment over time. His progressive attitude was the key to his success.

4.   After working with Sir Coxsone, Cecil Bustamente Campbell set up his own sound system, Voice of the _____. Before long, it was considered one of the best on the island.

6.   Having grown up in Jamaica, Clive Campbell (a.k.a. D.J. Kool Herc) moved to New York and held huge outdoor parties on his own system, the _____ . . . and pretty much invented hip-hop.

53. SONGS FOR A WEDDING DANCE FLOOR

The trickiest gig for any D.J. is the wedding: so many people to please, all with different tastes and opinions, all in the same venue and all desperate to have a good time. While no puzzle can guarantee ballroom bliss in these situations, this puzzle includes songs that bridge the gap between old and young, happy and sad, drunk and sober.

ACROSS

2. Most people will hear what they want to in a song, so wedding guests will happily chug around the floor to the chorus of "Stay with Me" by ___ _____, hearing a different meaning to the one that Rod Stewart intended.

4. "Have Love Will Travel" by the _____. There are several versions of this ode to the power of attraction that you could choose for the post-nuptial shindig. The Black Keys' recent cover is great, but this one edges it.

6. "_____" by Chaka Khan is a bold, direct song about the unmistakable onset of burgeoning love and is guaranteed to get people dancing.

7. The _____ _____'s "In the Name of Love" has another perfect sing-along chorus, which, at the right time of the evening, will even get men of a certain age on the dance floor, even if it is to air drum to the percussion break.

8. _____ Wilson's beautiful song, "I Get the Sweetest Feeling," has the beat, the melody, and the lyrics to get people smooching at a wedding.

10. "Young _____ Run Free" by Candi Staton. While the message may be that men will ultimately let you down, the unbridled optimism of the song's chorus is enough to have people dancing and singing.

DOWN

1. "Shack Up" by _____. This taut funk monster is one for the unmarried couples at a wedding.

3. _____ _____'s "We Are Family." By the end of the night the bridesmaids can be arm-in-arm, singing along to this, while a tearful bride tells them all that she feels like they're all her sisters, before bursting into tears.

5. The lyrics for John Paul _____'s "Love Is in the Air" could have come out of the cards on the gift table, but hey, a wedding's no place for cynicism.

9. After the bridal waltz, everyone needs to be encouraged to take to the floor. "I Want Your Love" by ____ does the job.

54. D.J.s

The best D.J.s don't just play records, they use music to dictate the emotional curve of the night. It's not about carefully pre-planning a set to show off skills, it's a responsive talent, one that involves watching the crowd, reading the situation, and responding with the right record. Even when it's something people might not know they want.

ACROSS

3. When Argentinian-born _____ Fiorito started DJing on the terrace at Ibiza's Amnesia club in 1976, his eclectic mix of disco and European pop wasn't an immediate hit. Given time, it was to define the Balearic sound.

6. Finding a home—and fame—at New York's Paradise Garage club at the height of disco, _____ _____ had an eclectic palette and a talent for incorporating live elements and high drama into his sets.

7. One of the most important and progressive D.J.s on the Northern Soul scene, Ian _____ had tunes that others could only dream of.

8. With a complete respect for the music, _____ Mancuso was famous for letting records play in their entirety.

9. It was New York D.J. _____ Grasso, legend has it, who invented the idea of beatmatching to create a continuous flow of music.

10. Frankie _____ invented house music. Chicago club the Warehouse, where he was resident, even lent its name to the new underground style.

DOWN

1. As well as having the Herculords sound system, D.J. _____ _____ was the first to switch between the drum-led passages in funk records—the breaks—to create an entirely new piece of continuous music.

2. The only royally endorsed D.J. on the list, _____ ___ (M.B.E.) set up the Good Times sound system with his brother Joey after trips to New York, which became a Notting Hill Carnival staple.

4. _____ Bassett's now-legendary nights at London's Gardening Club (Moist) and Blue Note (New Hard Left) were followed by his Stateside Sarcastic Disco venture, which saw his star, and legend, rise.

5. His recording career has pulled focus away from his DJing, but it's worthwhile taking a closer look at _____ Flash.

55. CITIES

"A change is as good as a rest," they say, and certainly a shift in surroundings has been an inspiration to countless musicians as they trek around the globe playing to audiences far and wide. The cosmopolitan charge of a city's streets has provided the perfect backdrop to some of music's finest moments, and the following have been practically paved with gold.

ACROSS

2.   In the Clash's "London _____," the band's contention that "London is drowning" may mark them out as the environmentalists of punk.

4.   It's probably best to remember Elvis Presley from the film ____ ___ _____ than his later years in the city.

7.   Lou Reed: _____. While the version on the Velvet Underground frontman's album of the same name may get the plaudits, it's the rough and ready one on his debut LP to which we turn here.

8.   _____ _____'s "Across 110th Street" is from three films: Barry Shear's thriller of the same name, Quentin Tarantino's *Jackie Brown*, and Ridley Scott's *American Gangster*.

9.   While his plan of an album for every U.S. state hasn't quite panned out, _____, off Sufjan Stevens's *Illinois* album, is a two-for-one as it also stops off in New York.

10. In Frank _____'s take on "New York, New York" there's a passion in the delivery from Ol' Blue Eyes that goes a long, long way.

DOWN

1.   If Frank Zappa were to deliver a TV news bulletin over a backing of beats, random noises, and cut-up snippets of stuff, it might sound a fraction as odd as _____ ____—from the Steve Miller Band.

3.   Gil Scott Heron: _____. The poet and soul singer confronted the problems in South Africa with a politically charged, unifying piece of music that spoke more eloquently than politicians could ever hope to.

5.   Simple Minds' "Theme for _____ _____" is, at first, all haunting dread, like a post-apocalyptic vision—then the bass kicks in.

6.   Blossom Dearie sees beauty where others would see the need for a sturdy umbrella. She also feels compelled to express this over a thunderous drum break in "I Like _____ in the Rain."

56. CARS

What is it about cars and pop music that makes them such perfect companions? Could it be the sense of freedom and abandon associated with them? The ability to dictate your surroundings that both of them allow? Whichever, cars and driving are themes as prevailing as love, death, and heartbreak in popular music.

ACROSS

3. _____ by the Ides of March possesses a blistering horn riff that pushed it firmly into the fast lane.

5. "Little Red _____" is Prince's bid to convince a woman to settle down with him—perhaps not likening her to a car might be a start.

6. Gary Numan's "_____" was written after he had to take refuge in his car to avoid a road-rage incident.

8. Written from the point of view of someone who's just along for the ride, the instantly recognizable riff and chorus (featuring guest vocals from David Bowie) make "The _____" an irresistible choice.

9. Although __ ___ ____ _____ was originally recorded by blues great Floyd Jones, Canned Heat's version has the distinctive falsetto vocal that sits comfortably on the band's rolling accompaniment.

DOWN

1. In the same way the Beatles may have wanted to do more than hold hands, it sounds like something euphemistic is going on in "_____ __ ___."

2. "_____ Benz" is among the last recordings that Janis Joplin made. It's a rejection of consumerism that has since been co-opted by advertising companies to sell cars!

4. Electronic rhythms propelling "_____" by Kraftwerk ever further forward without once feeling the need to check in the rear-view mirror.

7. The Beach Boys: "___, ___, ___." With Brian Wilson's ear for a melody and Mike Love's ear to the ground when it came to what the kids wanted, this story of one girl's freedom is enduring.

8. "No _____ Place to Go," the 1964 single by Chuck Berry, is the ultimate ode to carefree cruising.

57. YEAH YEAH TO YÉ-YÉ

Primarily associated with France, the distinctive, early 1960s yé-yé European pop sound is unmistakable—as is the look. Although deeply rooted in its time, the almost overpowering allure of this simple and direct music never strays too far from popular culture, and still turns up today on film soundtracks and television series.

ACROSS

2. Francoise _____ brought a grown-up glamour to yé-yé as well as sophistication. Le Temps de L'amour, in part written by her husband, Jacques Dutronc, is all smoky haze and lingering, longing looks.

6. Gillian Hills: "___ _____ _____." Familiar due to its appearance in HBO's hit series *Mad Men*.

9. France Gall: "Laisse Tomber les _____." The spy-theme twang of this 1964 single gives it a distinctive edge, which Tarantino recognized.

10. Sylvie Varan's "Cette _____ La" is a very good example of immediate pop that gets the killer hooks in you without sacrificing class or quality.

DOWN

1. _____ Laume: "La Musique et la Dance." This is a great example of the carefree, youthful exuberance that all truly great pop music has as its hallmark.

3. Jacqueline Taïeb: "7 Heures du _____." Sounding like a yé-yé version of the Who's "My Generation."

4. _____ _____'s "Va Toujours Plus Loin" was released in England as "Around Every Corner," but the French version of Tony Hatch's relentlessly optimistic song is about a million times better.

5. Abandoning the saccharine strings for a fuzzy blast of guitar, Anna Karina's 1967 song "_____," from the French TV movie *Anna* is a bit late to be considered classic yé-yé, but it still has that unmistakable pop nous.

7. _____ ____ —"Poupée de cire, poupée de son"—this Gainsbourg song translates as "Wax Doll, Rag Doll," and proved a hit at Eurovision in 1965.

8. Jacques Dutronc—"J'ai Mis Un _____ Dans Ma Guitare"—possibly, the coolest man on the planet was Jacques Dutronc (Ms. Francoise Hardy), who put a tiger in his guitar, apparently.

58. DUTCH BEAT GROUPS

While all eyes and ears were on Britain and America in the 1960s, there was something happening over in Holland. Taking their inspiration from the sounds heard on pirate stations like Radio Veronica, a generation of Dutch kids picked up guitars and quietly got on with starting their own noisy scene—Nederbeat.

ACROSS

2. Although Golden _____ are known around the world for the hit "Radar Love," the band had a penchant for writing 1960s guitar pop.

4. The _____. Favoring original material over cover versions, they had a distinctive style right from the get-go. Their 1968 album *C.Q.* is an absolute classic of the genre.

5. _____ were Holland's answer to the Rolling Stones. With a much more R&B sound to tracks including *Groovin'* and *Second Sight*.

7. A result of Nederbeat rather than practitioners of the sound, _____ _____'s best-known tracks include the huge hit "Venus."

9. Q__ took their cue from the Pretty Things rather than the Beatles and were purveyors of sharp-edged tunes like the awesome "The Life I Live."

10. Google __ _____ and the first thing you'll see is a collaboration with Chubby Checker. The results aren't so great, but turn to the blistering 1966 single "Three's a Crowd" and be impressed.

DOWN

1. The _____. One of the biggest bands on the Dutch scene. Guitarist Robbie Van Leeuwen eventually left to form Shocking Blue.

3. How does a band such as _____, who only released two 45s, make it onto this list? By making songs as wonderfully inventive and weird as the offerings from their 1968 self-titled LP.

6. Featuring Jan Ackerman, the _____ released a handful of great singles between 1966 and 1968. Of these, "Russian Spy and I" is perhaps the best.

8. After forming in 1965, _____ released a few singles with a heavy U.S. influence, including "Roll the Cotton Down" and the fantastic "Kicks and Chicks," all raw melodies and confident swagger.

59. BALEARIC BEATS

There's a huge amount of debate as to what constitutes a Balearic tune, never mind what the best examples may be. Eclectic pop oddities that sound great in the right setting is as good a definition as any, so with that in mind, this puzzle attempts to pinpoint the very best of the inimitable island sound.

ACROSS

3. Bocca Juniors' _____ opens with a beefed-up version of the Thrashing Doves' "Jeu on the Payroll" piano part. Andrew Weatherall, Terry Farley, Pete Heller, and Hugo Nicholson write a Balearic anthem with ease.

5. Surprisingly fast for a track that is so blissfully on the edge of sleep, "The Sun Rising" by _____ is an exceptionally onomatopoeic achievement.

9. The _____ _____: "La Passionara." Take one part Michael Viner's "Apache," one part flamenco flamboyance, and one part pop smarts.

10. If there's one song that's capable of making you feel like you're on vacation when you're actually unable to leave the house due to the rain outside, it's "Frontera del Ensueno" by ___ __ _____.

DOWN

1. Izit: "_____." "Butt, you've got to feel it in your gut, Get up and move your butt . . ." introduces an improbably funky journey into an aural montage.

2. Of all the new wave bands, _____ _____ had big ambitions and an even bigger sound, as in "This Fear of Gods."

4. "Going Back to My _____" was a disco hit for Odyssey; Richie Havens wakes the song up the morning after and takes it down to the beach.

6. "_____ (Stop Bajon)" by Tullio de Piscopo is a gem of a song that sees the bass and drums locked into a functional, metronomic task that provides a core from which the song unfolds.

7. Manuel _____: "E2-E4." The former Ash-Ra Tempel guitarist released this hourlong track in 1984.

8. The sweeping emotion of the introduction to "La Ritournelle" by Sebastien _____ gives way to a glorious release and a declaration of love steeped in honesty and integrity.

60. PSYCHEDELIC SWEDEN

Perhaps it's something in the fjords, but bearing in mind that Sweden is a country populated by fewer than ten million people, it punches well above its weight when it comes to rock music. And not just any old rock, either—this is rock with the words "progressive" and "psychedelic" stamped all the way through it.

ACROSS

1. One of Sweden's first big psychedelic bands, Mecki Bodemark's band, _____ ____ ___, made the kind of music you'd expect at the tail end of the 1960s.

3. During the mid-1980s and 1990s, S.T. _____ released five albums of incredible psych before going off the radar.

6. __ _____. His fantasy prog opus "Lord of the Rings" charted in the UK, and he followed this with the astounding "Attic Thoughts."

7. Hansson & _____ (the band's name was the result of a misprint) included the track "Tax Free," covered by Jimi Hendrix.

8. Singer Pugh _____'s debut album, *Ja, dä ä dä*, recorded with drummer Janne Carlsson, is full of big ideas and playful production.

10. _____ Sound created huge, extended pieces of music that left audiences agog, like the near half an hour of the Eastern-infused "Skrubba."

DOWN

2. Counting guitarist Reine Fiske among their number, the _____'s 2009 self-titled debut was released on Subliminal Sounds.

4. Baby _____ is the band that (with the addition of Mecki Bodemark) was to become Mecki Mark Men.

5. Imagine if Doctor John, rather than Kid Creole, had been backed by the Coconuts . . . voodoo guitars over infectious, polyrhythmic drums. ____'s 2012 debut LP is great—live, they're even better.

9. Singer/composer Gustav Ejstes gained international acclaim with 2004's "Ta Det Lungt." It raised the bar for psychedelic rock so high that, at times, only _____ themselves seem capable of reaching it.

61. EASTERN BLOC PARTY

The mid-twentieth century was a time when many Eastern European countries were under the authoritarian rule of Russia, so it's tempting to think that lives were played out in monochrome or, at best, sepia. However, the music in this puzzle shows that there were dashes of color and creativity as people got on with the business of making music.

ACROSS

4. ___ _____: "Słońce W Chmurach Łazi." Brilliant girl-band action from their 1969 debut album. Make room for the dancing!

6. Alla _____: "Tiredness." The Russian singer has had a huge number of hits in her career, but this track on her 1983 album *How Disturbing Is This Way* has the disco beat to get any party started in style.

8. Novi Singers: "_____." All parties need to warm up, so it's just as well that we've got their 1970 album of the same name, which oozes quiet cool.

9. Hungary's _____ had recorded "A Bolond Lány," a psychedelic monster of a record earlier in their career.

10. Proving that our Eastern European cousins can do English-language pop is the Czech band the Flamingo Group with "___ _____," a cover of Aretha's "A Change." They might have misheard slightly, but it's a killer version.

DOWN

1. Kati _____: "Add Már Uram Az Esöt." Hungarian funky rock that hits the right notes and the solar plexus at roughly the same time.

2. _____ Und Das Electrecord-Orchester: "Omule." Their name may be bit of a mouthful, but the psych leanings of this meaty, beaty, big, and bouncy Romanian band are very easy to swallow.

3. _____Kubisova's *Songy a Balady* album was banned by occupying forces in Czechoslovakia. Presumably, they were worried about the enormity of the bass line, which is big enough to stop tanks in their tracks.

5. The solo drum break that opens the song "Rytm Ziemi" by Poland's all-time greats _____ _____ pretty much sets the pace.

7. With almost as many versions of "Ringasd el magad" by _____ ___ as there are stars in our galaxy, we're spoiled for choice and go for the funk-filled breaks of their 1974 disco(ish) remake.

62. KRAUTROCK

The name "krautrock" is far from the best describer that this strand of experimental music from Germany could hope for. Kosmische, perhaps? Whatever your preferred terminology, one thing is for certain—the lasting legacy of the industrious, industrial, and inventive music is assured.

ACROSS

2. Ash Ra _____ are often seen as purveyors of wonky space-rock, but there were more strings to their bow than that.

4. The album *Father, Son & Holy Ghosts* sees _____ blend their more high-minded jazz tendencies into a compelling, coherent whole.

5. _____ mixed elements of musique concrète, the avant garde, and krautrock on their self-titled album to come up with a sound that remains compelling listening.

9. Cluster was the second incarnation of avant-garde pioneers Kluster, and their LP _____ represents a massive change in direction.

DOWN

1. Klaus Dinger and Michael Rother left Kraftwerk to form a new band. One side of this magnificent last LP, "___! 75," pretty much invented punk rock.

3. Although their first album marked the beginning of the end for Tangerine Dream's creative peak, the album _____ is where all the drifting space debris forms a heavenly body of work.

6. _____'s first album may have been hailed as revolutionary—and with good reason—but So Far boasts the pounding pop of "It's a Rainy Day, Sunshine Girl."

7. Formed when Cluster's Dieter Moebius and Hans-Joachim Roedelius were joined by Michael Rother of Neu!, their band name, _____, was heavy with irony as the musical differences surfaced.

8. Following the improvised craziness of their debut LP *Phallus Dei*, ____ is a much more considered record for Amon Duul II.

10. Tempting though it is to go for the back-to-basics of "Delay 68," as the group ___ began to play with primitivism, it is "Tago Mago," recorded three years later, that is essential.

63. ITALO DISCO

Few genres have had as profound an effect on modern pop culture and sounds as Italo disco. The late 1970s and early 1980s proved a fertile time for budding producers, spurred on by the success of luminaries such as Giorgio Moroder. Synths, sequencers, and singing (usually in English) were the key elements, as was a good ear for an irresistibly upbeat tune.

ACROSS

2. Bringing the boogie back to the Italo disco, "Bad Passion" from 1982 by _____ _____ has more swing than many others in its class.

3. Kirlian Camera's sound took a much darker path as the 1980s progressed. But the 1983 release "_____" (instrumental version) remains one of the pinnacles of their career and of Italo disco as a genre.

6. Mr. Flagio's "____ _ _____." This wonderful cover version of Material's 1982 song is a disco track that sparkles, shines, beeps, and has a melody that stays just the right side of cheesy.

8. _____: "Secret Agent Man." With both male and female vocal mixes on this 1983 mid-paced tale of voyeurism and espionage, we are really spoiled for choice.

9. After someone suggested there was money to be made in dance music, Alexander Robotnick took them at their word and came up with the seminal disco track "_____ D'Amour."

10. ___: "That's the Game" (instrumental version). If the game was to create a proto-house monster in 1983 Belgium, then they seem to have secured an impressive away win.

DOWN

1. Capricorn's "_ ____ ____" has nothing to do with the LL Cool J track of the same name.

4. "End Title" (Blade Runner) is the B-side to "Pulstar," and there's a distinctly electro feel to this track. It's slower than many by _____.

5. "Waiting for a _____"—Moonbase take the Flash and the Pan song, and beef it up with more richly textured instrumentation.

7. _____: "Spacer Woman." When it comes to the themes of Italo disco, there's love, obviously, then space . . . and robots.

64. GAINSBOURG'S GALLIC GREATS

Singer, songwriter, composer, writer, actor, director . . . there were many strings to the bow of French visionary Serge Gainsbourg. One of his chief talents—aside from smoking, drinking, womanizing, and courting scandal wherever he went—was to compose timeless songs at the drop of a hat. And quite possibly other items of clothing too.

ACROSS

3. With Brigitte Bardot as a singing partner, you can't to go far wrong—especially when there's not actually a lot of singing in "_____ and Clyde."

4. Flash _____. The 1976 album *L'homme à Tête de Chou* shows a more reflective approach, though not to the detriment of the songs.

7. In "Contact!" a zither strums away while a bass picks out a 1960s sci-fi funk groove and _____ _____ tries to communicate with extraterrestrials by spea-king. One syll-a-ble. At. A. Time.

10. "__, __, ___ ___." Taken from the score for the 1969 film *Mr. Freedom*, about an American nationalist who travels to France to help the fight the Communist threat.

DOWN

1. It takes a special kind of bravado to record a new version of your country's national anthem. Still, if you've got top reggae men Sly and Robbie on board, who cares? "Aux Armes __ _____."

2. "_____." A collaboration with longtime arranger Jean Claude Vannier, this song was from the film score for the 1970 movie of the same name.

5. Initials _._. No prizes for guessing which beautiful French actress provides the inspiration for this release.

6. "Je T'aime . . . Moi ___ ____." Originally recorded with Brigitte Bardot, Gainsbourg re-recorded it with lover Jane Birkin.

8. __ _____. The penultimate track on what is probably Gainsbourg's most complete album—and certainly his most well-known—*Histoire De Melody Nelson*.

9. "__ _____." A keyboard sound that could have come from the Middle Ages introduces unlikely stablemates—including galloping drums and a banjo.

65. TRAINS

As we continue on our world tour, we turn to the good old reliable train, whose rattling rhythms and percussive propulsion has ended up gaining it a special place in the popular music songbook. Whether it's as a narrative or directly musical device, the number of potential passengers lining up to ride this express makes for one hell of a rush hour.

ACROSS

5. Little Junior's Blue Flames' "_____ Train" is a blues standard in which the singer is waiting for a train to arrive—on board one of the sixteen coaches is the woman he loves.

7. The Clash: "_____ __ ____." The sleeve to *London's Calling* didn't list this track, so it came as a welcome surprise when Paul Simenon's distinctive bass introduced one of the band's most instant and emotive songs.

8. Despite appearing on *The Kinks Are the Village Green Preservation Society*, the track "Last of the _____-_____ Trains" has a particularly American blues feel to it.

9. ___ ___'s "Down in the Tube Station at Midnight" is a cheerful ode about a man left for dead after being attacked in an underground station.

DOWN

1. The Monkees' "Last Train to _____" is glorious pop done with panache, style, and wit.

2. "I hear a train whistle blow, In the night and I feel so low, And I know I have to go, 'Cause I've got a wanderin' soul." So begins Gary _____'s "Wanderin' Soul," the story of one man's battle with the Devil for his soul.

3. _____'s "Train Song" manages to be successfully onomatopoeic and provide a real sense of movement—although, given the band's folk roots, in a suitably gentle fashion.

4. Dispensing with both destination and journey, in "____-_____ Express," Kraftwerk turn their attention to the mode of transport itself.

6. The feel of Graham Nash's song "Marrakesh _____" as he and his bandmates travel in harmony is one of a breezy, smiling journey.

9. James Brown steers the course superbly in his 1961 recording of the blues standard "Night _____."

66. DIGGING INDIA'S FUNKY SIDE

As producers and record diggers traveled farther and farther afield looking for the perfect beat, India proved very fertile ground. Rich in offbeat breaks and soundtrack curiosities, the musical heritage of the country was far more varied than the big-hitting Bollywood soundtracks would have you believe.

ACROSS

1. _____ _____, nephew of sitar hero Ravi, blends frantic drums, electric guitar, moog, and boundless energy on "Dancing Drums" to thrilling effect.

4. Not one person but composer duo Sapan-_____ wrote the infectious funk floor-filler "Sote Sote Adhi Rat."

8. Despite a big budget and high hopes, 1980's *The Burning Train* wasn't a cinematic smash. The soundtrack however, by legendary composer R.D. _____ contains the inventive titular masterpiece.

10. The piercing voice comes in and makes a bid for being precisely the best thing you've ever heard in "Dharmatma Theme Music" by another talented composer duo, Kalyanji-_____.

DOWN

2. "___ ____ ___" by Asha Bosle was a huge hit when it was released. From the 1971 film *Hare Rama Hare Krishna*.

3. In "Tum Jaison Ko Toh Paayal Mein Baandh," ____ ____ trills over a delicate bass groove while synthesizers and strings wrap themselves around her.

5. "Sansani Khez Koi Baat" by composer _____ Bosle has a beat to match any house record, and ethereal, drifting synths.

6. It's probably safe to call Atomic Forest India's best psychedelic rock band. "_____ '77," off their almost impossible to find album, is a sprawling beast of a song in the best possible sense.

7. Ananda Shankar: "Streets of _____." A more traditionally Western feel, but the sitar and flute melodies bring the flavors of India with them.

9. Complete with choppy, wah-wah scratch, and propulsive bass, "Pyar _____ Hai" by Kalyanji Anandji is part of the soundtrack to 1978's box-office smash *Muqaddar Ka Sikandar*.

67. SKA

In 1962, a nation was born as Jamaica gained its independence. That wasn't the only new arrival, however, as 1962 also heralded the birth of a whole new genre of music, ska. The exact circumstances surrounding this landmark delivery are unclear, but its name seems to stem from the trademark guitar scratch.

ACROSS

2. Robert Marley: "_____ ____." The first single "Bob" ever released.

4. The year 1963 saw the release of "Honour Your Mother and Father," the first single from the soon to be legend Desmond _____.

5. Originally recorded in the mid-1950s by Barbie Gayle, it took Jamaican teenager Millie Small to make "My Boy _____" a smash hit nearly a decade later and establish Island Records in the process.

6. Also known as the Godfather of Ska, self-proclaimed Boss Skinhead Laurel _____ was revered by mods, skinheads, the West Indian community, and pretty much anyone with ears.

8. Bob Marley and the Wailers, plus producer Clement "Coxsone" Dodd, all contributed to the track "_____ ____," a plea for calm among the more excitable members of the Jamaican community.

9. Released on Prince Buster's legendary label, the 1962 record __ _____ marked a golden period of success for Derrick Morgan and helped to usher in the shuffle of ska.

10. Derrick & _____: "The National Dance." Singing the praises of the genre itself, Derrick Morgan and Millicent Todd's 1965 love song to ska references its popularity not just in Jamaica but also in London.

DOWN

1. Of all the versions of the song "_____ Yourself," no one has managed to stamp their personality on it with quite the authority of Prince Buster.

3. "____ ___ __ ____" is a defiant roar of resilience from Prince Buster and the Voice of the People as he refuses to be brought down by "bad-minded people."

7. Prince Buster's 1962 track "____ ____" drinks deep from music's redemptive and spiritually cleansing waters.

68. REGGAE

As the 1960s drew on, something new was stirring in Jamaica. While giving a nod to both ska and rocksteady, heads began to move in a new direction. Reggae. Faster than rocksteady, more complex than ska, it was a new and persuasive beat.

ACROSS

3. Taking its lyrics from Psalms 137: 1-4, and its melody from the traditional song "How Dry I Am," "River of Babylon" by the _____ is literally a mash-up of biblical proportions.

6. With a social message delivered in Junior Murvin's beautiful falsetto, "Police and _____" wasn't just a hit with the reggae audience. The Clash also covered it on their debut album.

7. _____ _____'s debut album is regarded to be his finest work, and "Blackheart Man" tells the story of a sinister, mythical figure that children came to fear.

8. Eric Donaldson found himself suddenly famous after the song "_____ Oh Baby" exploded in 1971.

9. "___ ____ (People Get Ready)" was originally recorded by the Wailers as a ska song.

DOWN

1. In "Bumping and _____," Gregory Isaacs's beautiful, crystal-clear tones sit perfectly on top of the gently bobbing backing.

2. Big Youth's 1975 "Knotty No _____" showcases considerable linguistic ability and highlights the production skills of Clive Chin.

4. The heavy, dubbed-out feel of "Some A Weh A Bawl" by the _____ sits surprisingly well against the hints of mento (Jamaican folk music).

5. If Bob Marley says you're his favorite singer, you know that you're doing something right! _____ _____'s career was prolific, and "Money in My Pocket" shows why his popularity is so enduring.

6. John Holt's "_____ ___" was released on the legendary Channel One label in 1974. Despite its slow, dubby feel, it's actually a considerably faster and brighter take than the original.

69. SAILING

We've had planes, trains, and automobiles, so now we're searching for a soundtrack to sail the seven seas. Music's rarely about the destination, it's all about the journey, and what better way to get from A to B than in the laid-back glamour of a private yacht? Not all the songs featured here are lying in the lap of luxury, but they're all seaworthy.

ACROSS

2. Whether it's with the brutal rock of "Birthday Party" or beguiling ballads like "The ____ ____," Nick Cave always manages to connect with devastating simplicity.

4. A high point of the *Morrison Hotel* album, the rock shanty "____ __!" was one of the songs that saw the Doors rescue their reputation after the critical failure of *The Soft Parade* album.

8. Fairport Convention: "_ _____ ____." While not actually as long as the life in question, eleven minutes is still something of an odyssey for a folk song.

9. "_____ ____" by Crosby, Stills and Nash may well be the only song in this puzzle to actually have been composed on a boat.

10. It would be a snub to leave out Rod Stewart's 1975 chart topper, "_____," especially after all the effort he went to dressing up for the video.

DOWN

1. Madness, a.k.a. the Nutty Boys, were renowned for infectious pop and silly videos, and "Night Boat to _____" is a prime example of both.

3. Written by Elvis Costello, the beautiful song "_____" by Robert Wyatt addresses the difficulty in marrying the newfound prosperity of the UK's shipyards with the Falklands War of the time.

5. Starting with the sound of creaking wood and crashing waves, a whip's crack, and the heave-ho rhythm of the bass, "Ship ____" by the O'Jays addresses the dark subject of slave transportation.

6. "_____ _____ and the Grey Goose" by Wings documents the attempts of a person to contact the *Grey Goose*, a ship in distress.

7. The Beach Boys' "_____ ____ _" sees Brian Wilson take a West Indian folk song and transform it into an expansive pop song.

70. AFROBEAT

In equal parts traditional Nigerian music, jazz, funk, and righteous political anger, there's a spirit to Afrobeat that is identifiable yet indescribable. Here are some key names who headed up the vanguard in 1960s Africa—ready to confront leaders, play music, dance with abandon, and entertain with ease.

ACROSS

2. ____ _____ Plays with Afrika 70: "Afro Disco Beat." Perhaps the single most important figure when it comes to the development of the Afrobeat sound.

4. Listen closely to the "Mama-say, mama-sa, ma-ma-ko-sa" vocal line from "____ _____" and it becomes apparent that Michael Jackson was a fan.

6. _____ Kuti: "Truth Don Die." You can hear much of Fela's phrasing in his eldest son's sound.

8. _____ was a band of South African and Nigerian musicians who recorded in London. "Akasa," from their 1971 album *Zimbabwe*, has grand ambition in its musical aims.

9. Arguably ____ ____'s strongest album, *Expensive Shit* boasted the magnificent eleven-minute song "Water No Get Enemy" on the B-side.

10. Oscar _____ & the Uhuru Dance Band: "Olufeme." With a flute in one hand and a bag full of jazz and funk in the other, the Ghanaian flutist strode forward looking for new paths for African music to take.

DOWN

1. One-time keys player for Ginger Baker's Airforce, the former Modern Aces singer Joni _____ recorded "Wake up Your Mind" in the late 1970s.

3. _____ _____ & His Modern Aces: "Ise Owo." One of the formative albums in Afrobeat history, the 1966 album *Super Afro Soul* blended American funk and jazz influences with traditional African rhythms.

5. Afrobeat is a style that still resonates today, and this is best illustrated by Brooklyn-based twelve-piece _____ with "Dirty Money."

7. Seun started singing for Africa 80, aged just fourteen. There is a continuation of sound and feel from Seun Kuti and Egypt 80 that few could manage. Try listening to "Mr. ___ _____."

71. TROPICÁLIA

The year 1968 saw worldwide political upheaval including, in Brazil, the birth of Tropicália, an arts-based movement vocal in its opposition of a repressive and brutal dictatorship. Fusing funk and psychedelic rock with avant-garde experimentation, the genre lasted just a year, yet worried the dictatorship enough to exile two of its leading figures, Caetano Veloso and Gilberto Gil.

ACROSS

2. Sampled, remixed, borrowed, "Jimmy Renda-Se" has been something of an underground hit since it resurfaced in the 1990s, along with its creator ___ __, after a spell in relative obscurity.

4. While enjoying success with Os Mutantes, Rita Lee tried her hand at a solo career. The first album didn't end well, but her second—from which the funk-filled song "_____ Tratar Da Saude" is taken—is fantastic.

5. While Os Mutantes recorded a great cover version of "___ _____," it's Gilberto Gil's original that has the looser feel, and the massive congas.

7. Showing the way in which art, literature, and music fed into each other in this movement, "_____," from Caetano Veloso's 1968 debut album, takes its name from an art installation by Hélio Oiticicia.

8. "Take It Easy My Brother Charles" by _____ ___ has an easy-going charm that marks it out as a Tropicália classic.

9. From Os Mutantes' second album, "____ ____" shows the band on absolutely scorching form.

10. __ _____: "A Minha Menina." If the 13th Floor Elevators had ever tried their hand at upbeat, sunshine pop instead of eating LSD for breakfast, there's a strong chance that it would have sounded like this.

DOWN

1. Gal Costa: "_____." While the introductory percussion and accordion line can make you wonder where the song is going, the assured funk of the drums soon makes this crystal clear. From the 1974 *India* album.

3. _____ ___: "Geleia Geral." A screaming statement of intent of the Tropicália movement, this is a manifesto as music.

6. "Tuareg," off ___ _____'s 1969 eponymous album, is full of Eastern promise and Western hooks.

72. FLYING

Perhaps it's the sense of awe in seeing the world laid out in front of you—perhaps it's the feeling of mortality that presents itself when you're 30,000 feet up in a really heavy metal tube. Either way, flying has inspired more songs than budget airliners could cram onto a single flight.

ACROSS

1. The expansive sound and elaborate arrangement of the Neil Young song "Expecting to Fly," from _____ Springfield's second album, are enough to make you think they'd just teamed up with the Walker Brothers.

5. Judy Henske's husky vibrato on "High Flying ____" was backed by a full band for this flight and showed the shape of things to come.

6. "Hey _____." This will be a new one on most, taken from Peaking Lights' critically acclaimed 2011 debut album *936*.

8. "___ __ __ ___ ____" The combination of Quincy Jones, Count Basie, and Frank Sinatra make this a classic, exploding with energy and verve.

9. The Byrds: "_____ _____ ____." Despite the song's overtly psychedelic nature, Roger McGuinn maintains that it was simply about a plane journey—a claim dismissed by David Crosby and Gene Clark.

10. There's barely a thrift shop that doesn't have a record by the Bradford band _____ available for pennies. Sadly, it's unlikely to be "We're Flying High."

DOWN

2. The sound of a plane landing is the point at which "Back in the ____" takes off. It's a fantastic rock 'n' roll song.

3. From the opening, delayed chords of "No _____ Bird," it's quite clear that the Creation didn't need an airplane to achieve optimum altitude.

4. There's a definite sense of flight in the rising keyboard lines that drift in and out of the epic track "Fly Like an _____" by the Steve Miller Band.

7. It may be one of Dave Grohl's least favorite songs from ___ _____'s third album, *There Is Nothing Left to Lose*, but "Learn to Fly" certainly had wings as far as everyone else was concerned.

73. PRODUCERS

Producers have to tease the best from musicians and songs, while working out what will work best and, crucially, which ones are likely to be the commercial big hitters for the record company. In short, in a room full of children and toys, they have to be the grown-up. They may as well try to herd cats.

ACROSS

5. Leaving his contemporaries open-mouthed in his wake as he rode the crest of his own creativity, Beach Boy _____ _____ continually pushed himself and the boundaries of pop music.

6. After a career in jazz and film scores, _____ _____ met Michael Jackson and went on to produce *Off the Wall, Thriller,* and *Bad.*

8. The first name on everyone's lips when the words "Fifth Beatle" are mentioned, Sir _____ _____'s legacy is assured.

10. Having redefined disco, Chic guitarist _____ _____ could have been forgiven for resting on his laurels.

DOWN

1. Marsha Hunt, Osibasa, and T.Rex were all lucky enough to work with Tony _____.

2. _____ ___. A musical magpie, but with a penchant for more extravagant plumage, he introduced Bowie to krautrock and took African rhythms to Talking Heads.

3. Operating in parallel to ordinary people, but quite clearly in a world all of his own, Lee "Scratch" _____'s productions are a delight of dub and delay.

4. Taking charge of the whole process of production, _____ _____ achieved exactly the results he wanted, creating the famous "Wall of Sound."

7. D.J. _____. His work for Gang-Starr, M.O.P., Jay-Z, and Nas shows his encyclopedic knowledge of music and his ability to incorporate real feeling into his beats.

9. Joe _____'s interest lay in sounds rather than tunes, and his pioneering use of homemade equipment to generate delay and reverb gave his productions an unmistakable sonic signature.

74. DEBUTS

While music lists are, by their very nature, controversial, a list of the top debut albums is likely to provoke a strongly worded email—or a mild nuclear rebuke. Like *Sophie's Choice* but for music nerds, trimming down the field can be an agonizing process and impossible to get right. Having said that, this is a very strong lineup.

ACROSS

3. _____ ____: *Licensed to Ill.* Not everyone got the joke or disliked the cartoon creations. In reality, this was a funny, literate, and musically sharp album, mixing punk, metal, rap, and humor with style.

4. From the inspired cover versions ("Police and Thieves," "I Fought the Law") to their own incendiary songs, the _____'s self-titled album was the perfect calling card.

7. The _____ put their collective foot down and sped through their 1976 self-titled offering safe in the knowledge that they'd stripped down rock to its bare essentials.

8. The first hip-hop album to boast a team of "super producers" including D.J. Premier, Pete Rock, and Q-Tip, _____ was musically assured.

9. *The Velvet Underground and* ____. If commercial success were directly proportional to the cultural influence of a band, the members of the Velvet Underground would be Bilderberg rich by now.

10. ___ _____: *Unknown Pleasures.* The cover art is iconic and a good indicator of the music that lies underneath.

DOWN

1. The Beatles' _____ _____ __ is the sophisticated pop premiere that changed everything. They recorded this all in a day.

2. Guns 'N' Roses: *Appetite for* _____. By 1987, heavy metal had stagnated. Enter Axl Rose, Slash, and company to give it a swift kick.

5. ___ _____: *Never Mind the Bollocks.* Some albums are like old friends— they become part of the furniture.

6. *Are You* _____? by Jimi Hendrix was an album that knocked people backward, forward, and side to side.

75. "DIFFICULT" SECOND ALBUMS

While the debuts can take years of under-the-radar work to perfect, bands are not afforded the same luxury when it comes to their under-the-spotlight and against-the-clock follow-up. With record companies breathing down their necks and fans waiting for more of the same, many bands fall at the second hurdle. Here are ten that beat their personal best.

ACROSS

4. ___ _____: *Astral Weeks*. Unhappy with 1967's *Blowin' Your Mind*, jazz, blues, and folk combine to create something extraordinary—and a world away from the light breeze of "Brown Eyed Girl."

5. *Everyone Knows This Is _____* was a debut in some respects as it was Neil Young's first outing with backing band Crazy Horse.

8. If 1987's *Yo! Bum Rush the Show* was a warning shot, *It Takes a Nation of Millions to Hold Us Back* was a full-on tactical assault for _____ _____.

9. Carole King's _____ is one of the most successful albums of all time.

10. While early songs like "About a Girl" and "Spank Thru" had hinted at Nirvana's potential for writing a pop hook, it wasn't until _____ that this potential fused with their devastating live show dynamics.

DOWN

1. Radiohead's second album, *The _____*, marked their first collaboration with engineer and producer Nigel Godrich. Dark and brooding, intense and intriguing, it spawned no fewer than five singles.

2. Black Sabbath: _____. When your first album is as good as their debut, how do you follow it? These concerns were more than answered by the end of side one.

3. ____ _____: *Axis: Bold as Love*. In "Little Miss Lover" and "You Got Me Floating," this has the heavy guitar grooves that made his debut so popular.

6. The Beastie Boys wowed the world when they came back from the frat-hop of *Licensed to Ill* with *Paul's _____*.

7. The _____ *Bob Dylan* is the album that marked Dylan out as the best songwriter of his generation and also brought folk music out of the clubs and to the radio.

76. CONCEPT ALBUMS

For some bands, releasing albums that were effectively a collection of unconnected short stories wasn't enough. They craved the kudos and creative respect commanded by great art with grand themes—they wanted to write a novel. Inevitably, many bands would stall at the first chapter, but this list is populated by wholly satisfying stories.

ACROSS

1.   The life of the fantastically named *S.F. Sorrow* provides the focus for the _____ _____' musical biography.

5.   _____ _____: *Ogden's Nut Gone Flake.* Getting Stanley Unwin to narrate this tale of a young boy's search for the missing half of the moon was genius.

6.   In some respects, all ____ _____'s records had been conceptual, but *Dark Side of the Moon* is the first time that we see a structured narrative, sensitively addressing death, greed, humanity, and mental illness.

7.   The _____ *Sgt. Pepper's Lonely Hearts Club Band* is certainly the most famous concept album of all time, even if the concept is a loose one.

10.   In *The Kinks Are the* _____ _____ *Preservation Society*, we find the Kinks in mourning for an England that seems to be lost.

DOWN

2.   Pink Floyd: ___ ____. This story of rock star isolation, despair, and the loss of humanity was Roger Waters's crowning achievement.

3.   The Who's _____ is a terrific tale of teenage identity and tribalism played out against a Mods and Rockers backdrop.

4.   _____ _____: *The Rise and Fall of Ziggy Stardust and the Spiders from Mars.* Bisexual rock star from another planet comes to Earth to deliver a message of hope to mankind before it consumes itself completely.

8.   Rock opera was the perfect vehicle for ___ ___'s Pete Townshend, whose storytelling prowess saw deaf, dumb, and blind *Tommy* journey out of a semi-catatonic state.

9.   Only in the mind of Serge Gainsbourg could a crash between a Rolls-Royce and a bicycle lead to an obsessive love affair. *Histoire de Melody* _____ is set to Jean Claude Vannier's exceptional scoring.

77. ROCK AND POP INSTRUMENTALS

"A little less conversation, a little more action," sang Elvis, and it's a sentiment that we can all get behind. There are times when we need the brain to be in neutral to really lose ourselves in music, and words can keep us grounded while we're trying to drift away—much like an unwanted conversation at bedtime. Pray silence please, for these instrumentals.

ACROSS

2. There's absolutely no reason for Scottish rockers to be scared of the Devil— if he ever heard _____ "Fear Satan," he'd duck and cover.

3. _____: *I Did It Just the Same*. Hiding in plain sight on the 1984 album is this unexpected gem. Annie Lennox does feature, only in a wailing way.

7. _____ was banned from the airwaves despite being an instrumental; this delightfully distorted offering from Link Wray is aptly titled.

9. ____ _____'s work on Bond films is widely known, but his talent extends to dreamy, flighty music more associated with 1960s shindigs, and "This Is How You Dance" is a prime example.

10. You'd think that narrowing down Pink Floyd's oeuvre to a field of one would be difficult. Yet _____ is a masterpiece that stands in a field of its own.

DOWN

1. Incredible Bongo Band: _____. Those drums! That guitar! Even if the jury's out on whether this is the best instrumental of all time.

4. The _____: "Machine Gun." Hello? Is it Lionel Ritchie you're looking for? It is, but don't expect any schmaltzy balladeering.

5. With the same sort of lush, orchestrated feel David Axelrod brought to American rock band the Electric Prunes, "_____," like the William Blake poems that inspired it, was largely ignored at the time.

6. "Green Onions" may be the default setting, but "_____ ___" by Booker T & the MG's is the one you want—preferably the album take.

8. The _____: "Telstar." For a song inspired by science fiction and recorded in a tiny flat on London's Holloway Road, this space-rock satellite transmission punched well above its weight.

78. POST-BEATLES TUNES FROM THE FAB FOUR

When they weren't taking barely concealed pot shots at each other from behind the gossamer-thin veil of lyrical conceit, the post-breakup of the Fab Four showed the world exactly why they had been the biggest band for years.

ACROSS

4. Paul McCartney's "Check My _____" is a wonderfully off-the-wall experiment. It was the first thing he recorded on the *McCartney II* sessions.

6. George Harrison: "___ ___." Hang on? No "My Sweet Lord"? No. On the *All Things Must Pass* album, you'll end up slap bang in the middle of one of the best moments of his entire career.

8. "_____ _____!" Lennon is on unusually optimistic form on this Plastic Ono Band single, which, as he rightly identified himself, is a "monster."

10. "My _____ _____," from the *McCartney II* sessions, was originally hidden away on the B-side of a limited-run 12".

DOWN

1. Off the same album as "Imagine," John Lennon's _____ _____ _____ is a superb snarling, vicious, angry pot shot at politicians and everything that's wrong with the world.

2. ____ _____'s "Uncle Albert/Admiral Halsey" from *Ram* was panned on its release, but it's a patchwork quilt of song fragments superbly stitched together to make something beautiful, warm, and comforting.

3. _____: "Live and Let Die." From the opening moments of the James Bond theme tune, we are taken on a ride as thrilling as any spy movie.

5. The title track of the triple album *All Things Must Pass* sounds like _____ _____ is coming to terms with recent events in a beautiful, elegiac song, originally given to Billy Preston to record.

7. "Maybe I'm _____" is a classic, with telltale McCartney melodies and an effortless elegance in its lyrical simplicity.

9. "Working Class ____" was the B-side yang to the yin of "Imagine." Once again, it's when Lennon's angry that he's at his best.

79. ODD TIME SIGNATURES

While most songs follow a basic rhythmic pattern, there are only so many times that four beats can walk into a bar without the setup getting a little tired. The desire to have a bit of fun with time signatures is perfectly understandable then, but it needs to be done well, otherwise everyone ends up feeling lost in music.

ACROSS

2. Waltzing to Jimi Hendrix is almost too bizarre to contemplate. "_____ Depression" might not feel like a classic waltz, but that's mainly thanks to the impossibly dexterous drumming of Mitch Mitchell.

7. The king of oddball swing, jazz legend Dave Brubeck gave entire albums over to his experiments in rhythm. "_____ _____" is his best-known song.

8. In the _____'s "Golden Brown" there's a waltz-time keyboard with a harpsichord playing in 6/8 time.

10. Dionne _____: "I Say a Little Prayer." With a meter varying between 10/4 and 11/4, this looks more like long division than musical instruction.

DOWN

1. In Pink Floyd's "_____" the bass line sounds so natural that it's a while until you realize odd time trickery is at play.

3. Putting to one side Robert Plant's dreadful James Brown impression in "The _____," when Led Zeppelin went funk they did a pretty good job.

4. To be honest, the _____'s "All You Need Is Love" just stinks of showing off.

5. Outkast: "___ __!" It's an odd time signature, veering between 4/4 and 2/4, but the fact that almost no one who bought or loves this record realizes there's anything untoward is its genius.

6. Lalo Schifrin: "Mission _____." Managing to smuggle an odd timing under the radar, the song's 5/4 beat is perfect for the job in hand.

9. "_____ ___" is one of the only times Nick Drake used a normal tuning and he makes it difficult for students of folk everywhere by employing the tricky 5/4 timing.

80. COUPLES

Although they say that those who play together stay together, many of the doomed pairings in this puzzle go to show that "they" may not have a clue what they're on about. That said, there have been some fantastic records—not to mention headlines—made by some of these musical marriages over the years.

ACROSS

2. _____. Four people, two couples, one band. What could possibly go wrong? Until Agnetha and Bjorn and Benny and Anni-Frid called it a day.

4. Johnny Cash and June _____ Cash. After Johnny proposed to June during a live performance, the pair married and stayed together for thirty-five years, until June's death in 2003.

5. Jack and ___ White. What do you do if you're a recently divorced couple in one of the hottest bands of the moment and reporters are sniffing around? You claim that you're brother and sister, of course!

6. _____ and Jay-Z. It's fair to say the couple didn't marry for money. The sound of their newborn daughter, Blue, crying is audible on Jay-Z's single "Glory," for which she was credited.

9. While the much-documented bust-ups and violent arguments made headlines, it's easy to forget just how big Ike and Tina _____ were.

10. John Lennon and _____ ___. Seen by some as the relationship that broke up the Beatles.

DOWN

1. John and Beverley _____. The folk duo met in 1969 and recorded the albums *Stormbringer!* and *The Road to Ruin*.

3. Ronnie and Phil _____. She was a stunning, stylish singer while he . . . looked a bit creepy.

7. Sonny and _____. They famously had each other—right up to the point where they divorced. Until then, they had a string of pop hits in the 1960s and a hugely successful TV career in the early 1970s.

8. Anyone who's listened to *Rumours* will presumably know that this didn't end well for childhood sweethearts Lindsey Buckingham and _____ _____.

81. TROUBLED SOULS

On closer inspection, the notion of the tortured artist channeling despair into great art is a convenient myth. It promotes an idealized, iconic image—and icons are easy to market. In reality, lives are cut short, talent wasted, and the promise of what could have been looms large. Some make it through . . . others aren't so lucky.

ACROSS

2. While the success of *Nevermind* never sat easily with ____ _____, his troubles were significantly more deep-rooted.

4. The precocious talent Amy _____ displayed on her first album, *Frank*, was prodigious by the time *Back to Black* was released.

6. Soul singer _____ ____'s addictions have been well publicized, as has his troubled personality. There was also conflict in the relationship with his fundamentalist father, who shot him dead during an argument.

8. While rock stars push out their chest and strut, ____ _____ hunched his shoulders and hid. Famously shy, he also battled depression for much of his life. He recorded three beautiful albums, including *Pink Moon*.

10. Elliot _____ was taken at the age of thirty-four. Despite rumors surrounding the exact nature of his death, the lingering thought is of huge, wasted potential.

DOWN

1. _____ Houston's problem with drugs was the subject of intense media scrutiny. Sadly, it came to dominate a career remarkable for the pure quality and breathtaking range of her voice.

3. Following the death of his bullying father and huge demands made of his terrific talent, something had to give. _____ _____ took to his bed for three years with cake and cocaine.

5. When Pink Floyd's former bandmate Syd _____ turned up at the recording of *Dark Side of the Moon*, no one recognized him.

7. At a time when homosexuality was illegal in Britain, being gay probably didn't help ___ Meek's spiraling paranoia.

9. A complex character, Ian _____ inspires devotion in fans like few figures can manage. His lyrics paint a picture of a tortured and introspective soul who found it impossible to carry on.

82. REVOLUTIONARIES

Popular music has a deep and rich history of anti-establishment songs. It has been used as a positive voice for peace, a nihilistic scream into the void, and an anarchic call to arms. Over the years it has, in equal parts, empowered, enraged, and engaged, but what are the best songs to soundtrack a mutiny?

ACROSS

3. ___ _____ _____'s "The Revolution Will Not Be Televised" is a devastating, stripped-bare attack on the media's coverage of civil unrest.

5. ___ _____'s "Get Up, Stand Up" is a direct order to the disenfranchised.

7. _____ _____ Animals: "The Man Don't Give a Fuck." This sweary, two-fingered dance of dissent laments a generation pacified by media and reminds them what side they're on.

9. ____ ____'s "Coffin for the Head of State" is a deeply personal musical missile launched against a government whose troops lay siege to the Kalakuta Republic, beating residents—including his mother, who later died.

10. _____ 3: "Revolution." A revolution of the mind, rather than one that requires running through the streets.

DOWN

1. ___ _____: "Guns of Brixton." Written and sung by bassist Paul Simonon, the intense and insular feel of this song mirrors perfectly the discontent felt at the time in 1979 South London.

2. _____ Guthrie's "This Land Is Your Land" is one of the greatest protest songs of all time.

4. While ____ _____' sound might not have been revolutionary, the 1980s rock revivalists' live shows were certainly riotous—just listen to "Revolution Stone" from 1989's *Live'r Than God* album!

6. _.___: "Children of the Revolution." Marc Bolan won't have had figures of authority cowering in the corner, despite some concerns that the song promoted a communist agenda.

8. Released in 1968, the year of the student uprising in Paris, Vietnam War demos, and anti-government protests in Poland, the _____ questioning the validity of revolution caused outrage on the Left.

83. MUSICIANS-TURNED-FILM STARS

From the recording studio to the film studio—it's a well-worn path as musicians try to spread their wings, find their feet, and chance their arm in the world of acting. It's a fairly safe bet, too, as an established musician is likely to attract a few moviegoers, even if it's just people desperate for a fix of schadenfreude.

ACROSS

2. Having taken the Fresh Prince from records to TV with alarming ease, _____ _____ had already proved he had the chops for acting.

4. After two albums, Kris _____ was cast in Dennis Hopper's *The Last Movie*. More followed, including *A Star Is Born*, with Barbra Streisand.

6. When he first bounded onto the stage with his Funky Bunch, Mark _____ was better known as New Kid on the Block Danny's younger brother.

8. After getting a taste for acting opposite Susan Sarandon in *Desperately Seeking Susan*, _____ struggled to replicate her assured debut.

9. Beginning her film career with husband Sonny in 1967's *Good Times*, there wasn't a sense anyone was watching a future movie star. Yet ____ was to get three Golden Globe awards as well as an Oscar for *Moonstruck*.

10. The movies seemed just another part of _____'s career rather than an artistic choice. Starting with 1956's *Love Me Tender*, _____.

DOWN

1. Hip-hop star ___ ___ was that rare thing, an underground act who achieved mainstream success by being good rather than selling out. His film career saw standout roles in *16 Blocks*, *Be Kind, Rewind*, and *The Woodsman*.

3. If TV talent shows are prosecuted for crimes against entertainment, _____ _____ will be the case for the defense, going on to win a Grammy for her debut album and an Oscar for her role in the film *Dreamgirls*.

5. Frank _____'s perforated eardrum—which kept him away from active service in World War II—left him free to embark on an Oscar-winning career on the silver screen.

7. The reason David _____'s stage personae were so successful is because he inhabited them so well.

84. FACTORY RECORDS RELEASES

Not so much ripping up the rule book as just not bothering to find out whether there was one in the first place, Tony Wilson's legendary Manchester label valued high-minded ideals over commercial viability every time. While this ensured a fair deal for bands and some of the most vital music of a generation, it also led to the label going bankrupt in 1992.

ACROSS

1. The _____. Factory's great folly, the money poured into the club was paid for largely by New Order's record sales.

3. Before M People, Hacienda D.J. Mike Pickering headed up electro dance band Quando Quango. Produced by Bernard Sumner, "____ ____" also includes Johnny Marr.

4. It seems fitting that Anthony H. Wilson's "_____" was the last object to bear a Factory catalog number (FAC 501).

7. Joy Division: "____ ____ _____". With this on one side and "Atmosphere" on the other, this is the best 12" record the label ever released.

9. It's so good that the _____ _____ dusted off *Bummed* for a twenty-fifth anniversary tour.

DOWN

1. If you should find yourself looking for the perfect example of what happens when former punks go electro, Section 25's "Looking from a _____" is it.

2. Only released on cassette in 1980, "The Graveyard and the Ballroom" is the incredibly accomplished debut for _ _____ _____.

5. ___ _____: "Blue Monday." In true Factory style, the biggest selling 12" single of all time ended up costing them money.

6. *The Return of the Durutti* _____. In an act of conceptual genius, the cover of this debut LP was made out of coarse sandpaper, to ruin the records next to it in the racks.

8. "A Factory _____," a double 7" single, was the first Factory record released and, as opening gambits go, it's a fairly bold one: Joy Division, John Downie, and Sheffield's Cabaret Voltaire had a side each on which to shine.

85. MUSICIANS-CUM-ARTISTS

With the number of bands formed at art college, it's not surprising to find that many musicians are frustrated artists at heart. Why this marriage of audio and visual? Maybe it's the flighty creative impulse looking for any suitable spot on which to settle, or maybe it's the fact that art class was laid back and the homework was easy.

ACROSS

1.   While tragic bandmate Stuart Sutcliffe was an artist who picked up a bass, Paul _____ has taken the opposite route.

3.   Having established herself with classic albums including *Horses* and *Easter*, poet and songwriter ____ _____ has also earned a reputation as an accomplished visual artist.

5.   Having started painting to alleviate the boredom of touring, ___ _____ has shown a collection of pastel portraits at London's National Portrait Gallery.

7.   Jazz musician _____ Davis used painting as therapy, saying, "It keeps my mind occupied when I'm not playing music."

9.   A student of Ealing Art College, London, guitarist _____ ____ was actually taught how to draw. His paintings often depict the Stones themselves.

10. The Stone Roses' iconic covers were all the work of guitarist John _____. While the earliest were Pollock pastiche pieces, his later work hinted at a confident and clever artist.

DOWN

2.   An advocate of amateurism, musician, artist, and maverick spirit Billy _____ sees art as a way of preserving the joy he takes in what he does.

4.   With his work in the permanent collections of several galleries and the Smithsonian Museum, it's fair to say that ____ _____ is no amateur.

6.   Not content with simply being one of the most inspiring singer/songwriters of all time, ____ _____ is also a talented artist, as seen on the cover of her album *Clouds*.

8.   _____ was an artist first who then went on to find fame in drum and bass. His graffiti pieces were featured in the street art bible *Spraycan Art*, and he now exhibits around the world.

86. SONGS AND ARTISTS INSPIRED BY ART

There's a vivid connection between art and music. In both you start with a basic sketch to which, over time, you give depth by adding new tones and splashes of color until you step away and decide that it's finished. Then it's time to unveil it to the world and let people judge your creation. The following ten are all masterpieces.

ACROSS

4. This song by ___-_, referencing one of the most famous artists of all time, itself became a work of art through the video *Picasso Baby: A Performance Art Film*.

5. The Modern Lovers: "_____ _____." Jonathan Richman's proto-punk rockers recorded this song for their debut album, but it didn't make the cut.

9. In *Time Further Out: Miró Reflections* LP, the pianist ____ _____ and his band interpret the Catalan painter Joan Miró through jazz.

10. David Bowie: "____ _____." The artist, whose work is shot through with references to transitional fame and pop icons, was a huge inspiration for Bowie.

DOWN

1. The Manic Street Preachers' "_____" is one of the lighter moments on the *Everything Must Go* album.

2. _____ ___: "Venus." The figure of Venus has proved an inspiration for artists throughout time, and the Dutch band was not immune to her charms.

3. The matchstick men in the title of _____ ___'s "Pictures of Matchstick Men" refer to the figures in the paintings of L.S. Lowry.

6. Despite its seemingly acronymic title, John Lennon always insisted that his son's painting was the creative spark for "Lucy in the Sky with _____."

7. "Every Picture That I Paint—Escher," from _____ Fanclub's album *Thirteen* is an irresistible choice.

8. Nancy _____'s beautiful song, from the sublime 1968 album *You've Come This Way Before*, was written for her daughter, actress Christina Applegate.

87. SONGS AND ARTISTS INSPIRED BY BOOKS

Songs are rooted in a strong tradition of storytelling and, as such, it's only natural that books should be a huge source of inspiration for musicians over the years. A picture, as we know, is worth a thousand words, but there has as yet been no count to determine what literary value a piece of music has. The following ten, however, are priceless.

ACROSS

2. The literary number-one hit "Wuthering Heights" was written by ____ ____ in only a few hours when she was just 18.

4. The _____'s 1980 single "Don't Stand So Close to Me" contains the phrase "That book by Nabakov," a reference to *Lolita*.

6. The Velvet Underground: "_____ __ ____" takes its cue from the book of the same name by Leopold von Sacher-Masoch.

9. _____: "Banana co." Although not explicitly cited as an influence, *One Hundred Years of Solitude* by Gabriel Garcia Marquez provides the background.

10. _____ _____'s "Oh You Pretty Things." *Anthem*, Ayn Rand's 1938 tale of a dystopian future, isn't a book that screams "chart hit," but that didn't stop this classic from 1971's *Hunky Dory*.

DOWN

1. ___ ____: "Killing an Arab." Robert Smith's attempt to condense Albert Camus's *The Stranger* into a three-minute pop song was not without controversy.

3. "Turn! Turn! Turn!" Many musicians have turned, turned, turned to that biggest of books for inspiration, but few with the success of this folk adaptation of passages from the *Book of Ecclesiastes* by Pete _____.

5. _____: "Tales of Brave Ulysses." The lyrics were, as the title suggests, inspired by Homer's epic poem *The Odyssey*.

7. _____: "Scentless Apprentice." Famously thought of as an "unfilmable novel" (though that didn't stop them), no one wondered whether you could successfully write a song about *Perfume*, Patrick Suskind's 1985 book.

8. Musically, Devo's 1980 single "____ __" was indebted to the sound of krautrock. Lyrically, songwriter Gerald Casale cites Thomas Pynchon's vast novel *Gravity's Rainbow* as the main influence.

88. INFLUENTIAL RADIO D.J.s

In an age of multimedia platforming and social media marketing, the radio can seem something of an anachronism. Like seeing someone popping the kettle on in the middle of *Star Wars*. At one time the D.J. had the power to make or break a record, but the role is a constantly changing one—this puzzle celebrates those who led from the front.

ACROSS

5. When the BBC first went on air, they didn't see any value in having a program with someone playing records. It took Christopher _____ to convince them, in 1927.

8. Described as one of the most influential kingmakers in American pop, _____ Bingenheimer was given a show in 1976.

9. A towering figure in Jamaican radio, the J.B.C. show _____ *Dread at the Controls* was wall-to-wall reggae and proved such a hit that listeners sent cassettes of it to family and friends back in England.

10. A fan of Alan Freed, Robert Weston Smith, a.k.a. _____ ____, became a legendary voice of rock 'n' roll during the 1960s.

DOWN

1. Although to some the street schtick can be off-putting, there's absolutely no doubting Tim _____'s dedication to the cause of hip-hop.

2. The UK's Kenny _____ pioneered a different kind of DJing altogether, using effects, skits, and invented characters to create an anarchic atmosphere in the studio.

3. Generations of English kids—and adults—relied on ____ ____ to hear the sort of music they simply wouldn't get to hear otherwise.

4. ____ _____ invented rock 'n' roll. After organizing a wildly popular rhythm and blues concert in 1952 that ended in chaos, the popularity of his radio show soared.

6. The first female presenter on the UK's BBC1, Annie _____ has been broadcasting for over four decades.

7. _____ _____ worked as an announcer on a New York radio station, then started playing records in between announcements. He soon had his own show, *Make Believe Ballroom*.

89. GROUNDBREAKING VIDEOS

Video may not have killed the radio star, but it did make them at least put a comb through their hair and have a quick look in the mirror on their way out. As the video age drew on, more musicians realized that their song's shiny, moving advertisement could be a work of art in itself, at which point creativity—and budgets—took a sharp upturn.

ACROSS

1. It's testament to the design of ____ _____'s "Money for Nothing" 1985 video that it's dated so well.

6. Peter Gabriel's "_____" was stop-motion on a grand scale. Gabriel lay there for sixteen hours among the plasticine chickens and toy trains while animators did their bit.

8. _____ was possibly the first Beastie Boys video to truly capture the feeling of unbridled joy in their music.

9. The _____ _____: "The Hardest Button to Button." This staccato, stop-motion vision of drum kit, guitar amps, and band snaking a perfectly-in-time path through a city is simply stunning.

DOWN

2. OK Go: "Here It Goes _____." As the track plays, the band performs an unbroken dance routine on treadmills that begs the question, "How many takes?" Answer: seventeen!

3. A-ha: "____ __ __." With its inventive blending of the real world with an illustrated, comic book narrative, a woman, beckoned by illustrated singer Morten Harket, enters a cartoon strip.

4. _____ ____: "Windowlicker." By far the most powerfully unsettling video in this puzzle, director Chris Cunningham's mind must be a dark, dark place.

5. Fatboy Slim's "_____ ___" is part music video, part performance art as Spike Jonze employed actor-dancers to dance in front of onlookers.

7. Herbie Hancock's video for "_____," his foray into electro, earned him no fewer than five MTV awards.

10. With a budget that would put most films of the time to shame, Michael Jackson's horror spectacular, "_____," boasted amazing special effects and dance routines.

90. SHOCKING VIDEOS

Well aware of the power of a controversial video and the sales it can generate (that's real shock value for you), many musicians go to great lengths to provoke and titillate in the hope of getting noticed. Some of the following may have softened over the years, but all of them hit hard at the time.

ACROSS

5. Nine Inch Nails' _____ features a laboratory with a dismembered pig's head, a naked woman, and a monkey tied to a cross!

6. Eminem: "_____." An obsessive fan, possessed by rage and anger, ends up killing himself and his pregnant girlfriend.

9. In _____ _ _____, Madonna witnesses a murder then hides in a church where a statue of a black man starts crying and then comes to life when she kisses his feet. Oh, and Madonna has stigmata.

10. M.I.A.'s _____ _____ depicts a world in which redheads are persecuted, rounded up, beaten, tortured, and ultimately killed.

DOWN

1. In "_____ Incest," it's no surprise to see Serge Gainsbourg cavorting on a bed with a young woman, but that "woman" is his 12-year-old daughter, Charlotte, and the song is about incest; controversy is bound to follow.

2. "I Want Your Sex" by George _____ was the subject of controversy back in 1987; the video featured shots of full-frontal female nudity.

3. In "_____," Lady Gaga plays a surrealist Madonna with an aversion to clothes, bailed from prison by Beyoncé to go on a killing spree.

4. If the title of ___ _____'s song "Smack My Bitch Up" wasn't enough to fuel the fire of righteous outrage, then the video of a debauched night out, including drugs, sex, and violence, was sure to cause a national uproar.

7. Causing consternation in 1981 because of the female flesh on show, _____ _____'s video for "Girls on Film" was promptly banned.

8. Despite a massive disclaimer at the beginning of the "____ __ ___" video saying that Nas isn't depicting Jesus, he's wearing a crown of thorns while carring a cross to a hill where he's crucified.

91. GOOD MORNINGS

Music, like all art, has the potential to be truly transformative. At its most powerful and intoxicating, it can alter the way we perceive the world around us. But can it get us out of bed and into the shower at 6:30 a.m. when the weather is gray and rainy? Here are ten songs and artists to wow us awake.

ACROSS

2. Alexis Korner's C.C.S. released "_____" a jazz-infused, horn-heavy blues number on their first album. It starts off with a piano and polite percussion before the voices grudgingly herald the dawn of a new day.

5. Lee Hazlewood and Nancy Sinatra's psychedelic pop song "Some Velvet _____" is one of the best-known tracks that the duo recorded.

6. _____ ____'s "Good Morning" is a wake-up call in more ways than one; this track introduces the *Graduation* album.

8. One for the insomniacs among us, "25 or 6 to Four" by _____ is about that time of the day when night becomes morning.

9. The _____ Underground's "Sunday Morning" represents an unusually gentle moment for the band, full of sober reflection.

10. From the 1957 *Jazz Mood* album, "Morning" by Yusef _____ might not get you out of bed in a hurry, but it's just about the perfect way to ease you into the day.

DOWN

1. ____ _____'s "Chelsea Morning" should put a spring in even the heaviest of steps, with lyrics such as "Oh, won't you stay/We'll put on the day/And we'll talk in present tenses."

3. From the first, fuzzy blasts of guitar to the soaring choral voices, "Wake Up" from _____ ____'s debut LP *Funeral* is enough to power the windmills of the mind into action.

4. Despite a beautiful melody and lightness of touch, Bonnie Dobson's "_____ ___" is actually set in a post-apocalyptic society.

7. "Friday Night, Saturday Morning" is the brilliant, but often ignored, B-side to the _____'s "Ghost Town."

92. DRESS TO IMPRESS

Music and fashion have always gone hand in hand. Every new movement brings with it a dress code—from rock 'n' roll through mod to punk and beyond. It's an identifier, a way of picking out someone from the same tribe, but it's also a personal statement, a way of saying, "This is who I am." Here are ten that are dressed up to the nines.

ACROSS

3. Run-D.M.C.'s "My _____" must have seen Run, D.M.C., and Jam in trainers for the rest of their lives; surely no one has ever displayed their brand loyalty quite as unequivocally as this.

5. Starting life as an advertisement, "_____ ___"—David Dundas's 1976 ode to workwear—is thought of by many as a guilty pleasure.

6. "These _____ Are Made for Walkin'," Nancy Sinatra's empowering stomp all over the reputation—and quite possibly body—of her good-for-nothing fella is a joy from start to finish.

7. _____: "Raspberry Beret." One of the more sober items in his Purpleness's wardrobe, the hat in question was on the head of a woman.

8. OK, so "_____ ____ ___" isn't actually about royal headgear. One listen to this superb track from Brian Eno's 1977 album and you realize that the title is actually an anagram of Talking Heads.

9. A bowed bassline leaves the picked guitar and banjo to provide the counterpoint rhythms for the funky folk drums on "Wedding Dress," a track from the _____'s *Reflection* album.

DOWN

1. The best psychobilly band ever to stalk the planet, the Cramps ratcheted up the reverb, fuzz, and echo to near-dangerous levels for "_____ After Dark."

2. "_____" is a good indication of the direction in which David Bowie was heading after "Ashes to Ashes." All dressed up for the disco.

4. There are many versions of Tommy Tucker's "Hi-Heel Sneakers"—but we're ignoring those in favor of the funky makeover by _____ _____ Jr.

6. Carl Perkins's "____ _____ Shoes" is possibly the most archetypal of all rock 'n' roll songs.

93. SONGS ABOUT FOOD

"If music be the food of love, play on." Orsino's plea for more music, hoping it would sate his appetite for love in *Twelfth Night,* was never likely to work— what he needed was a good book. Having said that, the link between music and food is a strong one and the following ten all cook up a storm.

ACROSS

3. There's a real sense of fun about "Rock _____" by the B-52s, which takes the energy and experimentation of the new wave scene and adds a concentrated stock straight from 1960s rock 'n' roll.

5. The Rolling Stones' "_____ _____" clearly isn't about unrefined sweetener, but no matter—an analogous reference to food is still a reference to food.

6. There were a host of James Brown recordings referencing popcorn (actually a dance) and "_____ Popcorn" is the best of the bunch.

7. "_____" is a defiantly simple track. It gives Kelis full rein to be at her coquettish best—an opportunity she doesn't waste.

9. "The _____ _____" is one of the high points of *Led Zeppelin II*. Robert Plant is having a spot of kitchen trouble while the band are locked into one of the best grooves of their career.

10. Nightlife Unlimited's "_____ and Prunes" is the perfect musical dessert— supremely fruity and sugary sweet harmonies layered over a firm bass.

DOWN

1. When Brian Wilson heard "_____ Fields Forever," legend has it he gave up on the album *Smile* that he was working on.

2. __ ____: "Gris Gris Gumbo Ya Ya." Gumbo is a traditional one-pot stew, which provides a good analogy for the wonderful mix of New Orleans rhythm and blues, psychedelic rock, and jazz that the band serves up.

4. The J.B.s: "____ ___ ____." The intro to this tune makes an important connection—food makes people happy; music makes people happy.

8. In _____'s "Pulling Mussels (from the Shell)," Chris Difford and Glen Tilbrook—two of the best songwriters to come out of the UK—paint us a picture of seaside vacations as detailed as any photo.

94. SONGS ABOUT LOVE

It's the big one. Where themes are concerned, they don't come any bigger. Whether it's literature, music, film, or art, everything comes down to love in the end. So, in celebration of the fact, here's a list of songs about love for that special someone—whether mixtape, vinyl, C.D., or online playlist, these will get straight to the heart of the matter.

ACROSS

2. When Roy _____ tells you that "Love Will Bring Us Back Together," you can't help but believe him.

4. The 1961 release "_____ of Love" features an absolutely stunning vocal performance from Wanda Jackson as she details the spiraling madness of head-over-heels love.

8. Why ___ _____'s "Get It up for Love" isn't absolutely massive is a mystery. The opening track of *Hard Candy* is highly polished, but in a way that doesn't sacrifice character for sheen.

9. _____: "Love Loves to Love." Managing to use the word "love" as noun, transitive verb, and infinitive in the same sentence deserves an award.

10. The _____'s blues-tinged hard rock song "I Need Love" was released on the Sun label in 1969 and may not be quite what you'd expect from Elvis's former home.

DOWN

1. _____ _____: "This Must Be the Place (Naïve Melody)." Although David Byrne sees this as a love song, it's certainly not in the "crazy fireworks" tradition, more a gradual reveal.

3. As well as being Minnie _____'s most famous song, "Lovin' You" is also the one that made most extravagant use of her incredible vocal range.

5. _____ teamed up with hubby-to-be Jay-Z for "Crazy in Love," an absurdly funky tune that defined the 2000s like a dictionary defines words.

6. _____'s "Crazy Little Thing Called Love" is unusually simple for the masters of the pop opera.

7. Taking the beat from Public Enemy's "Security of the First World" and laying a Lenny Kravitz-composed song over the top, Madonna's "_____ My Love" is the stuff of pop legend.

95. HEARTBREAK SONGS

Heartbreak isn't the other side of love's coin . . . it's knowing that coin's being spent on dinner for someone else while you're sitting at home eating a microwave meal you haven't even bothered to put on a plate. We all need to wallow sometimes. Thankfully, music's well aware of this and has given us the best tools for the job . . .

ACROSS

2. One of Burt Bacharach and Hal David's most well-known songs, Dionne Warwick's version of "____ __ __" is a plea for quiet dignity in her crystal-clear tone.

3. ___ _____'s "Different for Girls" is an achingly perfect pop song about a boy looking for love from a girlfriend content for a carnal, commitment-free arrangement.

7. In ___ _____'s "Dry Your Eyes," Mike Skinner talks us through the end of a relationship from a devastated ex-boyfriend's point of view.

10. "Love Will Tear Us Apart" by ___ _____ is another stripped-back confessional, as Ian Curtis documents the breakup of his marriage.

DOWN

1. In ____ ____'s "Say Hello, Wave Goodbye," when Marc Almond sings "Take your hands off me, I don't belong to you," it's a hairs-on-the-back-of-the-neck moment.

4. "I Will _____" is the breakup song for those with an eye on the future. Gloria Gaynor's done all her crying and is now empowered and confident.

5. "Cry Me a _____" was originally written for Ella Fitzgerald, but Julie London's distinctive version gives very little wriggle room for anyone else to make it theirs.

6. Carole King's remarkably honest breakup song "___ ___ ____" is full of resignation and acceptance, making it the saddest thing ever recorded.

8. When Jimmy _____ tells us "All is lost, there's no place for beginning/ All that's left is an unhappy ending," it doesn't bode well. Luckily, "What Becomes of the Broken Hearted?" picks up toward the end.

9. At nineteen minutes, Isaac Hayes's version of Jimmy Webb's stunning "By the Time I Get to _____" gives nearly enough time to make the state line.

96. CHRISTMAS SONGS

The tree's up, the stockings are over the fireplace, and the house reeks of whatever it is they put in those mulled wine sachets—cinnamon and mold? There's just one thing missing, and it's not Father Christmas, it's music! Where would the season of goodwill be without some good tunes? The following are guaranteed to bring festive cheer.

ACROSS

2. The Pogues with Kirsty MacColl: "Fairytale of ___ ____." There's not a lot of Christmas spirit evident in this curse-filled call and response between two lovers who are arguing on Christmas Eve.

4. "_____ Christmas Time" shares two things with other songs from the *McCartney II* sessions. Firstly, the presence of a massive synthesizer and, secondly, a lot of people hate it.

6. "Santa Claus Is Coming to Town" by the _____ is an utter adrenalin rush of pure excitement, galloping along like a magic reindeer.

8. Bing Crosby's recording is the best-selling single of all time, but the Drifters' doo-wop version of "_____ _____" has got it all wrapped up.

9. Take a standard song, add in some Christmas references and some bells in the background, give it to Bobby Helms, and you've got "_____ ____ Rock," a guaranteed Christmas hit!

DOWN

1. _____ ___ recorded the country-tinged Christmas pop hit "Rockin' Around the Christmas Tree" when she was just thirteen.

3. Bing Crosby and David Bowie's performance of "Little _____ Boy" on Bing's *Merrie Olde Christmas* TV special added a bit of class to Christmas.

5. Vera Lyn's recording of "The Boy That _____ _____ Forgot" is better known, but Nat King Cole's delivery brings tears to the eyes.

7. _____: "Merry Christmas Everybody." Like Father Christmas, Noddy Holder and company's song comes but once a year, but when it does, it screams "Christmas!" like nothing else.

8. _____: "I Wish It Could Be Christmas Every Day." Much has been made of the logistical nightmare of actually having Christmas every day, but here the sentiment is a fine one.

97. INSULTING SONGS

As well as spreading messages about peace and love around the world, music has also proved popular for those wishing to settle scores or launch an all-out attack. Being able to do so from the relative safety of the recording studio makes it easy, but you still have to make sure that the barbs hit their intended target. Here's a puzzle that really packs a punch.

ACROSS

2. _____ _____'s "You're So Vain" is thought to be directed, at least in part, at actor Warren Beatty.

6. The ___ _____'s anger-fueled attack on the monarchy, "God Save the Queen," has been seen as an assault on the very fabric of British society.

7. "___ ' __ __" pulls no punches. Directed at Tupac Shakur's former friend Biggie Smalls, it casts aspersions on the fidelity of his wife before making direct threats on his life. Three months later, Tupac was murdered.

8. In "Holiday in _____," the Dead Kennedys attack brutal totalitarian regimes and the West's sleepwalking complacency about world events.

9. Though clearly at the end of his tether with an acquaintance, in "Your Mind Is on _____" pianist Mose Alison is in no mood to raise his voice.

10. ___ __ _____'s "Fuck You"—re-titled "Forget You" to ease the path to worldwide release—is a resounding dismissal of a former love and her new, flash boyfriend.

DOWN

1. In the _____ _____' "Elizabeth My Dear," poor Liz has to face another angry mob, although a much quieter one, to the tune of "Scarborough Fair."

3. The raw emotion of Bob Dylan's bitter outpourings in the song "_____ ____" has led to near endless speculation as to who is the subject.

4. After taking umbrage at some pot shots on McCartney's *Ram* album, John Lennon responded with "How Do You _____?"

5. "Accident Waiting to Happen" by _____ _____ takes aim at a friend who has grown old disgracefully and manages to use the superbly worked, Kinks-referencing line "You're a dedicated swallower of fascism."

98. COVER VERSIONS

A musical acknowledgment, a nod of recognition, cover versions are a convenient way for musicians to acknowledge their influences and wear their heart on their sleeve notes. All bands have played someone else's songs at some point in their career, but when someone gets it absolutely right, it's like the song was theirs all along.

ACROSS

3. The biggest shock about "Try a Little _____" is discovering that Otis Redding's version wasn't the original.

6. The Jesus and Mary Chain: "_____' ___." Brian Wilson would never have foreseen the treatment meted out to his 1963 ray of sunshine pop by the Reid brothers.

7. My Bloody Valentine's surprisingly sensitive treatment of the John Barry classic "We Have All the ____ in the World" gives it a new lease of life.

8. Sharing a similar pop sensibility to Scottish band the Vaselines, Nirvana treated "_____ ____" with respect—before belting the hell out of it.

10. The Donovan folk-funk original "_____ _____ Man" was reasonably far-out as it was, but the Butthole Surfers managed to tease yet more otherworldly oddness from the song.

DOWN

1. The _____'s cover of singer/songwriter Suzanne Vega's song "Luka" reveals some surprising melodic similarities between the two.

2. In the Deidre Wilson Tabac's "___ ____," there's a driving, funky blues beat where Ringo would have played a fill.

4. Originally by Dandy Livingstone and called "Rudy, a Message to You," the _____ turned up, turned the title around, and . . . well, that's about it.

5. "All Along the _____." Dylan must be the most covered songwriter on Earth. Hendrix was a fan and put his stamp on the 1968 single so firmly that it's like listening to a completely different song.

9. Johnny Cash: "____." A country music legend covering a Nine Inch Nails song just shouldn't work, but it does.

99. UNEXPECTED SURPRISES

There's a special joy to be had in finding new music but, occasionally, the search can mean you overlook artists you think you already know. Most established musicians have tried their hand at different genres over the years, and many of them have great songs squirreled away, out of plain sight. Here are ten guaranteed to make you look twice . . .

ACROSS

2. Hidden away on the B-side to ___ _____'s "You'll Always Be a Friend" is "Go-Go Girl," a belting bit of poppy garage.

3. ___ ____: "On Time." This Maurice Gibb–penned folk funk gem begins with a slightly off-kilter lone acoustic guitar. By the end, it's been joined by drums, bass, piano, and strings for a rousing finale.

5. The former Stones bassist, ____ _____, unearthed the treasure "Beach Chase" in 1981 while composing the score for the film *Green Ice*.

7. It's not like _____ _____ has never recorded any good songs, but "The Girl Can't Help It" from the *Tracks 'n' Grooves* album is just such a departure.

9. "_____ _____"—before the kaftan and the film soundtracks, Demis Roussos and Vangelis were two-thirds of Aphrodite's Child.

10. Providing something of a twist in the tale of Chubby Checker's career is the unexpected experimentalism of his *Chequered* LP. "_____," recorded around the same time, is fast, furious, and funky.

DOWN

1. Gilbert O'Sullivan: "Too Much _____." Everything about this gem comes as a surprise.

4. Although known as an actor, Paul Nicholas started his career as a pop singer and recorded at least two jaw-dropping tunes. The Eastern-influenced, psychedelic "_____" is a monster.

6. Well known for occasionally managing a decent song, even "Crazy Horses" couldn't prepare you for "I, I, I." Bee Gee Maurice Gibb, on production duty, coaxes a disco classic out of ___ _____.

8. John Betjeman reads his poem "Late Flowering ____" to a pleasingly offbeat musical accompaniment. This unconventional offering was covered (well) in 2012 by the Asphodells.

100. SONGS ABOUT YOUTH

Before it was seemly for people in their forties to wear jeans, popular music in all its guises was largely the province of the young. That's all changed now, fifty is the new thirty or something. Pop's preoccupation with youth hasn't shifted however, as the kids look forward to a wide-open future and adults gaze wistfully back into the past.

ACROSS

5. _____ _____'s album *Daydream Nation* remains, for many, the band's artistic pinnacle, and "Teenage Riot" is right at the summit.

6. When it comes to blues-based rock 'n' roll, the Flamin' Groovies' 1971 album _____ _____ is right up there with the Rolling Stones.

9. There's no tantrums, no upsets, no call to arms on "_____," from Big Star's 1972 debut album *#1 Record*.

10. There's certainly a theme of stretching the elastic of childhood running through much of Kurt Cobain's career, including the unintentional anthem for youth, "Smells Like Teen Spirit," by him and his band, _____.

DOWN

1. Written specifically to emulate the feeling of breaking up for summer, Alice Cooper knew exactly how big his song "_____ ___" could be.

2. These days, Roger Daltrey presumably sings "Hope I die before I get too old," but back in 1965, "__ _____"—the Who's testament to youth—drew a line in the sand to mark "the kids" out from "everyone else."

3. "Teenage _____" by the Ramones is not the most straightforward of songs; it's about a boy who, following exposure to the insecticide DDT, is in need of medical attention.

4. Understandably, one of John Peel's favorite records, "Teenage Kicks" by the _____ was played twice in a row by the D.J. when he first aired it.

7. Supergrass: "_____." Though some people seem to reserve particular disdain for this joyful celebration of unfettered teenage abandon, it's difficult to see why they take such offense.

8. The touching song "A _____ in Love," dealing with the trials and tribulations of the fickle adolescent heart, was an enormous hit among post-war teenagers for Dion DiMucci and the Belmonts in 1959.

101. SONGS ABOUT ANIMALS

There are many things that separate us from the animals we share this planet with—the ability of abstract thought, the scope of our creative compulsion . . . and mustard. No animal would ever invent mustard. That aside, we love our furry and feathered friends, when we're not eating them, and we're prone to making a song and dance about it too.

ACROSS

5. _____'s first single, "Horse with No Name" has come to be a signature tune—which is surprising considering the fact that many people assume it was a Neil Young song.

7. Fleetwood Mac: "_____." The instrumental manages to convey the animal it references so well.

9. Robert Smith has tried to distance himself from the jazzy chutzpah of the ____'s "The Lovecats," and cited alcohol as the driving force behind it.

DOWN

1. Despite the odd allusion to crying birds, _____'s "When Doves Cry" is an enduringly brilliant piece of pop from the album *Purple Rain*.

2. ____ _____: "Johnny the Fox Meets Jimmy the Weed." The titular Johnny is actually a man who displays the characteristics of a fox.

3. Nick Drake's "_____ _____ ___" is an allegory for depression. Even at his most harrowing—and this is certainly harrowing—his music was always beautiful and captivating.

4. The Rolling Stones: "____ _____." The authentic sound may have been due to recording it at the legendary Muscle Shoals studio.

5. George Clinton's "_____ Dog" missed out on chart success when it was released in 1982, but didn't go unnoticed—most notably, Snoop Dogg sampled it for his 1993 single "Who Am I (What's My Name)?"

6. The Beatles' "_ __ ___ _____" takes its cue from Lewis Carroll's poem in *Alice in Wonderland,* but people are still trying to work out the meaning of the song.

8. Taken from *Doolittle,* the Pixies' track "_____ Gone to Heaven," is one of Black Francis's more straightforward lyrical offerings.

102. DISNEY FAMILY FAVORITES

For many of us, the first time we were confronted with music that enchanted and engaged us was on television or at the movies. Disney has a special knack for musical alchemy and seems to be able to score films with songs that bury their way into your brain and stay with you forever. Here are ten that show no sign of moving.

ACROSS

3. Randy Newman's theme tune for *Toy Story*, "You've Got a _____ in Me," perfectly captures the special bond between a child and a favorite toy.

4. 1941's *Dumbo* was an attempt to get back to the simple art of basic storytelling after the ambitious flop of *Fantasia*. Quite how they thought "Pink Elephant on _____" would achieve this aim is unclear.

7. 1967's *The Jungle Book* raised the bar when it came to soundtracks. The voice of Phil Harris as Baloo is key to the success of "Bare _____."

8. Proving that cartoons can be educational, it's good to report that "_____ _____," from *The Lion King*, does actually mean "no worries" in Swahili.

10. Disney's 1989 film *The Little Mermaid* contains the calypso classic "_____ ___ ___," during which Sebastian the crab tries to persuade mermaid Ariel to remain in her watery home. It won an Oscar.

DOWN

1. Another song from *The Jungle Book*, "_ _____ __ ____ ___" is a joint-jumpin' jewel. The scat duel between Baloo and King Louie is a particular high point in the film.

2. _____ _____ is a musical that relies as heavily on the music as the fantasy for its success. "Supercalifragilisticexpialidocious," based around a nonsense word, revels in the joy of language.

5. With actor Jason Segel delivering lines like "If I'm a Muppet, then I'm a very manly Muppet" in the song "Man or _____" meant 2011's *The Muppets* delighted old and young alike . . . and bagged an Oscar.

6. While traveling over the rooftops of Paris, our heroes meet up with a band, who break into the jazzy ditty "Everybody Wants to Be a ___."

9. With Peggy Lee writing the songs, it was a fair bet that *Lady and the Tramp* was going to be a cut above. Peggy takes lead vocals on "He's a_____."

103. MOVIE SOUNDTRACKS

The best soundtracks work hand-in-hand with their movie partner, creating tension, heightening emotion, and making us laugh, cry, and stuff ourselves full of popcorn. The very best can also stand alone without relying on bright lights, flashing colors, and huge explosions to make an impact. The following are stars of the screen and the surround sound.

ACROSS

3. The actors themselves wrote an entire album's worth of spoof songs for the 1984 mock "rockumentary," *This Is _____ Tap*.

4. While Curtis Mayfield's score for _____ ___ has become a funk staple, the film itself has blended into the background.

7. There's no denying the massive cultural impact the Bee Gees' soundtrack to _____ *Night Fever* had, turning a low-budget film into a worldwide, box-office record breaker.

8. ___ _____' six-song soundtrack to the 1967 film *Magical Mystery Tour* was, in some respects, more of a concept than their *Sgt. Pepper's* album.

9. Prince: "_____ ____." So entwined are the film and the soundtrack, working out which came first can lead to losing oneself in a chicken-and-egg catch-22.

DOWN

1. Charley Cuva's music to Robert Downey Sr.'s 1969 film _____ *Swope* only received a release in 2006, and even then, only 500 copies.

2. It's hard to imagine Ridley Scott's _____ _____, an epic interpretation of Philip K. Dick's *Do Androids Dream of Electric Sheep?* without the subtle and satisfying score from Vangelis.

3. The score to David Lynch's 1999 drama *The _____ Story* was written by his longtime associate Angelo Badalamenti.

5. While he composed edgier, more satisfying scores, Ennio Morricone's music for *The Good, the Bad and the _____* has managed to seep its way into the planet's collective consciousness.

6. The Monkees: ____. This stream-of-consciousness film may have gone over the heads of many, but the brilliant soundtrack shows what happens when ambition is allowed to run riot.

104. HALLOWEEN

Halloween is as good a time as any for a party, but what music to choose for the ideal rave from the grave? You need music good enough to raise the dead and keep the living on their feet, so once you've played "Thriller" ten times in a row, what then? Thankfully, popular music is full of horrific hits . . .

ACROSS

1.   Ronnie Cook and the Gaylads' "___ ___ ____" is so good the Cramps chose to cover it on their *Psychedelic Jungle* album.

5.   _____: "Season of the Witch." As a squad of cover versions lines up, desperate to be picked, we wave them all away for the clipped precision and haunting guitar lines of the original from 1966.

6.   German group ___ _____'s 1970 hit, "The Witch," would fall squarely into the novelty camp, were it not for the fact that, hiding beneath the screaming, cackling overdubs, is a good song.

7.   Believe it or not, *The _____ of Dartmoore's Dracula's Music Cabinet* LP is a sought-after pseudo soundtrack, full of breaks and beats.

9.   Screamin' ___ _____'s "I Put a Spell on You" is a combination of music hall exhibitionist schtick, hammy horror acting, and absolute anguish.

DOWN

1.   While the Specials' 1981 single "_____ _____" is more party political than party-till-dawn, it's still on the Halloween playlist.

2.   The _____ Country: "My Girlfriend Is a Witch." Boy meets girl, boy falls in love, boy realizes that girl is a witch.

3.   If, at any time during your party, the Halloween spirit seems to be flagging, one burst of the Cramps' 1979 song "_____ ___" will be more than enough to reanimate even the deadest of feet.

4.   Screaming Halloween in the way that Noddy Holder signals Christmas is "_____ ____," the 1962 novelty hit from Bobby "Boris" Pickett.

8.   _____'s distinctive blend of Native American voices and chants in "Witch Queen of New Orleans" certainly helps with the overall feeling of mystery and magic.

105. SPACE AND SCIENCE FICTION

The cosmos has long held a singular fascination for musicians—whether it's exploring the endless sonic possibilities that space suggests or looking to alien life-forms as a parallel with the marginalized outsider identities that pepper pop music. And then there's the big rockets and cool space suits of course . . . The following ten are all aiming for the stars.

ACROSS

3. _____'s "Balloon" is a lovely, lilting acoustic rock track that comes from the 1971 album *Space Hymns*, with the repeated vocal line "Balloon, just off the surface of the moon."

5. Marvin Gaye walked into the sessions for the *Here, My Dear* album intending to knock something out quickly, as his ex-wife was getting the royalties. One listen to "A Funky Space _____" is enough to see that professionalism soon took over.

6. Inspired by the science-fiction tales of Isaac Asimov, Alan Parsons set about making a concept LP. The title track, "_ _____," is the standout.

8. David Bowie: "_____ _____." An obvious choice but, just to be different, this is the version from his promotional film *Love You Til Tuesday*.

10. Sun Ra: *Space Is the* _____. If you came to this album with no knowledge of his reputation, one look at the cover would be enough to let you know this wasn't your ordinary musician.

DOWN

1. _____: *Ladies and Gentlemen We Are Floating in Space*. Most people had the band pinned as space cadets right from the start, but this album manages to float effortlessly while never lacking gravity.

2. The titular track "_____" is the best on the album by light-years. The eight-minute space funk sees band War take off into the cosmos.

4. ____ _____'s *The Piper at the Gates of Dawn* album contained a few surprises, but none of them quite as raw as "Interstellar Overdrive."

7. Apparently, the inspiration for "_____ ___," Elton John's launch into space, was lyricist Bernie Taupin's sighting of a shooting star.

9. Johnny Harris's brilliant lunar boogie "_____" was composed for an episode of *Buck Rogers in the 25th Century*.

106. SONGS ABOUT SPORTS

The competitive edge of sports is often glimpsed in musical rivalries; hip-hop, in particular, is stuffed full of them. The drive to compete fuels our passion for sports, and where better to wax lyrical about all of the beautiful games than in song? Like the competitors at a school sports day, these are all winners.

ACROSS

3. The soccer song "Ponta De Lança Africano (Umbabarauma)" gets a hat trick, scoring on groove, melody, and style. No surprise, then, that the architect is _____ ___, from his album *África Brasil*.

6. _____'s "Eye of the Tiger" or the theme tune to *Rocky III*, as it will always be known, is pretty much like the movie it soundtracks—full of emotion, cheesy as hell, but utterly irresistible.

8. Super Furry Animals: "Venus and _____." Although it takes its title from the Williams sisters, this is actually about a child and his pet tortoises.

10. Swiss band Yello stepped up a gear with "___ ____," their 1998 ode to motorsports.

DOWN

1. Kraftwerk got on their bikes this time. The result, "____ __ _____," was one of the most celebratory recordings the band ever made.

2. Despite being regarded as a stinker of a World Cup, Italia '90 gave England fans the best World Cup song ever: "World in Motion" by ___ _____.

4. Don Fardon's "_____ ___" was written to accompany a BBC documentary about soccer legend George Best.

5. _____ ____'s "Wide World of Sports" is a disco hit from 1979. D.J. Q saw it for the winner it is when he used it as the building block for his 1996 house classic "We Are One."

7. "When an Old Cricketer Leaves the Crease," from folk legend ___ _____, could make a pretty good case for being his best-known song.

9. 10cc: "_____ Holiday." Based on actual experiences while on vacation in Jamaica, the song highlights the power of sports—specifically cricket.

107. SONGS ABOUT TIME

The passage of time has proved a huge theme for musicians. As the clock ticks down and we all make our way to the same ultimate destination, it provides a truly shared focus, something we can all get on board with. And while philosophers and scientists try to work out the nature of this abstract concept, these artists and songs know what the time is.

ACROSS

3. The clever song "Time Becomes" by _____ consists of just a voice (that of *Star Trek* actor Michael Dorn).

5. The Rolling Stones' "____ __ __ __ ____" is sung as a message to a former lover, assuring them that they won't be able to stay away.

7. The Lemonheads' "_____ ___" is the high point from their 1989 album *Lick*. "Here I am outside your house at 3 a.m./Tryin' to think you out of bed/I whistle at your sill/It echoes 'cross the street instead."

9. If there's one track that really sums up the thrill of the _____ ____ first album, it's "Time to Get Ill."

DOWN

1. "Time of the Season" didn't achieve success until after the _____ had gone their separate ways in 1969.

2. _____ _____'s "9 to 5" is the theme tune to the 1980 comedy film of the same name, and a clock-watching classic!

4. In "___ ___ ___," Pop Will Eat Itself lean heavily on Alan Moore's *Watchmen* graphic novel and the U.S. Armed Forces' alert system to tell us we are minutes away from nuclear war.

6. Sparks got producer extraordinaire Giorgio Moroder to help with the urgent feel of their 1979 track "____ ___ _____." It was an inspired choice.

8. A monotonous, metronomic beat sets the pace on this low-key title track "_____ Seconds," from the Cure's second LP.

9. The most famous time-related song of them all, ____ _____'s 1954 "Rock Around the Clock" let teenagers know that *their* time had come.

108. SONGS ABOUT DEATH

And so we face the final curtain . . . The only certainty that life has for any of us is that it will end. Some broach the subject with gravitas and grave concern while others take a more lighthearted approach. And that's the key—the destination is fixed, but we decide how we face the journey. These songs are going to the grave in style.

ACROSS

3. In "Do You Realize?" Wayne Coyne's musings on our insignificance in the grand scheme of things never strays far from the artful and beautifully embellished pop that the _____ ____ have excelled at over the years.

4. Thought by some to be an endorsement of suicide, there's a far more poetic reading of the Blue Öyster Cult's 1976 single "Don't Fear the _____."

6. ___ _____'s "Knocking on Heaven's Door" shows what happens when someone really does shoot the sheriff.

7. _____ _____: "Always Look on the Bright Side of Life." The hilarious adult-Disney whimsy of Eric Idle's closing moments in *The Life of Brian* leaves everyone in stitches.

8. Whether or not ____ _____'s "Needle of Death" played a part in the inspiration for Neil Young's "Needle and the Damage Done," the two songs are kindred spirits of a kind.

9. The _____-___: "Leader of the Pack." This teenage tragedy tells the story of a girl whose relationship with the leader of a motorcycle gang is doomed from the start.

DOWN

1. Bobbie Gentry's storytelling outstrips most, with "Ode to _____ ___," a tale of a local boy who kills himself by jumping off the Tallahatchie Bridge.

2. The Bad Seeds' "Where the ____ _____ Grow," with Kylie Minogue, is the description of a murder from two points of view—the killer and his victim.

5. Following _____ _____'s suicide, the laid-bare, confessional cry of "King's Crossing" makes for very uncomfortable listening.

7. If claims that one in seven funerals feature a rendition of Frank Sinatra's "__ ___" are true, it's probably because the song speaks of a life well lived and (relatively) free of regret.

MUSIC
WORD SEARCH PUZZLES

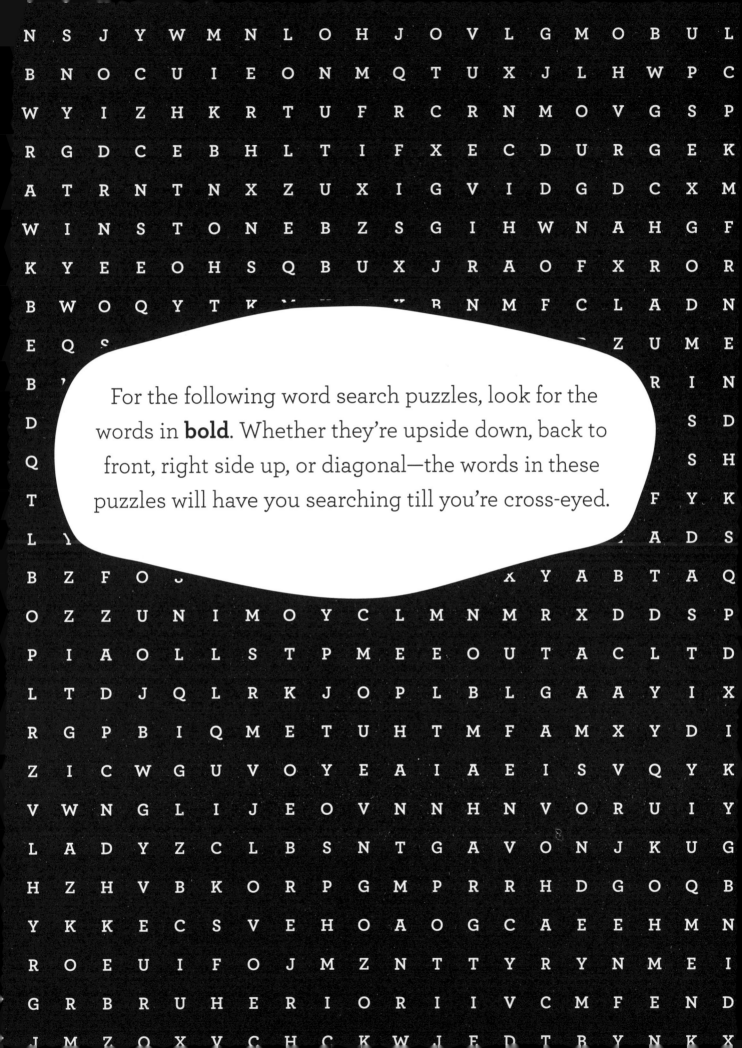

For the following word search puzzles, look for the words in **bold**. Whether they're upside down, back to front, right side up, or diagonal—the words in these puzzles will have you searching till you're cross-eyed.

1. FRONTMEN/WOMEN

```
P  V  Z  R  T  L  U  H  P  Z  L  A  C  I  O
Y  R  U  C  R  E  M  E  I  D  D  E  R  F  G
V  T  H  I  T  U  K  A  L  E  F  E  X  L  Z
H  Y  U  U  Z  J  M  M  B  C  U  Q  G  X  S
N  E  J  A  M  E  S  B  R  O  W  N  C  I  M
T  R  E  V  B  X  I  G  G  Y  P  O  P  M  K
B  T  F  T  F  E  T  H  F  O  K  S  H  I  G
W  L  F  V  H  O  Y  S  R  T  H  I  N  C  G
V  A  W  A  Z  G  P  U  B  H  H  R  Q  K  F
A  D  R  E  K  C  O  C  S  I  V  R  A  J  P
I  R  W  Q  N  C  X  R  E  T  P  O  D  A  X
Y  E  S  D  D  M  K  Z  J  U  K  M  K  G  H
X  G  S  Z  R  C  C  A  G  I  E  M  O  G  Q
V  O  J  A  N  I  S  J  O  P  L  I  N  E  G
T  R  W  E  M  V  Z  F  J  N  K  J  O  R  X
```

1. DEBBIE HARRY
2. JARVIS COCKER
3. FELA KUTI
4. IGGY POP
5. JIM MORRISON
6. ROGER DALTREY
7. MICK JAGGER
8. JAMES BROWN
9. FREDDIE MERCURY
10. JANIS JOPLIN

2. KEYBOARD WIZARDS

```
K X J F M Q R T V J L N B R F
H E V O Z N R L H I X O E E Y
F P R R N E X Q S E U T R D B
Y H M A K L F T R X Q S N N Q
J Y A O Z G O O C A X E I O G
T I O L T N G R L D V R E W M
N B J E S D A A D M F P W E Y
Q G W M Y H W M L S O Y O I Z
I L I R U B B G Y L Z L R V D
A T K S K F Y X G A P L R E S
H A A D F T S E G Z R I E T U
E G H A U S G X T U F B L S V
R I C K W A K E M A N Q L I G
N O S R E M E H T I E K G Y H
R I C H A R D W R I G H T J E
```

1. RAY MANZAREK
2. BILLY PRESTON
3. BOOKER T
4. RICK WAKEMAN
5. BERNIE WORRELL
6. LONNIE LISTON SMITH
7. KEITH EMERSON
8. STEVIE WONDER
9. RICHARD WRIGHT
10. JON LORD

3. LESSER-KNOWN GUITAR GREATS

```
N  M  A  E  I  D  J  V  S  T  G  Q  I  A  D
K  B  M  L  U  W  Z  Z  R  H  C  V  S  O  F
S  B  K  N  M  W  Z  H  Y  J  W  P  T  R  N
W  D  H  T  Q  C  E  M  M  M  S  Z  E  I  A
J  Z  L  O  K  C  K  N  Q  A  J  D  V  Z  N
H  S  H  E  N  M  Y  A  J  S  D  G  E  E  A
G  H  L  I  I  M  J  W  Y  I  Y  N  A  B  H
V  H  R  L  O  H  Q  E  C  G  C  L  R  C
G  P  R  V  X  P  S  S  D  S  I  G  B  G  U
X  S  O  G  A  I  T  N  A  S  I  L  I  L  B
R  E  Q  R  Q  O  H  Z  I  R  H  Q  N  A  Y
G  R  E  E  N  W  O  O  D  V  B  K  I  Y  O
B  J  P  E  Y  E  C  K  O  X  E  M  P  P  R
A  C  U  I  H  I  H  J  T  P  R  K  G  M  J
R  A  N  D  Y  C  A  L  I  F  O  R  N  I  A
```

1. RANDY CALIFORNIA
2. AL MCKAY
3. J. MASCIS
4. FREDDIE STONE
5. SANTIAGO

6. KEVIN SHIELDS
7. ROY BUCHANAN
8. PRINCE
9. GREENWOOD
10. STEVE ALBINI

4. DRUMMERS

```
R  H  E  V  H  O  D  T  R  M  H  C  R  G  H
A  U  Y  T  N  R  E  R  A  D  C  P  Z  C  I
D  A  V  E  G  R  O  H  L  H  I  L  N  C  P
E  O  E  D  R  I  N  X  I  X  R  Z  O  K  O
R  U  M  Y  L  O  N  F  E  K  Y  E  O  Z  T
R  C  C  V  B  E  N  G  B  R  D  Z  M  F  S
B  O  L  N  E  U  I  M  E  X  D  M  H  M  P
X  M  H  M  Y  M  K  F  Z  R  U  E  T  M  E
X  O  R  C  V  T  W  F  E  B  B  D  I  W  S
J  K  Z  I  A  X  O  Z  I  L  X  A  E  B  D
A  O  I  M  V  O  Z  U  T  G  B  I  K  X  O
X  Y  M  X  A  L  R  E  I  C  W  B  I  E  J
C  D  L  J  O  P  Z  X  N  P  R  O  U  D  R
V  J  F  P  T  O  N  Y  A  L  L  E  N  T  Y
W  K  O  A  B  G  J  Q  V  M  G  I  D  O  S
```

1. JOHN BONHAM
2. DAVE GROHL
3. TERRY COX
4. LIEBEZEIT
5. GINGER BAKER
6. BUDDY RICH
7. MAX ROACH
8. STUBBLEFIELD
9. TONY ALLEN
10. KEITH MOON

5. BASS PLAYERS

```
B  E  A  X  D  G  S  B  T  C  E  E  J  Y  O
Q  O  R  E  P  W  B  K  E  M  C  M  O  E  J
G  L  O  A  L  T  L  S  S  K  U  F  H  N  O
H  E  L  T  E  F  N  Z  H  D  R  O  N  T  N
Q  A  G  U  S  P  D  W  S  N  B  O  P  R  E
Y  V  O  C  W  Y  S  C  S  B  K  X  A  A  N
E  F  O  D  V  J  C  E  C  D  C  W  U  C  T
B  A  N  P  M  T  L  O  K  Q  A  G  L  C  W
K  Q  R  D  K  Z  R  Z  L  A  J  U  J  M  H
T  C  Y  F  V  R  B  N  J  L  H  M  O  L  I
Z  C  Z  D  G  F  F  Y  O  M  I  S  N  U  S
N  N  U  D  D  L  A  N  O  D  E  N  E  A  T
J  A  C  O  P  A  S  T  O  R  I  U  S  P  L
S  D  R  A  W  D  E  D  R  A  N  R  E  B  E
A  V  C  O  Y  A  I  Q  A  L  L  S  P  G  J
```

1.	BOOTSY COLLINS	6.	JACO PASTORIUS
2.	JOHN PAUL JONES	7.	JOHN ENTWHISTLE
3.	BERNARD EDWARDS	8.	DONALD DUNN
4.	ROBBIE SHAKESPEARE	9.	FLEA
5.	PAUL MCCARTNEY	10.	JACK BRUCE

6. RAPPERS

```
H  L  J  E  R  V  E  J  F  G  O  U  S  P  K
A  C  Z  U  C  N  N  J  G  G  X  A  Y  J  B
C  R  N  M  F  D  O  O  M  O  N  T  H  L  I
N  H  I  O  B  P  S  F  K  D  M  P  L  U  P
W  M  U  E  M  Q  R  C  W  P  O  C  B  F  S
N  W  I  C  O  E  K  C  X  O  O  X  H  I  S
O  P  N  K  K  M  H  Y  L  O  Q  Y  W  R  Z
T  E  W  U  A  D  U  A  L  N  C  O  V  W  E
O  T  U  J  Q  R  F  J  O  S  P  E  X  Q  P
R  A  T  V  N  M  N  R  D  R  C  X  B  E  Z
I  G  G  D  J  W  L  R  Q  W  A  L  N  K  E
O  E  H  C  K  R  M  X  F  Y  Z  H  G  V  N
U  W  J  X  K  P  B  H  O  L  A  I  P  S  I
S  J  Z  R  X  J  L  Y  H  M  F  Z  R  R  T
H  A  L  L  I  K  E  C  A  F  T  S  O  H  G
```

1. PHAROAHE MONCH
2. SNOOP DOGG
3. NAS
4. MF DOOM
5. CHUCK D

6. NOTORIOUS
7. LL COOL J
8. GHOSTFACE KILLAH
9. RAKIM
10. KRS ONE

7. COUNTRY FUNK

```
F  K  D  R  O  F  M  I  J  J  P  R  W  Z  N
I  D  E  N  N  I  S  T  H  E  F  O  X  N  D
R  O  N  R  L  X  J  E  R  R  Y  R  E  E  D
E  L  C  W  Q  S  C  E  B  A  X  B  N  R  D
B  B  N  S  Y  U  N  O  O  H  O  H  T  T  U
R  M  Y  F  I  E  D  F  P  B  B  F  B  I  F
I  B  N  R  L  C  V  O  B  T  I  R  H  H  D
M  X  W  O  D  K  N  I  N  T  L  B  M  W  Y
S  N  J  H  Y  S  E  A  K  C  L  Q  K  I  N
T  M  G  O  D  G  V  E  R  W  O  W  V  K  G
O  D  E  R  E  C  N  M  T  F  F  O  M  A  N
N  M  L  N  U  M  P  G  Y  H  L  R  P  J  Y
E  N  T  D  X  K  Q  K  H  G  S  U  H  E  W
I  R  B  W  Z  G  M  P  U  A  U  B  O  J  R
Y  M  V  K  J  L  R  S  N  B  W  J  F  S  B
```

1. JERRY REED
2. DON COOPER
3. FIRE & BRIMSTONE
4. BOBBIE GENTRY
5. JIM FORD
6. SOUL FRANCISCO
7. JAKI WHITREN
8. JOLENE
9. DENNIS THE FOX
10. BYRDS

8. FOLK ROCK

```
S T E E L E Y E S P A N U T T
E L D N A C W O L L E M Q H R
T A A Z E V U E H P N Q S E O
C T C O N S F W D L Y J L B P
H B O H E D P L Z A S W N Y R
E G U E E E A C Q F N Q E R I
O L R F S K G T J U H N G D A
N T G P F S L A V D Y N A S F
S S E N K A Y M E H X A A L D
I R F Q A Y L Y P S U L X W C
S O T H U T F O R L T Y Z Z W
L R H F O H N E A O I D W S Q
L N C N A R K E O E Q B E Y U
N E I R C N L L P O Q O F C F
N F F K S B B E A B Y B S K V
```

1. CLANNAD
2. BOB DYLAN
3. TREES
4. STEELEYE SPAN
5. **BUFFALO** SPRINGFIELD
6. THE BYRDS
7. ESPERS
8. MELLOW CANDLE
9. PENTANGLE
10. **FAIRPORT** CONVENTION

9. FUSION FLINGS

```
K  G  P  Z  X  B  D  G  P  N  V  E  X  C  T
U  C  O  G  B  H  K  K  O  B  L  K  Y  R  F
N  C  O  O  J  M  B  C  H  A  I  X  O  E  R
H  F  Z  C  D  F  Y  E  S  V  Y  P  T  N  A
S  L  C  Y  N  V  O  T  F  O  E  I  N  I  N
I  Y  Y  R  N  A  I  O  L  R  G  T  H  H  K
V  Q  X  G  Q  C  H  B  R  R  M  V  N  C  Z
A  S  Z  P  R  C  X  E  E  V  M  H  M  A  A
H  P  E  O  S  D  H  N  I  S  K  N  O  M  P
A  R  C  L  N  T  E  Q  O  B  R  O  Y  T  P
M  K  E  D  A  L  C  X  R  A  R  V  R  F  A
C  W  D  E  Q  O  Z  O  B  I  F  E  S  O  O
R  H  W  F  N  C  N  O  K  A  H  Z  H  S  V
P  M  S  J  B  I  L  L  Y  C  O  B  H  A  M
S  I  V  A  D  S  E  L  I  M  G  U  P  V  P
```

1.	HERBIE HANCOCK	6.	FRANK ZAPPA
2.	SOFT MACHINE	7.	ELASTIC ROCK
3.	WEATHER REPORT	8.	MILES DAVIS
4.	BILLY COBHAM	9.	MAHAVISHNU ORCHESTRA
5.	GOOD VIBES	10.	ENERGIT

10. GIRL GROUPS

```
O  L  N  R  K  R  T  N  R  Y  F  T  M  L  O
Y  D  D  C  V  R  U  W  S  V  D  U  L  D  G
S  G  I  R  L  S  A  L  O  U  D  L  E  L  N
S  A  R  Y  S  T  E  L  I  I  B  U  R  I  W
E  E  B  Q  E  L  Y  M  G  T  S  R  O  H  S
T  B  T  S  L  R  I  G  E  C  I  P  S  C  F
T  R  N  T  L  G  X  D  Z  R  C  A  R  S  W
E  Z  I  U  E  D  M  K  N  R  P  N  M  Y  K
L  P  C  E  R  N  E  N  V  O  G  U  E  N  H
E  C  Q  B  I  E  O  F  L  E  V  V  S  I  T
V  E  F  Y  H  U  E  R  D  N  F  K  F  T  D
R  R  C  H  S  H  A  N  G  R  I  L  A  S  K
A  P  P  S  Z  M  R  K  G  T  H  M  S  E  N
M  F  M  M  W  K  X  F  E  O  V  I  Q  D  B
W  I  H  J  Q  J  D  J  M  X  X  Y  Q  M  Q
```

1.	EN VOGUE	6.	THE **SHIRELLES**
2.	SUPREMES	7.	THE **RONETTES**
3.	GIRLS ALOUD	8.	THE **SHANGRI LAS**
4.	T.L.C.	9.	THE **MARVELETTES**
5.	SPICE GIRLS	10.	DESTINY'S CHILD

11. BOY BANDS

```
D M N S R D E J N H E T T E N
A N M D R D A F K P H C N U E
Y P O I Z F S K I E J O B D W
T X W K H V T E J L Z I R Y E
Q W N W M O H A T Y T K X X D
V L X E I S C R O E C S S T I
A E K N O K P B S I W L E M T
K R T E S T D O F Q O M B W I
E Y J O P L A R X A Q X E X O
C E N X H H S K Y S F H K K N
B K D N O I T C E R I D E N O
B A C K S T R E E T B O Y S A
T H E M O N K E E S H E Y O S
D A E M A O W R N Q F A B F T
P E T A Y W C H Z Y F Y T B M
```

1. BOYZONE
2. THE MONKEES
3. TAKE THAT
4. EAST 17
5. THE JACKSON 5
6. ONE DIRECTION
7. WESTLIFE
8. NEW KIDS ON THE BLOCK
9. BACKSTREET BOYS
10. NEW EDITION

12. POP PERFECTION

```
D  J  F  B  W  I  V  L  Z  K  E  R  I  A  S
F  D  J  K  H  Y  D  R  R  V  O  O  M  G  N
M  K  T  B  R  A  V  G  O  P  C  K  A  E  O
C  P  E  R  T  P  B  L  S  N  S  V  B  D  I
B  E  L  I  E  W  E  R  N  X  P  R  E  R  T
D  P  F  T  W  Y  M  D  A  L  S  D  L  R  A
P  U  M  N  B  O  Y  U  E  G  L  M  I  Z  R
J  C  A  E  A  Y  B  T  J  L  Z  B  E  F  B
F  Q  Y  Y  Y  M  A  D  E  K  K  B  V  W  I
L  B  S  S  K  Y  B  O  I  T  N  X  E  V  V
O  L  C  P  Y  T  Y  F  L  V  N  Y  R  Q  D
Y  S  F  E  U  G  A  E  L  N  A  M  O  H  O
L  O  H  A  E  U  R  B  I  P  S  D  N  S  O
J  U  I  R  S  N  J  Y  B  L  X  F  F  P  G
I  U  Q  S  M  I  M  V  Q  A  O  Q  J  D  J
```

1.	I'M A BELIEVER	6.	BRITNEY SPEARS
2.	DAVID BOWIE	7.	ABBA
3.	HUMAN LEAGUE	8.	GOOD VIBRATIONS
4.	BE MY BABY	9.	BYE BYE LOVE
5.	BILLIE JEAN	10.	HEY YA

13. MUSICAL PERSONAE

```
A  P  S  Y  D  R  D  L  D  M  S  I  Y  M  H
F  F  B  G  R  C  D  X  P  A  N  W  A  B  X
F  M  R  R  T  I  D  H  Z  S  X  C  S  Y  R
H  T  J  I  S  P  V  H  A  B  V  S  N  D  I
R  I  S  Z  K  J  E  N  M  B  P  S  J  A  A
X  C  D  U  P  A  E  P  O  P  Y  U  I  H  B
Y  S  D  P  D  C  B  B  P  U  D  R  M  S  J
W  R  D  F  L  R  A  A  E  E  E  L  F  M  K
I  E  K  O  S  N  A  O  M  G  R  Y  D  I  J
F  D  W  W  N  V  E  T  W  B  V  P  O  L  Y
Z  N  L  O  F  E  N  K  S  O  A  Y  O  S  M
B  X  D  T  C  K  T  Q  G  M  Y  A  M  N  J
E  A  K  Z  X  K  O  P  F  C  U  O  T  C  K
M  O  Z  Z  Y  O  S  B  O  U  R  N  E  A  I
K  I  S  S  R  E  P  O  O  C  E  C  I  L  A
```

1.	KISS	6.	STARDUST
2.	AFRIKA BAMBAATAA	7.	SLIM SHADY
3.	MF DOOM	8.	MADONNA
4.	INSANE CLOWN POSSE	9.	OZZY OSBOURNE
5.	ALICE COOPER	10.	SGT. PEPPER

14. MUSICAL FAMILIES

```
Q M I W R O F V P B U P T O G
G D S Z D F S A D P M U K Q H
D C I R S E Y M L M F Z F D M
B I S L E Y B R O T H E R S W
A Z T G S T K R P N D T D Y K
Y L E O S K N I K F D K M O I
R E R I Z U J E T H P S A B P
B J S R D Y E I P J J T I H K
M A L N I A H C K R A M E C X
O C E R M D M T T V A P U A O
R K D E W B I K T Q R C U E X
P S G N S A G D O E X S L B T
D O E S L Q N V C P V L R F Y
J N P U T S Z Y M E U N Q L X
N I A H C Y R A M S U S E J S
```

1. **ISLEY BROTHERS**
2. THE **CARPENTERS**
3. THE **KINKS**
4. THE **BEACH BOYS**
5. THE **JESUS** & **MARY CHAIN**
6. **SISTER SLEDGE**
7. **BEE GEES**
8. **OASIS**
9. THE **OSMONDS**
10. THE **JACKSON** 5

15. ROCK-STAR CHILDREN

```
C  N  Y  J  M  Q  M  W  E  C  S  F  O  Q  U
E  Y  E  L  K  C  U  B  F  F  E  J  H  V  Q
S  R  S  A  R  S  E  G  L  M  N  V  M  A  W
O  R  L  U  L  N  J  R  I  A  O  Q  J  N  P
D  E  P  F  R  R  E  K  D  Q  J  K  Q  A  W
W  H  A  Q  W  Y  U  C  O  W  H  T  S  N  S
L  C  I  A  A  T  C  N  R  C  A  N  F  C  M
M  H  K  Z  I  G  G  Y  M  A  R  L  E  Y  T
E  E  A  M  N  O  N  N  E  L  O  E  S  S  H
B  N  O  M  W  L  C  C  Y  L  N  K  L  I  X
Y  E  K  G  R  U  O  B  S  N  I  A  G  N  G
B  N  E  B  I  F  H  N  K  T  K  M  D  A  E
C  K  N  T  G  B  B  X  W  M  U  E  U  T  W
T  T  F  Z  H  M  H  G  X  Q  S  N  O  R  R
T  O  R  M  T  X  R  N  N  I  S  Y  V  A  N
```

1. FEMI KUTI
2. ZIGGY MARLEY
3. NORAH JONES
4. JEFF BUCKLEY
5. MILEY CYRUS
6. CHARLOTTE GAINSBOURG
7. MARTHA/RUFUS WAINWRIGHT
8. NANCY SINATRA
9. NENEH CHERRY
10. JULIAN/SEAN LENNON

16. GREAT GIGS

```
S P J U Y V V W H Z H I G B A
B E H S S L O T S I P X E S Q
R P L U P K L X J G O V T K S
J D U T N O E W B G V G D I A
A G R E A D I N G Y I A T Q F
E T K Y T E E T I S A R X L B
Z R J V C L B R L T X W K I L
P P Z J X P B I G A W F M V F
F R N B N S N O E R T B U E M
X D D U E P B J D D O E T A I
P Y D Y W G M R O U K U I I V
W K N S P I K E I S L A N D R
O L I J O W Q L R T I H O D O
A J X I R D N E H I M I J N C
B J X B T P Y Z X P P O I X G
```

1. THE **BEATLES**
2. **PULP**
3. VELVET **UNDERGROUND**
4. **ZIGGY STARDUST**
5. **SPIKE ISLAND**
6. THE **SEX PISTOLS**
7. **LIVE AID**
8. **NEWPORT** FESTIVAL
9. **READING** FESTIVAL
10. **JIMI HENDRIX**

17. LIVE RECORDINGS

```
A  S  X  I  O  V  M  E  M  O  Y  Q  B  D  S
Q  R  G  V  H  U  N  J  G  Z  R  A  E  I  M
R  F  E  A  W  L  Q  A  L  V  E  E  R  L  A
X  D  L  T  E  Y  H  M  O  S  L  O  F  O  J
O  T  A  A  H  W  P  E  I  R  U  X  W  X  E
Q  F  M  L  T  A  T  S  U  R  E  V  I  L  H
A  E  E  K  I  D  F  B  J  J  X  J  Q  N  T
Z  W  F  I  M  X  Y  R  N  L  K  M  A  H  T
K  H  F  N  L  C  D  O  A  L  V  Z  Y  K  U
U  F  O  G  A  O  M  W  L  N  H  C  V  R  O
J  J  L  H  Y  Z  O  N  Y  F  K  Y  B  W  K
I  X  L  E  T  J  A  H  D  J  K  L  I  I  C
K  I  E  A  Y  P  M  F  P  D  B  N  I  X  I
N  L  M  D  K  Y  J  N  M  Z  T  E  I  N  K
R  W  S  S  Z  I  F  U  K  M  R  W  T  P  R
```

1.	ARETHA FRANKLIN	6.	SMELL OF FEMALE
2.	THE WHO	7.	FOLSOM PRISON
3.	BOB DYLAN	8.	TALKING HEADS
4.	PINK FLOYD	9.	KICK OUT THE JAMS
5.	JAMES BROWN	10.	LIVE RUST

18. GIG VENUES

```
A  F  Y  Y  T  S  P  O  T  Q  W  U  R  F  R
F  M  R  J  C  R  V  H  C  B  G  B  B  B  M
U  H  S  E  D  H  O  M  Q  E  N  L  C  F  Z
I  U  W  T  D  G  A  U  S  R  H  A  S  T  Z
J  A  T  E  E  R  Y  U  B  U  K  C  A  C  S
X  N  P  A  I  R  O  T  S  A  F  K  A  E  Q
Q  C  F  H  N  H  D  C  L  J  D  P  R  P  Y
S  S  J  N  D  S  O  A  K  R  K  O  W  K  O
M  O  W  N  H  K  Y  A  M  S  M  O  U  K  V
S  Z  U  A  O  X  S  G  O  L  U  L  G  R  W
V  O  A  R  V  P  N  A  L  C  A  T  A  B  Z
R  B  R  O  E  R  J  I  U  J  C  S  D  U  H
F  X  J  G  N  V  F  Y  D  N  V  D  H  P  L
X  M  C  Y  R  T  O  C  S  J  E  Z  A  O  R
Z  I  R  D  O  D  T  Z  L  L  A  M  O  G  L
```

1. C.B.G.B.'S
2. PARADISO, **AMSTERDAM**
3. LONDON **ASTORIA**
4. **RED ROCKS**
5. EFFENAAR, **EINDHOVEN**
6. EMPRESS BALLROOM, **BLACKPOOL**
7. TROUBADOUR, L.A.
8. THE **ROUNDHOUSE**
9. THE **FILLMORE**
10. **BATACLAN**

19. SONGS ABOUT SMOKING

```
D  S  N  A  Q  N  X  J  E  Q  C  F  I  N  B
I  E  Y  P  L  C  I  G  A  R  E  T  T  E  F
L  R  Z  E  D  J  M  Y  A  N  I  M  A  L  S
N  K  R  I  K  O  O  E  J  X  T  O  C  L  H
L  P  L  A  L  N  V  M  H  I  Z  C  H  A  H
K  V  S  I  S  A  O  K  Y  I  P  Z  Y  F  A
X  V  A  M  K  M  U  M  Y  H  F  O  O  I  H
F  M  O  V  G  B  C  T  C  R  L  M  C  T  Y
Y  Z  Q  Y  B  P  O  K  I  I  B  S  E  Z  Y
P  H  I  I  F  A  F  G  P  R  T  W  C  G  F
P  L  E  K  N  U  F  R  A  G  I  C  V  E  X
X  H  E  Y  A  H  E  A  N  R  B  P  R  R  G
V  D  Z  Y  D  N  E  Y  A  R  T  H  S  A  L
L  K  T  M  K  H  A  A  A  L  R  X  A  L  I
Z  X  Y  D  A  A  E  W  C  F  E  G  R  D  L
```

1. **SPIRITUALIZED**
2. THREE CIGARETTES IN AN **ASHTRAY**
3. DON'T **BOGART** THAT JOINT
4. CIGARETTES & **COFFEE**
5. **ARCTIC MONKEYS**
6. **ELLA FITZGERALD**
7. **OASIS**
8. SUPER FURRY **ANIMALS**
9. **CIGARETTE** IN YOUR BED
10. SIMON & **GARFUNKEL**

20. DRINKING SONGS

```
E  Q  H  M  O  A  O  A  R  S  W  S  C  B  W
C  A  R  L  A  J  L  F  Q  U  H  K  E  R  O
I  E  D  C  Q  I  V  Y  C  G  I  A  P  N  I
U  A  R  D  U  S  G  H  S  S  S  R  E  M  P
J  X  F  Q  Q  N  O  M  N  T  K  B  B  A  T
D  T  E  B  R  E  D  R  I  O  E  A  U  K  W
N  T  E  N  T  O  M  E  T  E  Y  Y  Y  U  E
A  J  L  K  H  K  B  H  R  X  C  V  H  D  R
N  P  G  H  M  O  T  N  A  W  V  L  X  B  S
I  M  O  Y  Y  C  S  K  M  J  O  L  F  P  H
G  I  O  S  D  M  Y  M  E  D  K  R  D  K  G
Q  D  D  A  Q  G  S  G  S  I  F  R  L  K  J
A  I  Y  V  T  F  B  O  U  R  B  O  N  D  P
X  S  U  N  D  A  Y  M  O  R  N  I  N  G  V
K  Y  K  K  L  D  N  W  H  X  U  W  W  W  L
```

1. **BEASTIE BOYS**
2. **UNDERWORLD**
3. **TEQUILA**
4. **WHISKEY** IN THE JAR
5. **ONE BEER**
6. **DR. FEELGOOD**
7. THE **HOUSEMARTINS**
8. ONE **BOURBON**, ONE SCOTCH, ONE BEER
9. **SUNDAY MORNING** COMING DOWN
10. **GIN AND JUICE**

21. BLUES ROOTS

```
M U O W X D B R C O V I U X P
K Q M R O S L O P Z V S C E I
I A A X I V E B L E K B V N B
S G T L E V E E K X W X A O X
G Q T E T K C R H G Q U R G J
R I E A K C A T S E K O M S V
U I S D J N S J E B M R A I J
R W O B G G N O T W N X Q L V
E N R E K O O H S H B I M L C
V N L L X Q J N H R V J J I R
W I L L I A M S O N B Z J R L
F B H Y M W M O U P C J W H M
B E V R J V N G T K I Q T V
K G O F U Z G W T O V I H H A
W P E S Y Q Z Y I U V T T L N
```

1.	JOHN LEE **HOOKER**	6.	SONNY BOY **WILLIAMSON**
2.	**LEADBELLY**	7.	**SMOKESTACK** LIGHTNING
3.	LORD SEND ME AN **ANGEL**	8.	WHEN THE **LEVEE** BREAKS
4.	SISTER **ROSETTA** THORPE	9.	**THRILL IS GONE**
5.	**ROBERT JOHNSON**	10.	BIG BILL **BROONZY**

22. BLUES AND BEYOND

```
E  P  D  X  Y  A  B  T  A  Q  J  O  S  G  C
L  M  N  M  R  X  D  D  S  P  T  U  R  W  C
E  E  O  U  T  A  C  L  T  D  Q  K  E  M  N
P  L  B  L  G  A  A  Y  I  X  Z  D  K  L  N
H  T  M  F  A  M  X  Y  D  I  W  L  A  X  S
A  I  A  E  I  S  V  Q  Y  K  Z  H  E  N  Y
N  N  H  N  V  O  R  U  I  Y  L  B  R  O  W
T  G  A  V  O  N  J  K  U  G  D  Q  B  K  Z
M  P  R  R  H  D  G  O  Q  B  I  H  S  T  L
A  O  G  C  A  E  E  H  M  N  S  Y  E  S  U
N  T  T  Y  R  Y  N  M  E  I  P  B  U  F  V
R  I  I  V  C  M  F  E  N  D  O  G  L  M  S
W  J  E  D  T  B  Y  N  K  X  I  A  B  V  G
L  A  H  W  G  G  A  G  Q  C  W  O  N  I  R
C  G  A  R  L  M  U  Q  S  W  S  M  E  U  Y
```

1. **SALOME**
2. SEASON OF THE **WITCH**
3. **MELTING POT**
4. THE **GRAHAM BOND** ORGANISATION
5. THE **ANIMALS**

6. A LITTLE BIT **GROOVY**
7. GOT MY **MOJO** WORKIN'
8. **ELEPHANT MAN**
9. JOHN MAYALL AND THE **BLUESBREAKERS**
10. **MANNISH BOY**

23. TRIPPY TROUBADOURS

```
Y  P  Q  G  K  B  Z  F  O  S  B  M  K  N  T
B  A  S  X  C  O  Z  Z  U  N  I  M  O  Y  C
S  I  N  S  O  P  I  A  O  L  L  S  T  P  M
O  N  S  G  C  L  T  D  J  Q  L  R  K  J  O
R  T  Q  N  A  R  G  P  B  I  Q  M  E  T  U
C  A  P  I  E  Z  I  C  W  G  U  V  O  Y  E
D  L  T  R  P  V  W  N  G  L  I  J  E  O  V
I  A  B  A  E  L  A  D  Y  Z  C  L  B  S  N
V  D  B  E  T  H  Z  H  V  B  K  O  R  P  G
A  Y  G  B  T  Y  K  K  E  C  S  V  E  H  O
D  S  U  A  E  R  O  E  U  I  F  O  J  M  Z
P  U  N  N  N  G  R  B  R  U  H  E  R  I  O
E  O  T  F  N  J  M  Z  Q  X  V  C  H  C  K
J  Q  C  H  A  I  N  S  C  K  M  C  I  H  D
Q  Y  A  F  T  B  C  M  V  Q  X  M  T  R  W
```

1. JONATHAN WILSON
2. FULL MOON
3. BILL QUICK
4. PAINT A LADY
5. ANNETTE PEACOCK

6. FORGE YOUR OWN CHAINS
7. DAVID CROSBY
8. TIM BUCKLEY
9. RICHIE HAVENS
10. GET THY BEARINGS

24. EASY LISTENING

```
S  H  N  V  N  G  L  V  D  J  S  Y  D  J  C
U  B  I  Q  V  T  S  R  U  H  E  L  Z  A  H
O  Y  W  U  Q  C  I  G  W  S  V  F  S  M  K
I  K  L  Y  U  L  A  E  S  A  Q  Z  T  E  U
T  P  P  T  I  Q  G  Y  U  Z  I  S  D  S  B
I  H  B  K  E  P  D  Y  M  W  M  S  W  L  Y
T  V  N  P  T  O  F  L  M  A  D  A  P  A  A
S  W  N  N  V  W  X  Q  E  A  S  R  I  S  E
R  R  J  Q  I  K  W  R  R  I  G  B  C  T  W
E  T  A  S  L  X  D  V  T  E  F  N  J  O  L
P  N  E  L  L  Y  M  V  I  E  O  S  S  Z  A
U  G  Y  C  A  T  M  F  M  R  O  D  N  O  C
S  K  U  D  G  N  O  O  E  J  U  R  C  A  L
A  H  P  X  E  O  W  S  F  K  J  I  C  W  M
Y  H  M  S  P  J  X  R  U  W  C  B  L  R  P
```

1. 2001: A SPACE **ODYSSEY**
2. RONNIE **HAZLEHURST**
3. KEITH **MANSFIELD**
4. **BIRDS N BRASS**
5. THREE DAYS OF THE **CONDOR**
6. **SUMMERTIME**
7. **JAMES LAST**
8. **SUPERSTITIOUS**
9. **DAYDREAM**
10. **QUIET VILLAGE**

25. FOLK FINGERPICKERS

```
X  J  D  Z  F  B  Y  J  H  D  V  B  N  W  X
N  W  J  J  L  Q  E  K  A  R  D  K  C  I  N
X  G  B  X  Z  T  P  V  N  C  L  S  Y  Z  C
X  A  P  Q  R  V  Y  V  A  D  K  U  J  Z  X
S  M  Y  R  L  G  Z  C  J  M  E  S  O  J  Y
E  H  M  R  R  U  H  T  O  J  S  R  O  O  Z
T  X  Z  A  D  W  C  N  H  S  A  H  S  N  S
I  T  H  O  M  P  S  O  N  J  N  X  L  E  G
C  A  Z  F  I  H  N  C  F  M  D  M  H  S  J
M  Y  N  A  L  Q  A  A  A  A  Y  J  T  Y  A
R  W  O  J  P  I  J  R  H  H  B  R  A  Y  R
O  M  Q  I  Z  I  T  S  E  V  U  Q  E  I  D
F  T  R  C  B  Y  R  N  Y  A  L  B  D  D  M
U  K  E  A  N  I  E  Y  V  Y  L  P  Z  U  L
U  T  Z  R  E  N  B  O  U  R  N  Y  P  D  T
```

1. WIZZ JONES
2. DAVY GRAHAM
3. JACKSON C. FRANK
4. JOHN MARTYN
5. RICHARD THOMPSON
6. SANDY BULL
7. NICK DRAKE
8. BERT JANSCH
9. JOHN FAHEY
10. JOHN RENBOURN

26. SESSION MUSICIANS

```
G C R H L B B C H F K S X W A
N R H V B S I O L G M C P F L
B U W S O A L M O J D D V U A
F W S M T P L Y Q K T C A N N
B F E N K S Y Z C I E A H K P
W E I D R U P D R A N R E B A
S J H Z Y L R N L B E O T R R
A M U S C L E S H O A L S O K
X I J J O I S O L J Y K P T E
K Z D E U V T J R U L A A H R
U H V V J A O R Q Z N Y Z E P
F V D R F N N V O M Z E J R Q
K H E R B I E F L O W E R S M
G V R W E R C G N I K C E R W
H X H W Y X B L Z V J N C F F
```

1. BILLY PRESTON
2. BERNARD PURDIE
3. BOOKER T & THE MG'S
4. MUSCLE SHOALS RHYTHM SECTION
5. BIG JIM SULLIVAN
6. ALAN PARKER
7. FUNK BROTHERS
8. HERBIE FLOWERS
9. WRECKING CREW
10. CAROL KAYE

27. BRITISH JAZZ HEROES

```
R  E  Y  T  L  Y  T  M  H  Q  R  K  A  K  B
A  R  N  I  U  Y  B  I  I  N  E  E  Z  C  A
H  N  A  I  Z  B  F  I  E  J  A  N  V  I  S
Z  I  B  C  P  N  B  J  F  A  F  N  E  R  I
V  N  D  S  N  Y  V  Y  S  I  N  Y  Z  R  L
N  X  R  O  P  A  E  Y  H  W  A  B  E  A  K
L  K  P  F  B  T  I  N  Y  A  A  A  Q  G  I
L  Q  M  S  A  X  D  C  T  G  Y  K  D  L  R
H  T  W  K  E  L  Y  U  X  R  O  E  H  E  C
P  E  U  V  J  M  Y  N  T  M  U  R  S  A  H
E  N  O  T  S  N  I  W  A  M  R  O  N  H  I
Q  U  G  J  Y  C  O  O  T  L  S  W  C  C  N
G  R  A  H  A  M  C  O  L  L  I  E  R  I  W
K  O  O  R  B  T  S  E  W  E  K  I  M  M  B
C  T  J  O  H  N  D  A  N  K  W  O  R  T  H
```

1.	NORMA WINSTONE	6.	MIKE WESTBROOK
2.	COURTNEY PINE	7.	IAN CARR
3.	MICHAEL GARRICK	8.	JOHN DANKWORTH
4.	GRAHAM COLLIER	9.	TUBBY HAYES
5.	BASIL KIRCHIN	10.	KENNY BAKER

28. GRUNGE GREATS

```
S  C  R  E  A  M  I  N  G  T  R  E  E  S  Q
J  O  V  L  G  M  O  B  U  L  R  M  Z  H  N
Q  T  U  X  J  L  H  W  P  C  T  J  W  U  Z
R  C  R  N  M  O  V  G  S  P  L  K  G  O  A
F  X  E  C  D  U  R  G  E  K  M  V  U  G  K
I  G  V  I  D  G  D  C  X  M  Q  N  E  A  A
S  G  I  H  W  N  A  H  G  F  A  Z  E  R  F
X  J  R  A  O  F  X  R  O  R  N  X  Y  J  U
K  B  N  M  F  C  L  A  D  N  O  C  A  N  A
J  Z  E  Z  Y  B  Z  U  M  E  E  M  X  T  O
U  P  E  A  N  A  V  R  I  N  N  Y  J  T  G
O  R  R  Y  J  K  H  Z  S  D  G  Q  Z  L  V
X  V  G  R  X  Q  B  P  S  H  L  X  Q  F  I
K  I  O  D  E  G  G  F  Y  K  Q  K  O  P  C
L  E  M  O  N  H  E  A  D  S  V  L  Q  P  M
```

1. FLUID
2. SEX GOD MISSY
3. NIRVANA
4. AFGHAN WHIGS
5. MUDHONEY
6. GREEN RIVER
7. LEMONHEADS
8. SOUNDGARDEN
9. SCREAMING TREES
10. ANACONDA

29. MOD MOVERS

```
K I N J S Y L E D R U E L F E
W J J A P M A P C L Q P U Z V
D A C J Y F W A B M R A Q Q I
F C D T P E T U J V U Z A F L
F K K E T M D L N N F U T A A
I I S S I K J N O O U S F X M
A E G E C N J I Q P S K C W I
F E E Q C Q T C N Z T A M M E
Y D E V K A H H S L H T P V N
L W L D E F F O E P O A V Q T
U A E R U N J L W W M L W D B
F R C A H Z R A L W A I Z V T
M D V G Y K K S O A S T Z O W
I S P N I Q N Q N X M E E A D
T H E K I N K S D Q Y S I R R
```

1. THE KINKS
2. WADE IN THE WATER
3. CREATION
4. PAUL NICHOLAS
5. SMALL FACES
6. RUFUS THOMAS
7. SKATALITES
8. JACKIE EDWARDS
9. FLEUR DE LYS
10. I'M ALIVE

30. GOTH GROOVES

```
A  O  K  J  M  I  W  Y  G  L  D  H  Q  Q  O
N  I  N  E  I  N  C  H  N  A  I  L  S  A  E
I  M  X  H  S  T  R  E  N  G  T  H  L  I  E
C  D  I  S  L  E  R  I  O  N  J  Z  P  T  M
J  Q  V  N  X  T  E  Q  S  Q  Q  U  X  H  E
B  B  Q  K  I  L  L  I  N  G  J  O  K  E  O
T  A  M  B  L  S  D  O  A  T  R  R  R  C  W
G  U  W  E  G  Z  T  Q  M  N  Q  D  K  U  B
J  H  D  B  C  R  T  R  N  C  T  T  I  R  J
S  A  N  C  T  U  A  R  Y  E  N  C  P  E  J
X  U  P  R  C  B  D  B  L  J  B  P  Y  Z  C
Q  S  Y  Y  K  L  X  Q  I  Q  D  G  J  Y  U
Y  C  R  E  M  F  O  S  R  E  T  S  I  S  J
S  S  L  V  R  I  M  I  A  G  E  O  M  X  R
T  X  P  H  F  D  K  I  M  W  T  K  R  N  L
```

1. **DANIELLE DAX**
2. MISSION TOWER OF **STRENGTH**
3. **MARILYN MANSON**
4. **BAUHAUS**
5. **SISTERS OF MERCY**
6. **KILLING JOKE**
7. SHE SELLS **SANCTUARY**
8. **NINE INCH NAILS**
9. **MINISTRY**
10. **THE CURE**

31. NEW ROMANTIC CLUB HITS

```
K  M  J  Z  I  V  T  N  F  G  L  P  K  F  U
X  D  A  V  I  D  B  O  W  I  E  J  M  F  O
X  S  P  S  N  L  Y  I  H  Y  C  O  A  C  O
L  N  A  L  P  G  H  T  U  D  C  W  D  F  S
L  G  N  Y  X  A  A  C  R  L  P  F  P  W  T
E  R  S  P  A  N  D  A  U  B  A  L  L  E  T
C  D  W  J  B  O  X  E  N  T  O  Y  E  F  P
T  I  A  I  L  Q  K  V  S  C  H  O  H  K  U
F  E  S  V  I  U  P  O  J  X  W  J  S  V  K
O  C  Z  U  D  D  N  L  M  U  D  B  S  H  S
S  D  N  I  M  E  L  P  M  I  S  Y  R  X  C
V  Q  E  P  S  Y  J  R  O  R  B  K  Q  K  O
N  L  C  I  F  F  X  C  X  A  S  R  Q  G  D
W  X  W  J  Z  H  X  O  V  A  R  T  L  U  H
S  N  A  R  U  D  N  A  R  U  D  R  D  G  Z
```

1. JAPAN
2. VISAGE
3. SOFT CELL
4. ROXY MUSIC
5. SIMPLE MINDS

6. DURAN DURAN
7. ULTRAVOX
8. DAVID BOWIE
9. LOVE ACTION
10. SPANDAU BALLET

32. SHOEGAZE SWAYERS

```
I X V A E N X E B S U N C V M
C F M C S W G C T F W K H P I
V V I X D L P A E T E F A S G
H A T J Q M B K U Z R L P E K
V P H P K T U K B E E T T B T
F O O Q K A B P N S A E E A O
I U U G W H B F A O L L R M R
I R G O C D W I W O O T H B U
I T H G X P N D S N G M O W G
X R T W V T T B G V K E U H D
D A F H S I O G B U S W S F N
Y I O S R A E Y Y L R A E P V
U L R I C H S C H N A U S S R
S R M E S A W E G I Q G O V Y
B U S W Y Y Y W L W V W S E H M
```

1. CHAPTERHOUSE
2. PALE SAINTS
3. CATCH THE BREEZE
4. LORELLE MEETS THE OBSOLETE
5. SOON
6. ULRICH SCHNAUSS
7. VAPOUR TRAIL
8. THOUGHTFORMS
9. EARLY YEARS
10. BELONG

33. CHILL-OUT TUNES

```
G  L  O  B  A  L  N  B  N  L  C  I  K  L  V
Y  A  C  E  M  F  G  I  O  C  O  T  Y  D  D
U  M  H  F  L  F  W  B  I  S  N  C  C  C  E
F  B  V  L  P  T  R  N  S  O  T  C  U  U  J
Z  C  U  K  X  O  E  Y  E  E  A  E  Q  B  L
I  H  V  E  E  M  Y  T  M  C  W  S  U  A  I
Z  O  H  H  A  I  N  Y  P  J  A  G  X  B  L
S  P  T  T  S  S  N  Q  T  F  A  P  K  P  B
A  R  I  F  T  S  Q  Q  K  R  Z  H  S  X  X
K  C  P  Y  V  I  D  N  O  L  Q  L  A  Y  W
O  O  M  F  M  D  A  J  Z  P  Q  J  F  I  A
V  I  X  C  R  I  K  P  H  Y  O  K  Q  N  T
V  Z  T  X  N  L  J  R  E  W  C  O  O  U  E
M  B  R  T  F  O  T  L  E  S  S  E  W  E  I
P  J  Q  X  A  S  W  K  C  M  U  O  B  G  O
```

1. LAMBCHOP
2. GLOBAL COMMUNICATION
3. APHEX TWIN
4. THE KLF
5. ART OF NOISE
6. CINEMATIC ORCHESTRA
7. SOLIDISSIMO
8. BUGGE WESSELTOFT
9. SPACE
10. THE ORB

34. BRITPOP

```
N R U T E R T H G I L S D X G
Y C T D G M S I E X B E H Y B
D A E H O I D A R F I L J S U
R U K W S C T N B W Y P U Q J
S K Q A Z L M G A L A O T R J
B S O T R M E K K Y W E Z T U
T I A U P R I P M H E P P E I
J V E R P N S X O W C N I A I
R V E A G W D F S W H O R D L
I Y Y U J R G R J H I M V A E
R E P P F O E G H M N M I F B
O M K F S T Q P Y C O O A F P
Q H K B T O I H U H G C C A X
T J C I Q H J R P S K X L N M
E D B Z P J P O F N O Z J K M
```

1. SUEDE
2. SLIGHT RETURN
3. BARNEY AND ME
4. WAKING UP
5. RADIOHEAD
6. BITTERSWEET SYMPHONY
7. SUPERGRASS
8. COMMON PEOPLE
9. BLUR
10. OASIS

35. GREAT NIGHTS

```
O  O  N  S  P  S  W  L  N  D  P  N  E  L  T
Y  J  C  E  H  H  Y  O  I  U  I  V  H  I  C
G  O  N  N  E  Y  E  V  G  G  A  H  U  O  O
X  R  W  O  X  M  R  L  H  W  I  D  T  N  N
Z  S  T  T  S  C  R  T  T  U  E  G  Z  E  N
X  N  C  S  I  N  C  A  F  O  B  I  Y  L  E
E  Z  Q  G  Z  R  E  W  E  G  N  H  O  R  C
C  Q  S  N  U  H  V  B  V  D  J  J  P  I  T
J  L  W  I  H  A  C  F  E  Y  T  C  O  C  I
B  D  S  L  A  M  T  E  R  G  F  C  A  H  O
Z  E  O  L  Z  P  P  H  A  H  R  T  K  I  N
R  W  G  O  D  Q  J  O  X  R  U  O  T  E  Y
P  N  V  R  D  A  W  Y  K  O  P  S  E  V  J
C  D  C  A  D  M  Y  S  X  L  M  V  Z  G  X
J  I  H  V  C  I  S  Q  B  B  Y  A  J  P  I
```

1. AC/DC
2. NIGHT FEVER
3. GEORGE BENSON
4. ELTON JOHN
5. HEATWAVE
6. NIGHT CRUISER
7. T-CONNECTION
8. ROLLING STONES
9. INDEEP
10. LIONEL RICHIE

36. CLUBS

```
S  S  K  I  W  Y  O  N  W  A  W  N  L  C  U
E  T  M  P  J  C  I  H  A  D  J  O  O  V  S
D  I  U  X  E  A  Q  S  R  N  M  K  L  M  W
R  A  I  D  H  C  L  F  E  E  Q  O  M  J  Z
D  W  P  G  I  L  L  D  H  I  R  D  O  R  G
G  J  R  J  A  O  R  A  O  C  E  S  U  H  A
W  E  B  B  C  H  M  T  U  A  D  F  M  M  S
B  M  S  H  Y  S  R  S  H  V  M  N  D  F
Z  P  V  R  R  W  V  G  E  X  R  E  Q  P  H
M  I  N  I  S  T  R  Y  O  F  S  O  U  N  D
Z  E  G  A  R  A  G  E  S  I  D  A  R  A  P
K  C  F  F  O  E  Z  K  A  W  W  F  C  K  K
W  I  G  A  N  C  A  S  I  N  O  X  N  M  R
T  F  O  L  E  H  T  K  X  C  K  Y  O  D  F
X  L  M  M  U  W  I  J  N  K  Y  L  O  I  L
```

1. BERGHAIN
2. MINISTRY OF SOUND
3. STUDIO 54
4. WAREHOUSE
5. AMNESIA
6. THE LOFT
7. SHOOM
8. WIGAN CASINO
9. PARADISE GARAGE
10. HACIENDA

37. FUNK FLOOR-FILLERS

```
F  S  T  N  A  P  T  O  H  Z  R  B  W  R  T
R  E  B  R  O  C  O  D  A  U  F  C  U  I  C
M  S  O  P  F  I  W  Q  T  T  W  D  S  U  R
D  J  O  M  U  X  T  C  N  V  B  E  R  A  O
S  E  M  A  J  K  C  I  R  U  I  T  Z  V  U
K  Z  Q  W  W  K  N  L  T  S  I  X  O  X  C
D  R  B  L  M  E  T  E  R  S  P  P  U  L  F
J  S  S  F  Y  U  H  D  M  S  R  M  D  N  N
R  M  R  Y  J  M  Z  A  V  E  R  E  V  R  K
I  M  H  I  U  O  Y  K  N  A  H  T  P  P  V
K  I  K  Z  A  F  U  N  K  I  N  C  P  U  M
N  T  T  E  I  T  R  U  G  F  R  R  H  X  S
K  X  M  E  M  K  C  F  H  M  I  V  M  R  X
I  S  L  E  Y  B  R  O  T  H  E  R  S  M  N
E  D  D  I  E  B  O  S  O  I  I  Q  X  R  W
```

1.	RICK JAMES		6.	EDDIE BO
2.	FUNKADELIC		7.	THANK YOU
3.	CURTIS MAYFIELD		8.	SUPERSTITION
4.	FUNK INC.		9.	HOT PANTS
5.	METERS		10.	THE ISLEY BROTHERS

38. DISCO DANCE-FLOOR BOMBS

```
G  R  S  T  U  D  A  Y  D  A  N  C  E  R  J
P  R  E  B  R  C  X  S  I  H  W  N  R  G  M
P  T  P  R  G  S  I  P  N  W  A  L  W  G  Z
J  C  K  Q  U  S  Z  H  O  L  L  O  W  A  Y
E  G  E  Z  A  T  M  O  S  F  E  A  R  R  W
T  V  V  G  G  N  A  S  A  L  S  O  U  L  C
A  E  O  C  H  I  C  N  U  B  R  T  F  Q  L
D  R  S  L  A  O  H  E  R  A  W  Q  J  U  H
A  Z  B  U  L  J  I  R  L  E  J  S  B  Q  I
Z  J  U  A  Y  E  N  Q  B  Q  P  I  D  L  P
N  O  I  P  H  S  E  D  A  K  K  U  Q  Q  O
H  L  U  F  I  O  S  F  B  R  F  V  S  X  R
N  L  J  I  L  O  X  M  I  M  S  D  X  X  W
Q  R  J  C  I  L  C  G  U  X  S  V  L  V  W
B  S  C  D  K  X  Y  H  N  O  I  A  N  I  Z
```

1. SUPERNATURE
2. DINOSAUR L
3. ATMOSFEAR
4. MACHINE
5. LOLEATTA **HOLLOWAY**
6. LOOSE JOINTS
7. I FEEL LOVE
8. CHIC
9. SALSOUL ORCHESTRA
10. DANCER

39. JAZZ FINDS THE FUNK

```
S  S  S  G  F  G  M  D  B  A  P  K  K  N  C
N  P  E  N  R  R  J  J  K  J  L  D  E  O  S
O  C  B  L  S  A  A  T  S  O  A  Y  M  E  K
I  T  M  Q  N  N  A  G  M  H  C  A  U  L  U
S  P  Q  L  O  T  B  Q  U  N  E  L  H  E  I
N  S  L  J  I  G  N  H  L  N  B  J  J  M  Y
A  X  F  S  S  R  E  Y  A  Y  O  R  S  A  A
P  V  R  Q  M  E  M  T  T  H  Y  U  H  H  Q
X  E  V  U  A  E  I  I  U  A  T  S  Q  C  K
E  S  N  I  P  N  C  B  U  M  I  F  I  I  H
E  J  Z  R  X  R  I  Y  N  M  J  I  G  Y  R
H  Z  J  D  E  F  W  Q  S  O  D  J  Z  C  N
T  M  W  N  X  D  A  R  K  N  E  S  S  K  M
D  O  N  A  L  D  B  Y  R  D  G  N  T  A  D
A  I  M  T  O  A  B  U  A  Y  N  P  I  K  F
```

1. CHAMELEON
2. INNER CITY BLUES
3. DONALD BYRD
4. ROY AYERS
5. JOHNNY HAMMOND
6. THE EXPANSIONS
7. MARC MOULIN & PLACEBO
8. SLIPPIN' INTO DARKNESS
9. GRANT GREEN
10. MULATU

40. THE PHILLY SOUND

```
O  A  N  T  S  O  L  I  E  V  O  L  E  H  T
B  S  R  E  B  B  A  T  S  K  C  A  B  S  G
I  N  S  T  A  N  T  F  U  N  K  U  E  N  Z
L  T  G  X  Y  S  F  F  P  Z  V  N  F  B  L
Q  A  Y  E  J  S  T  H  O  Y  C  S  E  S  N
C  T  H  S  X  H  I  I  E  D  Z  Y  D  W  W
M  D  Q  A  V  V  M  J  S  O  M  R  H  C  K
N  B  J  N  K  T  U  F  J  L  B  I  X  M  B
X  O  H  A  D  E  B  V  F  O  T  A  K  C  T
Q  E  W  T  C  S  Y  J  Q  E  C  P  R  X  D
F  Q  K  N  E  K  D  B  H  W  V  V  V  T  O
E  C  I  O  H  C  S  E  L  P  O  E  P  C  Y
Q  T  L  M  S  F  A  O  V  F  P  M  U  W  T
G  Z  I  A  M  D  W  D  N  C  C  Z  N  A  I
S  Y  A  J  O  E  H  T  U  S  U  H  Z  H  Y
```

1. PEOPLE'S CHOICE
2. MONTANA SEXTET
3. EAST
4. JACKSONS
5. BACK STABBERS
6. MCFADDEN & WHITEHEAD
7. THE LOVE I LOST
8. INSTANT FUNK
9. MFSB
10. THE O'JAYS

41. LESSER-KNOWN MOTOWN MOMENTS

```
H  I  U  Z  V  P  D  R  U  N  A  X  A  B  D
C  A  E  Z  C  J  I  S  A  R  I  E  T  M  F
B  P  Z  E  V  I  L  E  V  O  L  T  E  L  H
R  T  F  S  B  W  A  A  D  C  H  L  F  R  W
K  R  Q  E  M  A  N  A  L  P  H  R  A  R  E
W  G  A  T  E  R  R  Y  J  O  H  N  S  O  N
C  Y  J  T  J  H  Z  B  H  P  D  P  I  S  C
D  Z  I  E  S  C  O  M  M  O  D  O  R  E  S
K  A  L  L  S  N  I  G  L  E  E  H  T  S  B
I  N  Z  E  H  U  I  P  V  B  H  B  H  S  V
I  R  A  V  C  P  H  W  C  W  Q  K  Q  U  N
F  N  F  R  K  W  E  P  D  P  Z  X  X  H  I
D  W  X  A  Z  Q  X  O  F  E  F  A  H  X  V
I  F  X  M  O  N  I  T  O  R  S  R  O  S  X
N  N  L  S  H  P  B  S  K  A  W  C  D  P  Y
```

1. EDWIN STARR
2. THE **MARVELETTES**
3. THE **MONITORS**
4. BEAT ME TO THE **PUNCH**
5. THE **COMMODORES**
6. THE **ELGINS**
7. BARBARA **RANDOLPH**
8. **TERRY JOHNSON**
9. BUTTERED **POPCORN**
10. **LET LOVE LIVE**

42. NORTHERN SOUL

```
W A Q S U X O G D B G R H E N
Z F T O N Y C L A R K E F Y I
Z Y M P A O Y N M E L K Y A T
Y L A M D F S X A A B O V R S
T F B R Z C R L I K T H V G U
V H X P A R I S I A N S Z E A
S J G Q N E M K I W L S F I I
Q K S I A B T N A A K M Q B T
C K N M N F T R W Y M N D O T
H O M T H E S N A K E A A D A
B R A U D D H A N I T I O R P
W A R L M E Y T N P C G W L F
S B O O H F T X I I S Y Q Z L
G V Z R I U Y X Q X I T E L J
E P T G Y A F F K F D T A L H
```

1.	DR. LOVE	6.	FRANK WILSON
2.	PATTI AUSTIN	7.	THE SNAKE
3.	BREAKAWAY	8.	PARISIANS
4.	DOBIE GRAY	9.	TONY CLARKE
5.	TAINTED LOVE	10.	THE NIGHT

43. ELECTRONIC PIONEERS

```
S  J  R  A  H  I  R  X  B  O  R  W  C  D  L
M  A  E  R  D  E  N  I  R  E  G  N  A  T  O
A  D  D  I  X  O  Q  Y  I  G  P  P  C  U  W
F  B  O  K  T  V  I  E  A  N  H  D  S  I  R
E  E  R  R  A  J  N  L  N  N  G  G  K  O  E
L  I  O  E  V  E  X  W  E  F  F  N  C  R  I
U  M  M  W  X  X  V  O  N  V  P  G  I  F  I
S  F  B  T  G  Z  R  C  O  W  S  H  N  Y  R
B  I  A  F  S  A  Y  K  K  Y  S  D  T  A  Q
W  G  L  A  M  W  K  C  L  Y  V  Y  O  I  L
F  T  N  R  T  A  A  I  B  D  Y  N  B  E  W
Y  E  R  K  Y  B  R  R  V  B  Z  S  O  F  Y
R  F  B  M  U  Z  E  T  X  M  K  L  R  G  O
U  D  W  P  S  D  M  A  M  L  R  L  A  E  X
L  M  V  Q  X  S  S  P  J  N  F  J  W  R  V
```

1. GIORGIO **MORODER**
2. **TANGERINE DREAM**
3. **MORTON** SUBOTNICK
4. **DAPHNE ORAM**
5. **KRAFTWERK**
6. **BRIAN ENO**
7. JEAN-MICHELLE **JARRE**
8. **PATRICK COWLEY**
9. DELIA **DERBYSHIRE**
10. ALEXANDER **ROBOTNICK**

44. ELECTRO

```
X  V  P  R  C  W  E  X  F  X  N  R  I  A  T
K  K  M  K  M  T  A  M  T  W  F  L  X  O  M
F  C  C  J  Q  Y  A  S  E  I  U  J  M  K  Q
P  G  O  O  Y  R  Y  R  G  C  Z  I  B  O  F
F  S  Q  R  C  O  C  I  H  E  H  V  R  W  Q
Y  S  B  X  T  N  M  W  Z  S  T  M  E  U  G
Z  T  T  Q  U  E  A  H  A  L  Q  C  A  M  L
H  O  F  Z  J  B  N  H  X  B  T  Y  K  D  V
S  B  N  X  S  R  P  A  E  V  Q  B  D  G  U
N  O  O  N  J  U  A  T  L  I  I  O  A  X  Q
J  R  H  F  K  N  R  H  E  P  B  T  N  E  N
R  E  B  S  Y  S  R  E  T  Q  E  R  C  G  A
C  H  M  W  P  O  I  X  G  B  C  O  E  H  S
E  T  P  G  O  N  S  T  P  H  O  N  K  H  Z
U  X  J  J  T  I  H  M  P  T  M  P  L  K  D
```

1.	JONZUN CREW	6.	TELEX
2.	TYRONE BRUNSON	7.	CYBOTRON
3.	THE ROBOTS	8.	PLANET ROCK
4.	HERBIE HANCOCK	9.	MAN PARRISH
5.	HASHIM	10.	BREAK DANCE

45. HIP-HOP'S DEF JAMS

```
S  S  D  C  B  E  C  P  X  I  W  D  L  S  L
D  L  I  Q  R  G  F  F  A  Y  L  G  D  S  F
U  J  I  M  O  F  J  J  Q  H  J  H  H  Q  S
D  L  L  C  O  O  L  J  Z  I  U  K  U  E  U
J  P  H  Y  K  S  F  D  B  P  T  B  E  U  U
O  I  J  R  L  R  J  Z  X  H  U  B  D  N  W
Z  A  P  T  Y  B  I  K  E  O  Z  C  X  P  Z
M  Q  G  A  N  L  T  C  P  P  V  G  K  G  Q
N  Y  E  D  H  N  H  Q  K  I  S  X  L  U  I
O  B  V  S  S  A  B  J  P  S  F  B  D  J  V
F  J  I  S  M  U  X  M  Y  D  C  P  Z  H  N
D  J  Z  P  U  B  L  I  C  E  N  E  M  Y  X
M  E  T  H  O  D  M  A  N  A  M  D  E  R  A
P  P  H  S  S  R  S  R  W  D  K  K  H  N  Z
E  J  Z  L  Q  U  B  L  M  R  U  E  O  V  M
```

1. SLICK RICK
2. EPMD
3. METHOD MAN
4. NO SLEEP TIL **BROOKLYN**
5. THE CHAMP

6. PUBLIC ENEMY
7. 3RD **BASS**
8. HIP HOP IS DEAD
9. LL COOL J
10. REDMAN

46. FOUNDATIONS OF GOOD HOUSE

```
T  B  A  V  V  C  Z  M  W  V  K  Q  P  X  U
U  N  C  D  P  V  S  R  Z  T  S  Q  P  P  N
N  V  N  N  O  R  U  F  K  I  M  J  J  R  D
Q  G  O  X  B  N  I  I  F  A  X  G  W  E  E
A  P  D  I  O  V  G  N  I  L  R  E  T  S  R
K  C  N  D  M  I  X  G  C  P  W  N  B  S  G
K  H  A  J  K  A  S  E  I  I  R  R  Y  Z  R
C  Y  N  C  R  K  R  R  P  U  P  J  A  C  O
Y  H  O  G  O  U  I  S  B  S  T  L  O  E  U
H  F  Y  P  T  G  O  P  H  C  W  Z  E  E  N
W  F  O  U  G  A  E  M  K  A  B  B  B  M  D
F  T  H  K  D  E  Q  V  J  B  L  S  Z  M  S
N  P  B  K  D  K  S  S  I  W  V  L  U  I  J
C  R  I  S  P  I  N  J  G  L  O  V  E  R  O
L  J  H  G  M  Z  W  O  Y  P  J  U  K  O  Z
```

1. **XPRESS** 2
2. **STERLING VOID** & PARIS BRIGHTLEDGE
3. **DEEP BURNT**
4. JAMIE **PRINCIPLE**
5. **MR. FINGERS**
6. **CRISPIN J. GLOVER**
7. **ON AND ON**
8. **MARSHALL** JEFFERSON
9. **PHUTURE**
10. **UNDERGROUND**

47. THE SYNTH-POP REVOLUTION

```
G  S  F  G  N  S  V  X  X  H  F  Y  Z  G  N
P  W  B  Z  E  D  O  M  E  H  C  E  P  E  D
B  M  G  G  V  V  Q  S  E  G  X  I  M  H  O
P  E  G  N  A  M  C  N  A  L  B  W  G  X  Q
V  E  I  R  E  R  E  D  R  O  W  E  N  N  F
Y  F  T  S  H  M  Y  C  H  G  E  U  J  F  J
I  L  F  S  C  J  P  N  C  M  T  G  S  C  J
U  E  L  F  H  I  E  Y  U  P  K  A  L  G  W
B  W  Y  E  S  O  M  F  L  M  P  E  M  F  N
Y  I  E  Z  C  R  P  H  I  O  A  L  C  C  H
U  D  F  Z  B  T  T  B  T  M  Q  N  A  V  T
C  X  C  T  Y  J  F  R  O  Y  W  A  H  A  Z
X  Y  X  K  Y  D  S  O  F  Y  R  M  Z  T  C
X  S  E  P  S  T  R  I  S  A  S  U  P  E  W
U  S  J  T  X  H  U  T  J  C  B  H  E  A  C
```

1.	ULTRAVOX	6.	NEW ORDER
2.	BLANCMANGE	7.	HUMAN LEAGUE
3.	DEPECHE MODE	8.	EURYTHMICS
4.	GARY NUMAN	9.	PET SHOP BOYS
5.	SOFT CELL	10.	HEAVEN 17

48. TOWERING TECHNO

```
P  R  F  E  M  U  A  S  Z  Q  E  C  E  M  H
F  O  U  S  A  O  B  S  N  E  L  M  F  K  G
A  N  X  B  E  Y  T  R  R  K  P  I  I  A  I
Z  T  V  W  U  N  D  E  R  W  O  R  L  D  Y
T  R  C  O  M  R  X  C  T  I  E  A  F  D  H
E  E  T  I  A  U  M  N  U  I  P  V  O  T  W
C  N  K  G  C  L  T  A  T  Y  P  E  S  N  F
M  T  O  S  G  E  L  D  F  Z  I  R  G  X  T
Y  N  K  U  Z  X  I  E  K  U  L  A  N  Y  Y
S  Q  S  A  F  I  Y  R  Y  T  C  H  I  V  L
T  B  X  P  S  O  U  P  Z  S  R  S  R  Q  D
I  C  E  X  I  K  S  Q  Y  S  E  H  T  R  N
C  Y  W  H  S  B  M  L  W  H  P  S  S  W  D
U  H  K  G  O  L  N  G  W  Q  A  Z  P  B  Y
Z  G  Y  X  F  J  X  W  A  G  P  V  J  N  S
```

1. JOURNEY OF THE DRAGONS
2. UNDERWORLD
3. STRINGS OF LIFE
4. E-DANCER
5. PAPERCLIP PEOPLE
6. AZTEC MYSTIC
7. NO UFO'S
8. ALLEYS OF YOUR MIND
9. SHAREVARI
10. RON TRENT

49. POST-PUNK

```
F  U  D  U  S  R  I  E  G  O  H  E  N  X  T
U  O  S  K  X  N  D  Y  D  Z  Y  H  I  Z  Q
N  K  U  D  V  X  V  Q  O  T  U  I  R  B  Y
O  H  C  N  A  O  W  Z  C  F  H  S  X  J  M
L  D  G  A  D  E  L  E  K  Z  I  A  Y  P  G
X  X  Z  A  B  A  H  T  A  F  G  G  Y  H  W
J  M  Q  Z  N  K  T  D  A  X  H  H  S  M  S
H  U  A  P  L  G  E  I  E  I  P  F  I  F  Q
X  H  W  G  F  B  O  I  O  R  R  S  G  K  O
K  L  K  C  A  N  S  F  R  N  E  E  R  B  A
K  Y  X  P  V  Z  A  T  F  H  S  V  H  W  H
D  E  A  T  H  D  I  S  C  O  S  C  E  G  L
E  L  M  A  C  A  A  N  X  G  U  S  T  S  D
J  L  C  Z  X  D  U  E  E  J  R  R  G  J  Y
G  O  Y  J  Q  P  W  E  D  W  E  X  U  J  S
```

1.	**DEATH DISCO**	6.	**MAGAZINE**
2.	BORN UNDER **PUNCHES**	7.	**SHRIEKBACK**
3.	**GANG OF FOUR**	8.	SHAKE THE **FOUNDATIONS**
4.	**YELLO**	9.	**SEVERED HEADS**
5.	**HIGH PRESSURE** DAYS	10.	CABARET **VOLTAIRE**

50. INDIE DANCE

```
Y  Z  S  M  R  F  X  S  U  U  Q  K  D  C  Y
S  N  Z  S  J  M  O  B  Z  V  J  H  W  H  T
U  Q  Z  H  U  R  K  Z  E  J  G  F  E  A  K
D  C  H  A  V  I  L  Z  O  Y  O  N  E  R  Y
V  H  U  P  A  B  A  N  D  O  N  Z  K  L  G
R  M  G  P  R  I  M  A  L  S  C  R  E  A  M
U  R  C  Y  K  F  B  S  C  M  U  F  N  T  A
L  B  Z  M  O  T  G  Y  Q  D  I  V  D  A  Q
B  J  F  O  E  O  B  P  S  V  H  F  E  N  C
I  J  Q  N  L  Y  W  L  P  E  J  B  R  S  E
G  A  K  D  R  S  O  D  H  I  G  O  O  J  W
C  K  V  A  T  M  V  C  Z  V  A  J  R  R  A
I  U  M  Y  D  J  J  N  J  R  X  W  Y  Y  Z
T  R  O  S  L  I  D  O  F  F  A  D  Z  I  R
Y  I  A  T  F  O  O  Z  E  T  U  F  G  K  Z
```

1. BIG CITY
2. BLUR
3. MBV
4. ABANDON
5. FOOL'S GOLD

6. PRIMAL SCREAM
7. CHARLATANS
8. HAPPY MONDAYS
9. WEEKENDER
10. NEW FAST AUTOMATIC DAFFODILS

51. ROCK COMES TO THE DISCO

```
T  B  C  S  H  O  L  R  G  Y  B  R  A  O  G
N  E  T  S  U  X  I  K  H  X  R  E  X  H  P
M  L  L  A  B  N  O  N  N  A  C  Y  H  Q  Q
Z  S  N  L  S  I  I  R  E  I  W  A  R  G  A
M  L  U  G  U  K  D  K  N  C  B  L  X  U  I
K  L  L  F  D  N  K  I  L  S  M  P  F  K  F
W  A  C  O  J  X  H  S  A  A  P  T  E  L  S
X  F  Q  T  W  T  V  C  S  R  T  E  T  X  B
Q  J  Z  R  Y  J  B  E  F  C  K  E  F  Y  U
M  R  U  A  W  W  N  R  N  B  I  R  V  O  Y
B  I  T  E  S  T  H  E  D  U  S  T  Y  I  Z
Q  A  R  H  P  M  Q  I  S  L  H  S  M  V  J
G  Q  S  U  C  R  I  C  O  C  S  I  D  N  W
V  L  L  A  W  E  H  T  N  I  K  C  I  R  B
M  B  N  A  B  I  W  L  M  U  I  H  C  U  K
```

1. CANNONBALL
2. JIVE TALKIN'
3. STREET PLAYER
4. HEART OF GLASS
5. MISS YOU
6. ANOTHER **BRICK IN THE WALL**
7. ROCK THE **CASBAH**
8. WALKING ON **THIN ICE**
9. **DISCO CIRCUS**
10. ANOTHER ONE **BITES THE DUST**

52. SOUND SYSTEMS

```
N  G  N  G  B  Y  B  B  A  T  H  M  S  Z  V
A  A  T  A  A  B  M  A  B  B  O  N  D  E  T
Z  S  G  N  J  X  D  N  S  V  O  O  R  N  I
S  E  A  V  A  O  R  W  K  X  W  S  O  C  L
F  H  E  I  H  I  R  O  Z  N  H  D  L  D  H
I  U  L  J  S  H  G  T  B  X  U  I  U  L  O
R  N  P  Q  H  P  Z  E  I  V  X  V  C  T  X
E  E  O  E  A  C  A  M  H  H  X  P  R  F  T
N  J  E  X  K  T  B  O  N  T  Y  R  E  Y  J
F  L  P  I  A  I  R  H  S  A  C  T  H  K  X
G  R  E  A  T  S  E  B  A  S  T  I  A  N  Y
K  L  H  E  Y  X  M  Z  I  C  E  X  R  E  O
J  V  T  O  T  N  Q  V  C  F  G  K  G  J  Q
J  A  R  J  N  B  Y  C  H  M  C  V  R  G  E
M  F  X  F  Y  Q  P  J  I  P  P  A  V  O  M
```

1. KING EDWARDS **THE GIANT**
2. **JAH SHAKA**
3. **DOWNBEAT**
4. THE **TROJAN**
5. **SAXON** STUDIO SOUND SYSTEM
6. TUBBY'S **HOMETOWN HI-FI**
7. TOM THE **GREAT SEBASTIAN**
8. AFRIKA **BAMBAATAA**
9. VOICE OF **THE PEOPLE**
10. THE **HERCULORDS**

53. SONGS FOR A WEDDING DANCE FLOOR

```
S  W  S  N  I  W  T  N  O  S  P  M  O  H  T
C  L  Y  E  D  N  J  E  O  E  P  J  V  S  V
I  C  I  H  C  P  I  I  V  B  M  C  V  J  I
N  G  N  W  G  A  R  R  A  B  N  A  B  H  G
O  U  O  Y  R  O  F  L  E  E  F  I  J  P  F
S  W  S  Y  X  Q  R  E  Q  R  B  S  W  I  Q
E  E  L  Z  K  F  E  M  H  G  F  L  U  L  Y
H  K  I  P  G  R  R  E  G  T  J  B  D  G  G
T  V  W  K  Y  L  A  L  B  N  K  X  M  C  I
X  R  E  W  I  R  B  H  N  I  D  K  Q  L  G
X  S  I  S  T  E  R  S  L  E  D  G  E  K  T
H  G  K  S  H  G  V  Y  L  A  P  T  Z  M  G
F  V  C  Y  G  K  V  T  J  M  D  D  M  Z  G
W  U  A  X  W  J  T  Q  H  O  Y  I  Z  E  W
X  R  J  O  H  N  P  A  U  L  Y  O  U  N  G
```

1. THE FACES
2. THE SONICS
3. I FEEL FOR YOU
4. THOMPSON TWINS
5. JACKIE WILSON
6. YOUNG **HEARTS** RUN FREE
7. BANBARRA
8. SISTER SLEDGE
9. JOHN PAUL YOUNG
10. CHIC

54. D.J.S

```
Y  D  F  N  B  Z  Z  L  F  Q  U  O  K  G  O
U  E  P  O  M  W  L  Y  K  U  O  M  I  L  P
D  A  V  I  D  M  A  N  C  U  S  O  D  F  R
V  F  F  R  Q  E  R  G  N  C  S  I  J  U  E
Y  A  J  N  A  M  R  O  N  P  A  L  K  U  T
A  I  D  S  J  H  Y  F  G  N  R  I  O  E  S
N  Z  W  R  T  Q  L  L  L  N  G  N  O  E  A
P  E  P  G  E  I  E  E  M  A  S  K  L  E  M
C  Q  D  C  Z  T  V  A  K  R  I  K  H  V  D
T  G  S  V  L  I  A  X  O  S  C  I  E  M  N
F  R  G  P  N  Z  N  R  P  U  N  S  R  G  A
I  B  Y  E  R  Y  W  D  N  Y  A  Z  C  Y  R
D  C  C  M  U  P  R  K  F  N  R  C  S  F  G
Q  B  J  H  N  F  Y  Q  S  U  F  N  S  D  X
W  M  D  X  H  D  P  G  U  R  P  P  K  L  S
```

1. ALFREDO
2. LARRY LEVAN
3. IAN LEVINE
4. DAVID MANCUSO
5. FRANCIS GRASSO
6. FRANKIE **KNUCKLES**
7. D.J. KOOL HERC
8. NORMAN JAY
9. HARVEY
10. **GRANDMASTER** FLASH

55. CITIES

```
K U A B Y L Q N Q E D X R R Q
L V D V T V S E B H K Q G I Z
O C G L I B H Q N Y B R P S F
N Y O G C V M S A E E K D G X
D X H O O T A M R A K B W R V
O U I N H F F L T C D S U U C
N X S U C H I C A G O Z A B P
C P M S A N I M N S Y T X S A
A C I L M T O D I Y V Z E E K
L C X X I W J U S N F E N N C
L S O E Y C Z Y K I O P G N C
I L S B W N I K N P O D Y A O
N L B J E X W L A F I X N H S
G O Y I W Z D D R E T M Z O Z
B X M E W I W V F A A W M J L
```

1.	LONDON CALLING	6.	FRANK SINATRA
2.	VIVA LAS VEGAS	7.	MACHO CITY
3.	BERLIN	8.	JOHANNESBURG
4.	BOBBY WOMACK	9.	THEME FOR **GREAT CITIES**
5.	CHICAGO	10.	I LIKE **LONDON** IN THE RAIN

56. CARS

```
M I E W P U E V X Y Z A H P T
G G L V N O L P P J N H A M H
K N W D I X C A R S E W I F E
P Y M R A O I S G T B M G Z P
A N P I G D H S T P S W Y W A
R F Q V A J E E C O E F L A S
T J V E D Q V M A I D Y R F S
I T X M A R E G J I E E M V E
C U J Y O V I E X G C I Q D N
U K X C R L N R Z Z R K F X G
L W D A E I A L Q A E J Z A E
A E R R H I P F W L M R X U R
R U L T T N U F N U F N U F C
B O F A N H A B O T U A M S K
A D Z U O Q U L A A P H L R B
```

1. VEHICLE
2. LITTLE **RED CORVETTE**
3. CARS
4. THE PASSENGER
5. ON THE ROAD AGAIN

6. DRIVE MY CAR
7. MERCEDES BENZ
8. AUTOBAHN
9. FUN, FUN, FUN
10. NO **PARTICULAR** PLACE TO GO

57. YEAH YEAH TO YÉ-YÉ

```
F  M  U  M  Q  Y  N  A  Z  A  T  N  Y  D  U
K  R  B  R  D  P  F  I  P  C  W  I  M  P  T
V  J  A  P  F  O  X  L  A  Q  E  O  G  H  L
A  P  M  N  S  J  P  K  Q  W  T  E  P  R  P
F  R  A  N  C  E  G  A  L  L  O  L  O  L  E
C  H  N  Z  R  O  L  L  E  R  G  I  R  L  T
F  Q  Y  E  B  B  I  L  D  S  E  S  T  Z  U
U  O  S  I  B  U  O  S  I  B  U  O  Z  G  L
P  C  J  R  W  S  A  K  E  F  F  I  Y  M  A
M  Y  I  N  K  G  W  C  A  H  W  T  V  A  C
O  C  H  R  I  S  T  I  E  L  A  U  M  E  L
F  M  C  E  T  T  E  L  E  T  T  R  E  L  A
J  A  U  N  Y  A  A  Q  I  D  S  Q  D  L  R
S  J  R  J  T  S  A  M  V  Z  Y  A  X  Y  K
L  C  O  J  Z  B  R  T  C  L  K  C  B  L  C
```

1. **FRANCOISE HARDY**
2. **ZOU BISOU BISOU**
3. LAISSE TOMBER LES FILLES
4. **CETTE LETTRE LA**
5. **CHRISTIE LAUME**
6. 7 HEURES DU **MATIN**
7. **PETULA CLARK**
8. **ROLLERGIRL**
9. **FRANCE GALL**
10. J'AI MIS UN **TIGRE** DANS MA GUITARE

58. DUTCH BEAT GROUPS

```
Q  L  Y  W  N  P  C  S  D  D  E  S  C  V  X
I  S  G  L  R  B  P  H  E  R  R  I  S  G  K
D  V  H  H  F  P  G  M  Q  E  X  X  R  N  L
O  K  Q  O  I  N  A  W  D  Y  S  T  E  I  C
R  E  J  Z  C  S  O  I  M  J  C  Y  T  R  J
E  Q  E  N  K  K  S  G  U  Q  C  F  N  R  F
Z  H  B  E  C  T  I  H  A  Z  D  I  U  A  W
T  Q  R  X  U  Y  B  N  I  R  D  V  H  E  V
V  S  U  O  A  X  N  H  G  K  D  E  E  N  R
P  S  E  I  X  X  T  T  Q  B  R  U  H  E  N
A  H  B  I  H  X  K  B  C  A  L  F  T  D  L
T  S  N  O  I  T  O  M  E  H  T  U  U  L  G
O  H  G  J  K  X  X  E  Q  G  C  W  E  O  A
O  S  D  Z  E  X  V  B  I  N  T  A  N  G  S
R  L  Q  G  Y  H  E  U  B  S  I  S  H  I  A
```

1. GOLDEN EARRING
2. THE OUTSIDERS
3. BINTANGS
4. SHOCKING BLUE
5. Q65 (SIXTY-FIVE)
6. DE MASKERS
7. THE MOTIONS
8. DRAGONFLY
9. THE HUNTERS
10. THE ZIPPS

59. BALEARIC BEATS

```
P  G  L  G  B  Q  A  K  G  X  P  B  H  Z  F
S  N  B  T  Q  R  R  R  L  Q  R  G  R  S  B
G  I  G  R  G  J  E  A  Z  B  I  G  Z  Z  A
J  H  V  H  S  S  I  I  B  G  M  B  T  P  C
F  C  N  L  F  D  K  X  L  J  A  Z  J  Q  K
H  S  U  Q  Q  U  N  X  O  L  V  B  B  O  T
T  T  A  O  H  C  R  I  W  D  E  B  B  C  O
X  T  F  P  L  O  A  V  M  L  R  T  B  Q  M
W  O  C  A  O  Y  I  V  O  E  A  L  D  W  Y
U  G  O  T  O  C  S  V  N  L  L  P  K  X  R
O  Z  D  B  M  L  E  W  K  C  E  P  T  X  O
S  T  A  M  K  D  H  D  E  K  Z  M  M  L  O
I  M  L  R  V  Q  F  Y  Y  I  Y  V  G  I  T
R  H  D  J  L  I  J  R  S  E  I  R  O  T  S
K  W  K  N  C  M  V  H  O  U  R  Z  Y  A  L
```

1. RAISE
2. BELOVED
3. BLOW MONKEYS
4. REY DE COPAS
5. STORIES
6. SIMPLE MINDS
7. GOING **BACK TO MY ROOTS**
8. PRIMAVERA
9. MANUEL **GÖTTSCHING**
10. SEBASTIEN **TELLIER**

60. PSYCHEDELIC SWEDEN

```
M R Q K O U G N W Z J P A N R
S E S R E H T O M D N A R G F
F P C I G Z H F A A B R V C Z
X W Y K Q G X I H T I S O I S
M Y K Z I U O T R V W O Q Z T
C P X I T M V U N E G N U D H
K Q A U U W A X N A F S M G E
R X K S O K A R L S S O N A A
H X R I E M Z K K T S U Z A M
F Q E H C Q B Y V M F N Z M A
W S N L Q P D U M I E D C N Z
G K Z Q O D K Q O K A N R S I
F L S L B E B O H A N S S O N
P U G H R O G E F E L D T L G
N W T E I E A C L L M D U A M
```

1. MECKI MARK MEN
2. S.T. MIKAEL
3. BO HANSSON
4. HANSSON & KARLSSON
5. PUGH ROGEFELDT
6. PÄRSON SOUND
7. THE AMAZING
8. BABY GRANDMOTHERS
9. GOAT
10. DUNGEN

61. EASTERN BLOC PARTY

```
I  H  O  P  A  W  C  W  R  J  Y  Y  K  T  A
Y  K  V  B  B  J  Y  P  A  P  N  Y  W  Q  Y
R  B  B  G  I  S  C  A  V  O  K  I  T  A  K
A  A  H  A  X  G  P  V  D  R  P  Y  V  V  B
T  X  R  Z  B  E  C  E  I  F  W  L  P  O  J
I  P  C  V  C  I  P  H  X  D  B  O  L  S  K
G  O  F  B  L  R  L  C  A  U  Y  C  M  I  J
E  V  Z  L  O  W  T  A  Z  I  Z  O  S  B  H
N  S  E  T  J  G  Q  G  E  A  N  M  F  U  T
O  S  I  J  N  W  M  U  U  D  P  O  E  K  H
W  M  S  R  O  X  S  P  I  P  Z  T  Y  A  R
R  O  J  Y  R  P  Z  A  G  G  Z  I  G  T  C
E  C  Y  F  Z  R  L  L  R  P  T  V  P  R  K
Z  Q  Q  Y  V  C  G  L  R  S  M  G  E  A  V
C  E  M  R  J  H  J  A  G  Z  V  T  F  M  E
```

1. ALI BABKI
2. ALLA PUGACHEVA
3. TORPEDO
4. ILLES
5. BIG CHAIN
6. KATI KOVACS

7. **MONDIAL** UND DAS ELECTRECORD-ORCHESTER
8. MARTA KUBISOVA
9. CZERWONE GITARY
10. LOCOMOTIV GT

62. KRAUTROCK

```
M  O  C  O  O  A  Z  C  R  E  M  G  D  P  T
L  Y  K  Y  T  V  X  S  W  A  F  N  Z  V  F
Q  E  E  R  J  Y  C  B  S  A  N  Y  Q  K  A
K  P  P  B  A  D  A  T  U  E  W  I  Z  I  K
M  L  U  M  S  F  K  S  A  G  D  U  N  M  P
F  P  I  E  E  A  T  L  R  R  C  O  L  Z  M
Y  M  H  A  N  T  Q  W  D  K  M  P  W  V  R
D  X  K  Z  Y  A  A  K  E  R  H  K  A  T  S
X  F  V  W  G  S  C  R  A  R  J  A  H  O  T
G  R  N  T  D  X  Z  H  H  T  K  F  I  T  E
H  K  G  B  D  E  Q  B  P  S  T  F  V  Q  Q
Z  Q  Q  A  I  Z  D  G  B  L  A  H  M  B  X
E  H  W  T  A  P  D  S  V  Q  G  I  G  W  X
K  V  E  U  H  I  R  M  V  X  B  U  U  Q  F
F  Y  O  O  Z  W  Q  Z  A  V  H  U  F  H  U
```

1. ASH RA TEMPEL
2. EMBRYO
3. KRAFTWERK
4. ZUCKERZEIT
5. NEU!

6. PHAEDRA
7. FAUST
8. HARMONIA
9. YETI
10. CAN

63. ITALO DISCO

```
I  I  K  C  Q  E  Z  B  Z  F  I  M  H  T  R
E  S  E  O  L  W  F  V  V  C  H  E  A  U  S
D  N  I  M  L  E  E  T  S  R  L  K  O  D  C
B  D  X  M  Q  T  X  Z  R  J  E  M  P  O  X
G  H  X  U  E  M  Z  U  Z  A  A  J  S  U  R
F  C  M  N  L  T  D  Z  C  D  I  O  A  N  S
C  H  Y  I  Z  E  I  H  S  P  F  N  U  Q  W
W  A  G  C  G  L  A  M  A  E  D  M  S  V  T
Z  R  G  A  Z  N  E  V  A  D  A  I  C  O  Y
I  L  D  T  C  L  S  O  W  W  S  Y  S  L  U
M  I  X  E  B  O  G  U  D  O  M  M  F  X  B
Q  E  V  O  L  D  E  E  N  I  L  A  V  U  R
E  Y  R  V  N  X  W  P  W  Z  F  F  Y  J  S
L  P  N  E  B  H  Y  W  T  Y  C  A  A  N  E
L  G  M  W  B  H  T  C  A  Q  J  W  Q  B  I
```

1.	STEEL MIND	6.	WET
2.	COMMUNICATE	7.	I NEED LOVE
3.	TAKE A CHANCE	8.	HYPNOSIS
4.	GAZNEVADA	9.	WAITING FOR A **TRAIN**
5.	PROBLEMS D'AMOUR	10.	CHARLIE

64. GAINSBOURG'S GALLIC GREATS

```
E  S  R  B  B  Z  F  Z  I  O  V  R  D  E  K
N  D  B  B  D  D  Y  Q  K  I  K  W  W  L  F
G  R  Y  S  U  L  P  N  O  N  I  O  M  A  G
K  A  D  L  I  H  D  H  Z  J  O  L  R  H  O
Z  W  O  A  C  Z  K  N  P  F  E  E  R  O  T
M  R  L  I  A  D  V  H  W  B  T  X  W  R  K
G  O  E  T  N  O  N  O  Y  E  S  Y  E  S  Q
I  F  M  I  N  I  N  A  A  V  Q  O  Q  E  X
Z  H  N  A  O  H  C  E  V  R  D  G  V  L
T  S  E  I  B  S  T  E  Y  I  V  V  C  F  Y
Z  A  Q  A  I  E  D  E  J  Z  N  Y  M  V  H
S  L  H  Y  S  U  V  K  Z  O  G  N  L  M  N
D  F  V  G  Q  C  Z  C  Y  W  O  O  O  A  S
T  O  D  R  A  B  E  T  T  I  G  I  R  B  A
Y  N  K  V  J  L  L  A  H  E  Q  X  I  K  A
```

1. BONNIE AND CLYDE
2. FLASH FORWARD
3. BRIGITTE BARDOT
4. NO, NO, YES, YES
5. AUX ARMES **ET CAETERA**
6. CANNABIS
7. INITIALS BB
8. JE T'AIME…MOI NON PLUS
9. EN MELODY
10. LA HORSE

65. TRAINS

```
D  E  R  E  W  O  P  M  A  E  T  S  D  C  M
S  I  Q  Q  L  B  W  P  A  R  D  G  E  J  Z
Q  C  Z  A  O  R  N  I  A  J  W  K  S  E  N
C  L  A  R  K  S  V  I  L  L  E  R  X  C  Q
E  L  G  N  A  T  N  E  P  I  T  H  P  A  U
O  W  F  U  I  I  Y  I  Y  R  N  Q  T  M  V
B  N  O  S  N  I  K  T  A  Y  R  A  G  X  P
Z  J  F  V  X  Y  L  N  B  X  I  B  F  P  Y
J  J  A  T  M  Y  S  T  E  R  Y  G  P  K  D
R  I  X  N  I  E  X  P  R  E  S  S  U  X  P
N  T  E  M  U  I  Z  X  S  Q  W  I  N  S  S
N  I  A  R  T  T  H  G  I  N  Z  J  P  R  Q
O  B  O  E  R  D  U  V  Y  O  F  A  H  A  K
Q  P  N  V  P  U  M  C  F  P  R  T  W  H  L
E  F  M  R  F  N  B  W  T  S  Y  U  K  D  D
```

1.   **MYSTERY** TRAIN
2.   **TRAIN IN VAIN**
3.   LAST OF THE **STEAM-POWERED TRAINS**
4.   **THE JAM**
5.   LAST TRAIN TO **CLARKSVILLE**
6.   **GARY ATKINSON**
7.   **PENTANGLE**
8.   **TRANS-EUROPE** EXPRESS
9.   MARRAKESH **EXPRESS**
10. **NIGHT TRAIN**

66. DIGGING INDIA'S FUNKY SIDE

```
R  L  D  W  A  H  Z  N  G  W  I  Y  A  N  K
E  A  V  U  E  T  A  N  L  O  C  Z  S  A  S
A  L  K  M  M  M  T  R  F  R  N  N  H  H  X
D  P  A  N  R  M  W  U  U  D  Q  E  A  O  M
D  N  K  U  A  I  A  L  C  Y  H  K  B  M  O
T  K  B  G  A  H  I  R  Z  L  B  H  H  G  W
R  D  Z  F  A  V  S  J  O  X  A  D  O  A  C
R  Z  Y  L  S  O  S  A  Y  D  U  C  N  J  O
U  Y  M  F  U  O  J  Y  D  O  U  Y  S  N  U
O  F  M  A  I  E  C  I  M  N  N  M  L  A  X
J  K  S  K  Y  E  O  D  P  D  A  J  E  P  G
N  O  I  S  S  E  S  B  O  Q  B  N  A  A  I
W  E  H  P  V  G  F  K  V  H  J  H  A  S  A
K  A  L  Y  A  N  J  I  A  N  A  N  D  J  I
P  Y  A  R  Z  I  N  D  A  G  I  H  A  I  V
```

1. ANANDA SHANKAR
2. SAPAN JAGMOHAN
3. R.D. BURMAN
4. KALYANJI ANANDJI
5. DUM MARO DUM
6. ASHA BHONSLE
7. HEMANT BHONSLE
8. OBSESSION '77
9. STREETS OF CALCUTTA
10. PYAR ZINDAGI HAI

67. SKA

```
T  U  L  X  K  G  D  P  H  M  I  U  B  H  G
H  Z  K  Z  D  N  M  V  G  G  S  E  D  S  N
E  A  P  Z  E  G  Y  M  D  M  S  P  P  A  N
Y  N  T  C  S  X  B  A  N  T  W  S  Z  W  D
G  E  G  I  M  Z  O  O  I  O  V  B  O  H  E
O  K  L  O  O  F  Y  L  T  X  F  D  L  S  R
T  T  U  W  N  D  L  T  S  G  R  P  Q  A  R
T  I  Z  M  D  U  O  R  F  E  J  A  K  W  I
O  A  M  R  D  N  L  Q  M  C  Y  A  N  L  C
C  L  J  R  E  T  L  M  G  G  W  Z  B  Q  K
O  E  N  G  K  M  I  H  S  U  U  F  O  X  P
M  R  D  J  K  S  P  A  T  S  K  K  U  N  A
E  U  D  N  E  D  O  J  A  Q  Z  F  C  V  T
J  A  J  O  R  F  P  L  N  F  E  Q  Y  H  S
F  L  E  S  R  U  O  Y  Y  O  J  N  E  W  Y
```

1. JUDGE NOT
2. DESMOND DEKKER
3. MY BOY LOLLIPOP
4. LAUREL AITKEN
5. SIMMER DOWN

6. BE STILL
7. DERRICK & PATSY
8. ENJOY YOURSELF
9. THEY GOT TO COME
10. WASH WASH

68. REGGAE

```
N  S  C  Y  R  O  Q  W  M  P  V  R  U  M  C
L  B  T  H  I  E  V  E  S  L  T  E  R  B  H
S  F  S  A  J  V  L  C  T  Z  E  T  U  C  E
D  G  V  F  R  O  L  I  Q  X  T  S  S  F  R
C  W  N  C  D  L  H  K  A  V  N  E  W  R  R
P  J  X  I  I  E  I  A  Q  W  I  J  Z  A  Y
Z  T  A  L  R  N  R  G  O  Y  Y  O  D  D  O
X  N  P  J  C  O  K  R  H  A  J  N  Y  V  H
S  R  A  W  L  A  B  I  R  T  B  Y  N  W  B
V  Y  K  H  F  S  N  M  X  P  S  T  Q  U  A
O  M  C  H  I  Y  S  R  S  N  H  T  A  T  B
K  D  Z  N  A  X  P  P  Q  S  I  O  W  Y  Y
U  H  N  X  W  N  S  X  T  M  P  N  F  H  M
K  E  S  F  T  F  G  D  L  U  C  K  P  J  H
D  F  N  E  J  F  L  V  T  Q  J  W  B  J  V
```

1.	THE **MELODIANS**	6.	BUMPING AND **BORING**
2.	POLICE AND **THIEVES**	7.	**KNOTTY NO JESTER**
3.	**BUNNY WAILER**	8.	THE **STARLIGHTS**
4.	**CHERRY OH BABY**	9.	**DENNIS BROWN**
5.	**ONE LOVE**	10.	**TRIBAL WAR**

69. SAILING

```
S  T  O  Y  I  W  N  E  B  V  H  Z  J  G  B
O  Z  T  K  P  K  Y  L  F  O  N  I  V  G  Q
S  W  O  O  D  E  N  S  H  I  P  S  O  N  G
K  D  E  E  E  M  R  D  U  P  R  E  Y  I  M
L  H  O  N  F  K  N  B  K  C  Z  G  C  D  O
G  N  I  L  I  A  S  W  K  U  L  E  N  L  R
X  A  J  H  L  G  P  Y  M  L  O  C  Q  I  S
R  D  H  K  S  J  H  W  F  F  K  Y  J  U  E
O  W  V  X  R  Q  O  T  X  N  T  U  K  B  M
F  G  Z  C  O  M  D  W  B  K  P  T  O  P  O
B  D  P  S  L  O  O  P  J  O  H  N  B  I  O
H  I  H  Y  I  E  S  Y  O  H  A  P  I  H  S
Z  U  N  B  A  D  Q  U  W  Y  K  T  U  S  E
K  Z  F  V  S  V  B  M  T  C  Q  H  O  T  M
N  S  Y  D  A  B  B  X  T  M  X  H  X  L  D
```

1. THE **SHIP SONG**
2. **LAND HO!**
3. **A SAILOR'S LIFE**
4. **WOODEN SHIPS**
5. **SAILING**
6. **NIGHT BOAT** TO CAIRO
7. **SHIPBUILDING**
8. **SHIP AHOY**
9. **MORSE MOOSE** AND THE GREY GOOSE
10. **SLOOP JOHN B**

70. AFROBEAT

```
K  B  S  A  L  A  B  I  T  N  A  Z  W  P  U
C  O  R  L  A  N  D  O  J  U  L  I  U  S  G
S  J  P  N  D  D  N  D  E  R  A  R  V  O  C
T  O  T  T  L  Y  Z  P  H  G  T  I  S  L  D
I  T  U  K  A  L  E  F  A  S  A  C  N  P  R
B  U  K  L  M  U  M  S  A  J  A  J  M  V  X
N  Q  L  C  M  Z  S  A  G  R  X  R  E  O  L
K  E  V  Z  Q  A  H  U  S  O  B  M  S  Y  G
N  N  F  E  M  I  K  U  T  I  X  T  K  E  J
R  S  X  M  N  W  L  O  G  Q  H  N  W  P  V
P  U  T  O  A  L  D  T  S  K  H  R  S  Z  M
W  U  J  T  E  D  H  V  V  S  R  Q  Q  Q  M
X  A  L  Y  Y  I  R  L  D  R  A  E  Y  A  T
S  G  A  W  E  S  D  X  T  S  O  D  N  H  E
S  L  B  F  B  J  H  Q  V  H  G  H  G  N  W
```

1. **TONY ALLEN** PLAYS WITH AFRIKA 70
2. **SOUL MAKOSSA**
3. **FEMI KUTI**
4. **ASSAGAI**
5. **FELA KUTI**
6. **OSCAR SULLEY** & THE UHURU DANCE BAND
7. **JONI HAASTRUP**
8. **ORLANDO JULIUS** & HIS MODERN ACES
9. **ANTIBALAS**
10. **MR. BIG THIEF**

71. TROPICÁLIA

```
T  H  M  P  H  C  R  O  K  K  C  O  R  B  J  T
P  U  Y  G  T  C  K  N  W  M  V  A  M  O  S
P  V  U  V  V  U  G  M  A  U  T  F  M  R  M
A  Q  G  H  H  L  J  O  P  M  C  Z  N  G  T
E  Y  M  G  N  E  C  N  A  L  E  R  M  E  E
Z  L  G  O  I  L  E  C  A  F  O  U  W  B  S
P  C  E  X  B  L  U  U  I  A  P  O  C  E  L
A  S  N  K  C  M  B  V  O  M  J  B  T  N  Q
P  G  I  W  B  P  G  E  T  O  I  N  S  W  L
A  I  L  A  C  I  P  O  R  T  A  R  G  J  M
R  M  R  P  M  Q  Y  Y  D  T  N  B  N  S  P
X  X  D  X  C  O  Z  T  U  B  O  R  I  V  U
V  I  L  D  W  O  G  M  T  K  H  G  I  L  P
V  D  K  Z  W  Q  S  L  M  R  Z  Q  I  N  L
C  G  A  L  C  O  S  T  A  A  M  A  G  L  L
```

1. TOM ZE
2. VAMOS TRATAR DA SAUDE
3. BAT MACUMBA
4. TROPICÁLIA
5. JORGE BEN

6. ALGO MAIS
7. OS MUTANTES
8. RELANCE
9. GILBERTO GIL
10. GAL COSTA

72. FLYING

```
P C C W Q W C M L E H W O R B
T O I C K A O J H R I O M U B
H O R K A M Q R V P I K F X B
M H N E J X Y L R D M F O S J
D B D K H Z J P X A A B X M D
U Q J G O H B G Y L P X O H S
T N V Q A U D S O X Q S M I N
D R I B R E V L I S O N Y A N
P F W Q J E K I R O M H F E M
D R I B G N I Y L F H G I H H
F L Y M E T O T H E M O O N B
H G I H S E L I M T H G I E V
B A C K I N T H E U S S R P T
F L Y L I K E A N E A G L E U
R S R E T H G I F O O F X F Y
```

1.	BUFFALO SPRINGFIELD	6.	SMOKIE
2.	HIGH FLYING BIRD	7.	BACK IN THE USSR
3.	HEY SPARROW	8.	NO SILVER BIRD
4.	FLY ME TO THE MOON	9.	FLY LIKE AN EAGLE
5.	EIGHT MILES HIGH	10.	FOO FIGHTERS

73. PRODUCERS

```
A N X L I M B K W T B N X J L
N I L E R O D G E R S A P A E
J T V L Q P I W I T Z S P Y E
J R K M J M T A V X C G J G S
F A D Q U I N C Y J O N E S C
G M X A Z W O Q O C K J O O R
C E M J I I C I B H X Y Z H A
X G B L K B S Y S P P W C B T
Y R S R R E I M E R P J D Z C
X O E L I D V D O M Z S H F H
N E S W H A Y Q S K U K D L P
E G A B O T N L M U Q B X B E
A U G M F J O E M E E K E M R
Y B D E Q M T L N O P K P O R
P H I L S P E C T O R W R D Y
```

1. BRIAN WILSON
2. QUINCY JONES
3. GEORGE MARTIN
4. NILE RODGERS
5. TONY VISCONTI
6. BRIAN ENO
7. LEE "SCRATCH" PERRY
8. PHIL SPECTOR
9. D.J. PREMIER
10. JOE MEEK

74. DEBUTS

```
D  B  S  S  S  L  O  T  S  I  P  X  E  S  R
E  G  Y  W  N  J  W  X  T  N  L  L  T  I  N
C  A  O  X  M  C  J  H  W  O  E  Z  W  C  S
N  X  B  G  Z  Q  E  B  N  I  A  Q  H  J  N
E  C  E  Z  O  C  I  N  O  T  S  S  D  M  O
I  R  I  L  L  M  A  T  I  C  E  E  M  Q  J
R  I  T  A  K  Q  A  A  S  U  P  S  A  S  L
E  R  S  C  W  M  U  G  I  R  L  S  Q  S  A
P  H  A  L  E  H  B  E  V  T  E  H  J  P  M
X  N  E  M  P  T  E  C  I  S  A  P  I  J  W
E  N  B  X  O  V  P  D  E  S  Q  E  Y  B
P  S  U  M  I  N  Z  Q  Y  D  E  J  E  O  D
F  E  J  Z  W  S  E  T  O  Z  M  C  E  F  T
X  M  N  L  Y  T  Q  S  J  N  E  C  Y  I  C
A  M  T  M  W  F  S  E  U  E  J  K  O  S  Q
```

1. **BEASTIE BOYS**
2. **THE CLASH**
3. THE **RAMONES**
4. **ILLMATIC**
5. THE VELVET UNDERGROUND & **NICO**
6. **JOY DIVISION**
7. **PLEASE PLEASE ME**
8. APPETITE FOR **DESTRUCTION**
9. THE **SEX PISTOLS**
10. ARE YOU **EXPERIENCED**?

75. "DIFFICULT" SECOND ALBUMS

```
U U N U P W M W M V J L W E D
W R O Q X N I C F T T B A U P
D O S N T P O M D C K M J Q F
U Y I Y F R E E W H E E L I N
A E R E H W O N S I S I H T D
P N R T H E B E N D S W U U X
Z E O N S H O C S S L J C O C
G Y M E N E C I L B U P A B T
S Y N V I R P E F O B A T S B
R K A E M J A A I O F R Q L N
E T V R K B Y F T E C A E U D
U X L M U I A F N A O N P A U
J I M I H E N D R I X O M P D
K D T N Y F J N G Q K I D X U
L L X D Q M O R H A L D N X W
```

1. VAN MORRISON
2. EVERYONE KNOWS **THIS** IS NOWHERE
3. PUBLIC ENEMY
4. TAPESTRY
5. NEVERMIND
6. THE BENDS
7. PARANOID
8. JIMI HENDRIX
9. PAUL'S BOUTIQUE
10. THE **FREEWHEELIN'** BOB DYLAN

76. CONCEPT ALBUMS

```
N  P  D  L  F  L  B  D  N  X  O  I  W  C  Z
F  J  A  W  S  Q  H  M  K  L  K  U  V  K  L
Z  Y  F  P  A  R  Q  W  F  G  P  R  Q  L  A
A  D  M  U  S  I  O  R  L  E  W  S  U  L  R
M  Q  N  U  E  I  W  O  B  D  I  V  A  D  H
S  X  C  B  H  D  I  R  A  S  R  N  D  C  P
S  G  N  I  H  T  Y  T  T  E  R  P  R  C  Y
O  G  T  Y  R  O  S  O  L  C  K  U  O  S  Y
N  X  V  P  U  W  M  X  L  A  I  P  P  F  R
C  O  C  M  E  M  M  L  Y  F  G  X  H  R  Q
X  P  S  W  Y  P  A  V  H  L  K  O  E  D  G
P  D  G  L  R  W  P  C  A  L  U  N  N  G  O
J  U  N  E  E  R  G  E  G  A  L  L  I  V  N
M  I  Q  H  I  N  H  K  R  M  H  J  A  P  K
Q  I  T  M  J  K  A  Z  F  S  N  A  Q  I  I
```

1. THE **PRETTY THINGS**
2. **SMALL FACES**
3. **PINK FLOYD**
4. **SGT. PEPPER'S** LONELY HEARTS CLUB BAND
5. **VILLAGE GREEN** PRESERVATION SOCIETY
6. **THE WALL**
7. **QUADROPHENIA**
8. **DAVID BOWIE**
9. **TOMMY**
10. **HISTOIRE DE MELODY NELSON**

77. ROCK & POP INSTRUMENTALS

```
Q  U  P  O  U  X  J  P  L  V  J  X  M  B  A
O  T  S  H  Z  B  Z  S  R  N  X  H  L  Q  C
S  E  N  E  V  S  M  B  C  Y  P  K  N  M  V
T  P  C  I  H  D  E  H  R  P  F  P  H  E  V
D  E  K  Z  R  C  X  R  H  O  F  J  C  L  R
D  Z  T  O  R  N  A  D  O  S  Z  I  U  T  O
Y  B  C  E  L  B  W  P  M  D  W  P  Z  I  B
R  Y  P  C  N  R  K  Z  A  V  O  E  T  N  I
A  B  M  H  W  E  B  F  B  M  S  M  O  G  M
Z  P  O  O  E  M  Z  Y  M  Y  H  D  M  P  R
G  J  G  E  D  C  U  I  Q  V  E  F  C  O  E
N  G  W  S  A  N  F  V  R  A  S  A  M  T  C
Q  R  A  L  L  M  L  U  C  U  S  C  C  Y  E
S  C  I  M  H  T  Y  R  U  E  L  B  M  U  R
D  H  I  Y  U  W  V  C  F  U  T  D  H  U  T
```

1.	MOGWAI	6.	APACHE
2.	THE EURYTHMICS	7.	THE COMMODORES
3.	RUMBLE	8.	URIZEN
4.	JOHN BARRY	9.	MELTING POT
5.	ECHOES	10.	THE TORNADOS

78. POST-BEATLES TUNES FROM THE FAB FOUR

```
D  K  N  M  D  Q  V  A  D  S  G  W  Q  V  W
E  A  E  R  N  Y  I  P  A  Q  I  O  M  N  B
Z  S  P  J  R  P  N  P  T  N  M  R  Y  O  P
A  D  A  T  D  Y  S  X  G  F  M  K  S  S  I
M  F  U  G  D  T  T  S  E  I  E  I  E  I  G
A  H  L  E  M  P  A  E  Q  B  S  N  C  R  B
M  U  M  L  J  M  N  H  Z  T  O  G  R  R  I
I  V  C  A  D  H  T  S  S  J  M  C  E  A  I
E  V  C  C  T  W  K  H  N  O  E  L  T  H  U
B  M  A  N  N  V  A  U  N  Q  T  A  F  E  W
Y  F  R  I  S  M  R  H  K  K  R  S  R  G  I
A  U  T  D  A  Y  M  B  W  X  U  S  I  R  M
M  L  N  Z  U  T  A  R  E  A  T  H  E  O  P
C  H  E  C  K  M  Y  M  A  C  H  I  N  E  L
A  E  Y  M  O  O  Z  Z  U  V  P  Y  D  G  V
```

1. CHECK MY MACHINE
2. WAH WAH
3. INSTANT KARMA!
4. MY SECRET FRIEND
5. GIMME SOME TRUTH

6. PAUL MCCARTNEY
7. WINGS
8. GEORGE HARRISON
9. MAYBE I'M AMAZED
10. WORKING CLASS HERO

79. ODD TIME SIGNATURES

```
M K Q Y G Z L V T Z H M E Y Y
D A V N C I G K A P J E E G X
K E N K A L L S K R X N Y Q V
C P E I K M T T E N O L Y Y R
I Z U N C P R C F M D M G S A
W R C V U D R E I E E H N F S
R Z L O V O E P V Q S D W Z H
A V E D U M Y P E I N Y O F J
W U R A M S Y L R X R Y X G J
E J Q H U J N H L E V G P F R
N F G Q R L Q U K A S U B A O
N Z S R E L G N A R T S E H T
O T H E C R U N G E K G I H C
I E L B I S S O P M I W A O F
D B W S M N O N E K G H C C N
```

1.	MANIC DEPRESSION	6.	THE CRUNGE
2.	TAKE FIVE	7.	ALL YOU NEED IS LOVE
3.	THE STRANGLERS	8.	HEY YA!
4.	DIONNE WARWICK	9.	MISSION IMPOSSIBLE
5.	MONEY	10.	RIVER MAN

80. COUPLES

```
I  I  T  I  Y  D  K  A  G  O  X  S  A  L  J
T  L  N  O  N  K  J  X  O  Q  E  I  B  I  U
L  Q  I  O  H  J  W  I  P  S  M  R  B  J  N
B  V  M  H  V  C  L  V  V  W  J  R  A  T  E
A  M  I  B  P  G  Q  M  H  B  I  C  E  L  C
R  H  F  V  H  D  J  R  V  K  K  B  U  G  A
X  V  U  O  Y  H  N  T  E  A  T  I  N  P  R
B  E  Y  O  N  C  E  A  N  D  J  A  Y  Z  T
S  Y  O  Z  T  Y  N  D  E  Z  M  X  T  Y  E
B  A  K  A  J  D  M  O  Y  I  F  W  R  K  R
G  N  O  M  T  E  R  Q  F  Q  N  U  A  R  S
P  D  O  I  G  G  U  W  L  M  I  N  M  C  Y
S  O  N  N  Y  A  N  D  C  H  E  R  O  C  T
S  A  O  J  N  D  O  X  U  X  X  A  L  R  U
G  D  Z  N  S  K  C  I  N  E  I  V  E  T  S
```

1. **ABBA**
2. JOHNNY AND **JUNE CARTER** CASH
3. **JACK AND MEG** WHITE
4. **BEYONCÉ AND JAY-Z**
5. **IKE AND TINA** TURNER
6. JOHN LENNON AND **YOKO ONO**
7. JOHN AND BEVERLEY **MARTYN**
8. **RONNIE AND PHIL** SPECTOR
9. **SONNY AND CHER**
10. **STEVIE NICKS** & LINDSEY BUCKINGHAM

81. TROUBLED SOULS

```
U  P  Z  Z  U  U  T  X  U  R  W  O  J  J  O
Q  Z  E  V  V  T  T  T  G  E  H  J  D  Z  N
B  K  S  C  V  O  E  X  K  L  I  R  F  Q  K
R  C  U  P  P  M  R  A  W  L  T  J  L  C  W
I  F  O  J  X  Q  R  U  A  I  N  L  G  R  B
A  P  H  G  W  D  A  E  J  O  E  M  E  E  K
N  V  E  V  K  I  B  Y  K  T  Y  H  M  W  M
W  G  N  C  B  A  D  A  E  S  H  H  H  V  H
I  Z  I  C  Y  H  Y  G  T  M  O  S  Y  D  U
L  N  W  Q  I  L  S  N  Z  I  U  H  T  F  G
S  J  Y  I  B  I  X  I  Q  T  S  M  E  J  G
O  W  M  Z  G  W  K  V  Y  H  T  Z  I  L  M
N  I  A  B  O  C  T  R  U  K  O  H  X  M  J
S  I  T  R  U  C  N  A  I  T  N  S  J  M  U
E  M  K  T  N  N  N  M  L  V  B  M  J  O  Q
```

1. KURT COBAIN
2. AMY WINEHOUSE
3. MARVIN GAYE
4. NICK DRAKE
5. ELLIOT SMITH

6. WHITNEY HOUSTON
7. BRIAN WILSON
8. SYD BARRETT
9. JOE MEEK
10. IAN CURTIS

82. REVOLUTIONARIES

```
H  K  C  C  T  S  U  W  U  A  V  V  X  R  Y
N  S  E  S  A  B  J  O  F  S  U  S  E  N  S
D  J  A  W  O  O  D  Y  G  U  T  H  R  I  E
T  U  H  L  B  F  N  O  U  P  F  F  T  X  L
G  I  L  S  C  O  T  T  H  E  R  O  N  L  T
C  T  E  W  S  E  B  D  Z  R  I  K  Y  T  A
A  U  J  L  J  Z  H  M  U  F  D  S  P  W  E
A  K  D  W  N  K  T  T  A  U  G  N  Q  C  B
J  A  O  I  E  Z  Z  R  G  R  P  E  P  F  E
K  L  T  S  V  L  N  T  W  R  L  M  P  Y  H
C  E  S  C  I  T  O  N  P  Y  H  E  E  H  T
C  F  D  M  P  G  L  B  Y  L  V  C  Y  J  M
M  I  F  A  W  G  Q  O  T  I  W  A  O  Y  O
F  Y  R  G  B  F  L  H  A  F  N  P  Y  H  P
P  N  H  Q  I  L  M  P  T  I  Q  S  T  J  Y
```

1. GIL SCOTT HERON
2. BOB MARLEY
3. SUPER FURRY ANIMALS
4. FELA KUTI
5. SPACEMEN 3
6. THE CLASH
7. WOODY GUTHRIE
8. THEE HYPNOTICS
9. T. REX
10. THE BEATLES

83. MUSICIANS-TURNED-FILM STARS

```
L  M  P  E  L  N  K  A  V  M  C  W  D  M  P
A  K  A  R  T  A  N  I  S  K  N  A  R  F  P
M  V  B  R  O  F  X  F  Z  B  V  Y  O  V  I
G  D  E  G  K  U  N  P  F  I  N  H  B  B  H
L  H  F  H  O  W  X  M  D  D  T  W  F  N  C
C  F  Y  T  Z  A  A  B  R  I  D  R  W  V  M
D  E  L  X  X  D  O  H  M  E  U  Y  A  O  P
L  R  W  B  O  W  H  S  L  F  L  G  S  J  G
J  C  O  N  I  A  L  V  Q  B  E  D  A  T  N
D  C  N  E  E  L  I  W  E  F  E  Z  V  M  U
N  A  K  R  I  S  T  O  F  F  E  R  S  O  N
V  L  I  W  L  F  Y  L  B  E  Q  G  G  B  N
J  E  N  N  I  F  E  R  H  U  D  S  O  N  F
R  U  A  H  N  G  M  H  M  B  C  A  W  I  Y
G  F  F  J  K  R  R  P  X  A  H  Z  J  V  D
```

1.	WILL SMITH		6.	ELVIS
2.	KRIS KRISTOFFERSON		7.	MOS DEF
3.	MARK WAHLBERG		8.	JENNIFER HUDSON
4.	MADONNA		9.	FRANK SINATRA
5.	CHER		10.	DAVID BOWIE

84. FACTORY RECORDS' RELEASES

```
M  S  B  A  T  C  N  H  F  G  L  T  Z  V  N
U  Y  N  A  J  J  M  S  Z  U  H  S  H  T  E
W  A  E  C  L  A  U  B  K  E  B  P  Q  Y  S
V  D  W  E  R  C  L  E  H  F  S  M  Y  R  M
D  N  O  R  N  R  O  A  T  I  O  F  M  E  D
L  O  R  T  N  O  C  T  S  O  L  S  E  H  S
A  M  D  A  W  I  I  O  L  R  C  L  Q  I  G
D  Y  E  I  E  M  T  M  F  V  P  R  T  V  Y
B  P  R  N  B  E  T  R  L  F  R  Q  I  O  H
O  P  D  R  K  J  U  O  E  W  I  P  M  M  P
E  A  W  A  I  H  R  C  P  N  G  N  V  J  S
X  H  L  T  J  E  U  K  E  Z  D  R  N  A  C
X  G  P  I  S  G  D  P  C  F  A  M  F  B  L
X  O  K  O  F  V  A  U  R  Z  G  X  J  L  T
E  L  P  M  A  S  Y  R  O  T  C  A  F  A  C
```

1.	THE HACIENDA	6.	LOOKING FROM A HILLTOP
2.	ATOM ROCK	7.	A CERTAIN RATIO
3.	TONY WILSON'S **COFFIN**	8.	NEW ORDER
4.	SHE'S LOST CONTROL	9.	DURUTTI COLUMN
5.	HAPPY MONDAYS	10.	A FACTORY SAMPLE

85. MUSICIANS-CUM-ARTISTS

```
D  X  T  L  B  G  D  Z  Q  E  R  F  H  J  U
A  B  J  J  F  O  O  L  C  W  Q  J  S  H  U
Z  I  O  A  O  N  O  L  S  B  F  C  I  R  J
W  T  N  N  V  D  W  Y  D  U  M  B  D  E  R
H  Z  I  Y  N  M  E  V  D  I  X  U  L  S  F
T  X  M  B  E  W  I  W  J  A  E  G  I  Q  W
I  V  I  E  F  O  N  V  O  R  P  V  H  I  X
M  S  T  M  Y  E  N  B  H  V  A  I  C  Y  H
S  I  C  T  W  T  O  Z  N  D  K  H  Y  O  D
I  G  H  R  U  B  R  H  S  L  F  W  L  N  R
T  Y  E  Q  D  Y  Z  E  Q  Y  U  A  L  M  S
T  S  L  Y  O  Q  L  G  U  L  V  U  I  Y  R
A  A  L  O  P  I  T  H  I  X  B  T  B  E  Y
P  A  U  L  M  C  C  A  R  T  N  E  Y  F  W
N  G  X  T  T  E  N  N  E  B  Y  N  O  T  O
```

1.	PAUL MCCARTNEY	6.	JOHN SQUIRE
2.	PATTI SMITH	7.	BILLY CHILDISH
3.	BOB DYLAN	8.	TONY BENNETT
4.	MILES DAVIS	9.	JONI MITCHELL
5.	RONNIE WOOD	10.	GOLDIE

86. SONGS AND ARTISTS INSPIRED BY ART

```
M  R  F  L  C  G  V  Z  B  O  G  P  G  M  I
F  L  O  H  R  A  W  Y  D  N  A  R  A  A  Y
O  L  D  A  V  E  B  R  U  B  E  C  K  T  U
J  V  K  I  K  V  M  F  L  M  D  U  U  C  T
A  I  N  T  E  R  I  O  R  S  A  X  O  H  Z
Y  N  A  N  C  Y  P  R  I  D  D  Y  W  S  W
Z  N  U  Z  P  I  H  R  O  N  D  Y  B  T  F
F  S  F  L  C  D  J  H  M  O  A  U  K  I  S
M  F  V  A  X  M  L  I  N  M  R  J  H  C  J
H  N  S  T  Q  W  N  C  V  A  X  A  G  K  V
F  S  D  Y  Y  W  J  V  O  I  F  L  J  M  A
O  G  S  M  R  T  B  K  L  D  W  W  T  E  Q
D  R  C  L  A  P  U  W  Z  G  W  N  I  N  N
Z  Y  G  K  O  M  V  C  U  W  C  L  K  E  F
T  E  E  N  A  G  E  F  A  N  C  L  U  B  K
```

1. JAY-Z
2. PABLO PICASSO
3. DAVE BRUBECK
4. ANDY WARHOL
5. INTERIORS (SONG FOR WILLEM DE KOONING)
6. VENUS
7. PICTURES OF MATCHSTICK MEN
8. LUCY IN THE SKY WITH DIAMONDS
9. TEENAGE FANCLUB
10. NANCY PRIDDY

87. SONGS AND ARTISTS INSPIRED BY BOOKS

```
P E T E S E E G E R W W P X D
M Z J Q A C I R B F T W K O D
O M G S A L W W U Q E Q S G B
H B U C N I O S L C A V G H E
B D A E G M B E Y G E P I M U
R L J N T V D C S L U H O X P
X I G T A R I L S T D T T Y Q
L C U L X N V K E Y M G L V M
H I I E S L A A S R I E U X B
E T K S Z T D C H X T W G O Y
C O G S E C I L O P E H T D S
K T B B I Y N M G B W I V Z G
S R U F N I S U N E V P Z C S
E S O Z Q V F M H U F I Q K S
H C M Q H W N S A F O T K P B
```

1. KATE BUSH
2. THE POLICE
3. VENUS IN FURS
4. BANANA CO.
5. DAVID BOWIE

6. THE CURE
7. PETE SEEGER
8. TALES OF BRAVE **ULYSSES**
9. SCENTLESS APPRENTICE
10. WHIP IT

88. INFLUENTIAL RADIO D.J.s

```
U  F  Y  T  S  L  C  P  O  H  N  W  S  X  Z
Y  U  K  K  E  G  O  Q  G  G  T  D  W  I  E
W  B  C  J  T  I  M  W  E  S  T  W  O  O  D
S  X  O  A  F  J  O  H  N  P  E  E  L  A  A
T  U  L  N  R  Q  S  K  D  U  R  P  F  I  E
O  T  B  B  I  N  G  E  N  H  E  I  M  E  R
N  U  N  O  B  B  E  N  I  Q  V  V  A  K  D
E  Y  I  B  B  R  Q  M  Y  P  E  P  N  Q  Y
B  G  T  W  F  Z  T  E  T  M  Y  O  J  X  E
I  Q  R  N  J  D  S  O  W  H  N  Y  A  W  K
E  L  A  G  N  I  T  H  G  I  N  F  C  R  I
D  L  M  V  B  W  F  H  N  I  E  T  K  O  M
A  J  B  D  L  V  Z  X  C  E  K  O  Z  Z  S
A  F  C  D  N  W  B  R  S  B  M  I  V  O  W
U  J  Z  O  B  U  Z  B  Z  J  U  J  S  N  D
```

1. CHRISTOPHER **STONE**
2. RODNEY **BINGENHEIMER**
3. **MIKEY DREAD**
4. **WOLFMAN JACK**
5. **TIM WESTWOOD**
6. **KENNY EVERETT**
7. **JOHN PEEL**
8. **ALAN FREED**
9. ANNIE **NIGHTINGALE**
10. **MARTIN BLOCK**

89. GROUNDBREAKING VIDEOS

```
D N F I U Y W K J Q D J V B K
N I U M W U O A C S I P D X F
V A R C X Y F Q A E X N K U H
E G E E F U A B T P H T T I J
I A M O S E O Z B I S H H L M
J S M Y I T M Y P R F T R H C
Y E A B A S R N E T T R I S K
N O H G K P P A O S R A L S V
C G E K P H T Y I E I A L R Y
C T G N Z O T H D T K A E F G
L I D X G C U O I I S A R B Q
V E E B T O L K D H V H T P B
W R L R E K C I L W O D N I W
M E S R A O J U S B E J L U S
W H I B R T L F X Z U T Q D T
```

1. DIRE STRAITS
2. SLEDGEHAMMER
3. SABOTAGE
4. WHITE STRIPES
5. HERE IT GOES AGAIN
6. TAKE ON ME
7. WINDOWLICKER
8. PRAISE YOU
9. ROCKIT
10. THRILLER

90. SHOCKING VIDEOS

```
A  F  V  N  N  F  F  F  Y  B  M  T  G  L  Q
R  L  B  N  L  D  D  A  C  L  T  W  L  H  X
L  E  E  E  R  F  N  R  O  B  E  E  X  H  Q
N  A  P  R  E  J  T  Y  G  S  M  G  S  Y  C
J  H  M  B  Y  L  J  Y  P  O  S  I  U  B  A
J  C  W  Q  A  K  W  G  N  Z  B  R  W  D  W
M  I  X  A  R  E  O  I  O  T  D  L  K  U  G
N  M  C  Z  P  A  N  D  T  S  G  S  D  O  H
P  E  C  I  A  C  E  O  U  Y  M  O  S  C  U
D  G  N  L  E  V  M  R  H  N  M  N  A  V  X
W  R  A  S  K  A  E  P  X  P  L  F  K  E  K
Q  O  T  K  I  W  T  E  H  S  E  I  Q  W  I
R  E  S  O  L  C  A  H  C  Q  N  L  M  C  C
O  G  E  N  L  L  H  T  O  E  C  M  E  R  Q
B  I  J  M  L  O  K  Z  E  E  W  R  C  T  M
```

1.	CLOSER	6.	GEORGE MICHAEL
2.	STAN	7.	TELEPHONE
3.	LIKE A PRAYER	8.	THE PRODIGY
4.	BORN FREE	9.	GIRLS ON FILM
5.	LEMON INCEST	10.	HATE ME NOW

91. GOOD MORNINGS

```
T  V  F  Y  O  V  M  O  Q  K  I  E  Q  C  N
H  F  P  E  O  C  S  N  N  Z  S  R  Z  W  D
E  H  M  D  S  B  R  A  O  W  L  I  M  N  F
S  I  L  N  S  L  D  V  G  K  L  F  A  J  K
P  U  Y  U  S  E  F  L  A  T  E  E  F  J  Q
E  K  N  O  U  I  H  N  C  E  H  D  N  J  I
C  F  W  R  I  Y  Y  I  I  Y  C  A  N  O  X
I  E  T  G  I  E  L  M  H  C  T  C  V  Y  A
A  O  B  R  W  S  T  Y  C  V  I  R  P  Z  O
L  J  V  E  L  V  E  T  Y  A  M  A  C  H  Y
S  B  S  D  G  W  E  D  G  N  I  N  R  O  M
O  T  Z  N  T  Y  K  U  Y  P  N  C  E  X  Z
X  F  C  U  Q  I  Y  Z  Y  M  O  H  F  L  I
I  T  V  Q  U  M  J  W  Q  X  J  P  J  X  R
K  D  J  Q  I  S  G  W  N  N  L  A  M  L  D
```

1. SUNRISE
2. SOME **VELVET MORNING**
3. **KANYE WEST**
4. **CHICAGO**
5. THE VELVET
   UNDERGROUND
6. **YUSEF LATEEF**
7. **JONI MITCHELL**
8. **ARCADE FIRE**
9. **MORNING DEW**
10. **THE SPECIALS**

92. DRESS TO IMPRESS

```
V  I  A  G  K  P  E  P  M  F  M  H  L  K  K
L  P  Z  Z  I  C  F  E  Y  H  A  D  P  X  S
U  I  U  Y  N  O  S  N  A  E  J  B  Z  T  X
Q  X  E  I  G  V  Q  T  D  D  T  I  O  B  N
I  E  R  K  S  G  D  A  I  Z  Z  O  E  F  F
Q  P  C  I  L  F  X  N  D  S  B  U  B  H  G
D  D  P  F  E  A  Q  G  A  E  P  M  A  B  S
S  U  A  O  A  H  M  L  S  S  G  S  P  B  I
U  O  K  N  D  S  Q  E  Q  S  I  B  B  Z  V
O  V  C  D  H  Q  H  U  F  A  V  X  J  X  I
F  R  N  Q  A  T  W  I  F  L  J  G  Z  Y  K
X  C  J  Z  T  C  L  F  O  G  V  E  P  M  P
V  C  S  G  U  O  U  Q  K  N  W  E  S  P  B
X  S  E  O  H  S  E  D  E  U  S  E  U  L  B
S  A  M  M  Y  D  A  V  I  S  J  R  P  W  G
```

1.	MY ADIDAS	6.	PENTANGLE
2.	JEANS ON	7.	SUNGLASSES AFTER DARK
3.	THESE BOOTS ARE MADE FOR WALKIN'	8.	FASHION
4.	PRINCE	9.	SAMMY DAVIS JR.
5.	KING'S LEAD HAT	10.	BLUE SUEDE SHOES

93. SONGS ABOUT FOOD

```
T  P  T  O  J  T  U  Z  B  N  H  O  J  R  D
H  M  T  J  F  O  N  Y  E  A  C  N  X  E  O
E  L  I  H  L  B  H  B  S  E  Q  N  J  R  C
Z  E  C  L  J  K  W  M  J  P  U  S  A  E  V
E  Y  I  L  K  J  V  O  R  K  E  G  K  Z  E
E  X  M  O  H  S  E  L  S  H  U  Q  Y  E  Q
U  T  V  L  F  L  H  Q  C  S  C  N  G  E  A
Q  W  S  E  S  D  S  A  N  R  U  L  Z  Y  Y
S  H  Y  M  G  H  E  W  K  O  Q  A  Z  Z  A
R  N  R  O  C  P  O  P  R  E  H  T  O  M  M
O  E  L  N  Y  R  R  E  B  W  A  R  T  S  O
R  E  T  S  B  O  L  K  C  O  R  D  K  M  G
Q  S  A  O  J  Y  B  I  H  B  V  V  M  V  M
N  X  R  N  P  A  S  S  T  H  E  P  E  A  S
T  Z  K  G  B  M  S  M  N  P  N  K  C  R  E
```

1. ROCK LOBSTER
2. BROWN SUGAR
3. MOTHER POPCORN
4. MILKSHAKE
5. LEMON SONG
6. PEACHES AND PRUNES
7. STRAWBERRY FIELDS
8. DR. JOHN
9. PASS THE PEAS
10. SQUEEZE

94. SONGS ABOUT LOVE

```
C  G  S  D  A  E  H  G  N  I  K  L  A  T  F
X  Y  J  R  V  B  H  C  Y  F  I  T  S  U  J
Z  H  T  F  E  Z  H  M  E  E  O  T  G  R  Q
A  M  A  N  W  Y  N  A  N  F  L  R  U  Z  R
M  N  E  Q  T  I  A  B  E  E  H  U  X  C  J
G  W  E  D  N  X  E  Y  H  T  D  X  L  F  Q
U  V  C  E  V  O  L  F  O  L  E  N  N  U  F
D  B  N  K  U  K  T  R  D  R  I  O  Y  L  G
A  X  O  X  H  Q  C  R  D  T  S  Z  G  U  X
J  S  Y  R  T  N  E  G  E  H  T  H  A  O  O
L  Q  E  T  S  A  T  F  N  P  Q  F  W  X  N
H  C  B  O  M  X  H  I  O  K  P  F  P  Q  S
T  B  Z  X  U  T  D  D  J  Z  N  I  O  M  F
K  F  G  P  Q  G  B  B  J  Z  K  R  R  N  H
I  W  F  L  Z  I  Z  A  G  H  I  U  K  Q  B
```

1. ROY AYERS
2. FUNNEL OF LOVE
3. NED DOHENEY
4. LULU
5. THE GENTRYS
6. TALKING HEADS
7. MINNIE RIPPERTON
8. BEYONCÉ
9. QUEEN
10. JUSTIFY MY LOVE

95. HEARTBREAK SONGS

```
S T E E R U O Y E E T S V I C
J E K Q F L B P X R X W V V W R
M N M U W N B L L T W F J I Y
H L P J O E J A C K S O N L M
S L O K D E B K X A Y H N L E
C F L H R G D J Y D O J I S A
E A M E C X L R I R P T F U R
W F C Z C U Y V M S S F F R I
C R L H O T I N M T Z D U V V
V J V M D S F M O R S D R I E
E Y G X I N E O H P O Q Y V R
N A H O Y Q L Q S K Y Y M E A
E D N Q I A H A V O T C M K C
O M K V T G C O V R Y L I S Y
G T H E S T R E E T S W J Q Y
```

1. WALK ON BY
2. JOE JACKSON
3. THE STREETS
4. JOY DIVISION
5. SOFT CELL
6. I WILL SURVIVE
7. CRY ME A RIVER
8. IT'S TOO LATE
9. JIMMY RUFFIN
10. BY THE TIME I GET TO PHOENIX

96. CHRISTMAS SONGS

```
K C G H D Z C E E N I S D R F
C V Q V H Q T S O W D A R W R
O T E J U J H J R K L F U Y Q
R W H I T E C H R I S T M A S
L E T A S C L X I O H C M J L
L X E L U J W S J E L O E K D
E F A E A K V Q C E Q T R N G
B D R Y L U F R E D N O W E S
E Q O M C A Y C X M Y U I Z N
L W H I A S D L V W S N Z M N
G G S L T I V N E D L L Z E Q
N E L A N P P N E Z S Y A D I
I P L Y A D M M Y R S T R R A
J S G Z S M J W F I B O D B L
G B G U M B O Z F S N D I C S
```

1. FAIRYTALE OF **NEW YORK**
2. **WONDERFUL** CHRISTMAS TIME
3. **THE CRYSTALS**
4. **WHITE CHRISTMAS**
5. **JINGLE BELL ROCK**
6. **BRENDA LEE**
7. LITTLE **DRUMMER** BOY
8. THE BOY THAT **SANTA CLAUS** FORGOT
9. **SLADE**
10. **WIZZARD**

97. INSULTING SONGS

```
C  Y  Q  N  W  V  J  O  M  P  W  K  O  H  T
U  E  X  N  S  N  B  N  U  N  T  F  G  O  D
S  U  X  J  E  C  N  M  R  U  A  M  S  W  X
I  R  P  S  X  M  E  U  B  W  D  M  E  D  M
D  O  K  P  P  T  M  E  I  I  D  Q  S  O  C
I  F  L  J  I  X  I  A  L  N  H  S  O  Y  G
O  O  Y  H  S  A  I  G  L  O  L  I  Z  O  C
T  O  R  B  T  D  L  A  Y  I  G  H  A  U  D
W  K  O  D  O  T  B  U  B  T  V  R  B  S  C
I  J  C  B  L  M  B  O  R  A  T  O  E  L  D
N  O  M  I  S  Y  L  R  A  C  R  H  T  E  R
D  A  H  C  W  K  B  B  G  A  R  B  H  E  N
C  C  E  Q  U  G  Q  W  G  V  I  U  I  P  W
J  W  F  P  T  K  M  U  T  I  A  O  E  R  M
S  E  S  O  R  E  N  O  T  S  E  H  T  T  H
```

1.	CARLY SIMON	6.	CEE LO GREEN
2.	SEX PISTOLS	7.	THE STONE ROSES
3.	HIT 'EM UP	8.	IDIOT WIND
4.	HOLIDAY IN **CAMBODIA**	9.	HOW DO YOU SLEEP?
5.	YOUR MIND IS ON **VACATION**	10.	BILLY BRAGG

98. COVER VERSIONS

```
A  O  P  S  L  A  I  C  E  P  S  E  H  T  J
Y  G  W  S  U  R  F  I  N  U  S  A  U  Q  S
Q  E  L  E  M  O  N  H  E  A  D  S  R  W  C
M  A  P  N  M  V  S  O  U  W  M  L  D  V  I
W  H  U  R  T  I  K  B  G  A  O  A  Y  K  N
B  E  C  E  A  U  T  T  P  T  L  L  G  V  R
P  E  S  D  S  E  Z  E  U  C  L  F  U  G  L
K  E  Q  N  E  Q  H  P  H  H  Y  R  R  N  O
E  D  G  E  T  B  A  C  K  T  S  N  D  M  M
E  L  S  T  L  J  Z  A  X  O  L  Z  Y  B  I
I  V  V  Q  G  P  T  M  Q  W  I  L  M  K  U
M  N  O  D  B  K  S  T  X  E  P  U  A  M  X
R  M  B  J  J  K  C  A  S  R  S  V  N  B  V
Y  F  L  W  T  P  P  P  W  F  B  O  B  D  V
R  A  G  V  C  I  Y  J  V  N  D  U  P  V  M
```

1. TRY A LITTLE **TENDERNESS**
2. **SURFIN' USA**
3. WE HAVE ALL **THE TIME** IN THE WORLD
4. **MOLLY'S LIPS**
5. **HURDY GURDY MAN**
6. THE **LEMONHEADS**
7. **GET BACK**
8. **THE SPECIALS**
9. ALL ALONG THE **WATCHTOWER**
10. **HURT**

99. UNEXPECTED SURPRISES

```
D  N  A  X  X  S  G  J  S  O  U  H  L  Q  T
G  X  O  J  X  M  V  V  B  B  O  O  M  M  T
S  D  N  O  M  S  O  E  H  T  R  Q  B  L  Y
F  Y  R  O  R  R  I  M  C  I  G  A  M  R  W
O  N  U  A  I  K  D  H  D  W  H  N  E  L  P
B  O  V  U  H  I  O  T  Q  Z  R  T  N  K  W
S  I  U  O  E  C  C  P  L  B  H  D  D  L  Q
E  T  L  S  O  V  I  B  Q  G  S  F  K  Z  R
E  N  F  L  O  W  E  R  I  N  G  C  W  Y  J
G  E  A  O  W  H  C  L  F  C  Q  G  H  U  E
E  T  F  Q  G  Y  P  S  Y  F  M  A  T  U  G
E  T  G  U  K  M  M  Y  J  Q  I  A  D  M  D
B  A  O  J  A  E  F  A  Q  X  V  L  S  M  O
E  C  G  L  Y  R  G  H  N  L  P  U  C  X  G
T  V  H  T  E  G  W  D  A  I  E  Q  Q  O  P
```

1. HOT CHOCOLATE
2. BEE GEES
3. BILL WYMAN
4. CLIFF RICHARD
5. MAGIC MIRROR
6. GYPSY
7. TOO MUCH **ATTENTION**
8. LAMPLIGHTER
9. THE OSMONDS
10. LATE **FLOWERING** LUST

100. SONGS ABOUT YOUTH

```
R  C  O  L  H  M  J  K  E  F  E  Z  O  W  G
W  Z  D  G  H  P  L  N  D  H  V  I  E  I  S
N  H  A  R  T  H  I  R  T  E  E  N  I  P  I
B  T  E  Q  F  U  N  U  O  P  K  I  L  H  A
C  M  H  P  B  S  O  I  X  K  L  R  O  J  V
V  N  E  U  Z  Y  I  S  A  O  K  V  M  Q  X
R  O  G  K  C  B  T  G  L  B  Y  A  U  B  O
K  B  A  I  N  S  A  Z  R  O  G  N  G  E  J
W  B  N  G  R  W  R  I  I  W  O  A  S  Y  E
Y  O  E  N  H  N  E  C  G  C  W  H  V  R  M
S  A  E  G  A  B  N  P  H  E  W  B  C  F  R
V  L  T  U  N  D  E  R  T  O  N  E  S  S  T
M  K  I  Y  S  Y  G  V  P  S  P  B  I  F  S
Q  T  X  M  Q  B  Y  M  O  T  O  B  O  L  D
B  Y  X  W  U  K  M  E  V  L  P  J  Q  X  S
```

1. SONIC YOUTH
2. TEENAGE HEAD
3. THIRTEEN
4. NIRVANA
5. SCHOOL'S OUT
6. MY GENERATION
7. TEENAGE **LOBOTOMY**
8. THE **UNDERTONES**
9. **ALRIGHT**
10. A TEENAGER **IN LOVE**

MUSIC PUZZLE SOLUTIONS

CROSSWORD SOLUTIONS

1. FRONTMEN/WOMEN
ACROSS:
2. HARRY
4. JARVIS
5. KUTI
7. IGGY POP
9. MORRISON
DOWN:
1. DALTREY
3. MICK JAGGER
4. JAMES BROWN
6. MERCURY
8. JOPLIN

2. KEYBOARD WIZARDS
ACROSS:
2. MANZAREK
3. PRESTON
5. BOOKER T
6. WAKEMAN
7. BERNIE
8. LISTON SMITH
DOWN:
1. EMERSON
4. STEVIE
6. WRIGHT
8. LORD

3. LESSER-KNOWN GUITAR GREATS
ACROSS:
4. CALIFORNIA
6. MCKAY
8. MASCIS
9. FREDDIE
10. SANTIAGO
DOWN:
1. KEVIN
2. BUCHANAN
3. PRINCE
5. GREENWOOD
7. ALBINI

4. DRUMMERS
ACROSS:
4. BONHAM
6. GROHL
7. COX
8. LIEBEZEIT
9. GINGER
10. BUDDY
DOWN:
1. ROACH
2. STUBBLEFIELD
3. ALLEN
5. MOON

5. BASS PLAYERS
ACROSS:
2. BOOTSY
4. JONES
5. EDWARDS
9. SHAKESPEARE
10. MCCARTNEY
DOWN:
1. PASTORIUS
3. ENTWHISTLE
6. DUNN
7. FLEA
8. BRUCE

6. RAPPERS
ACROSS:
3. MONCH
4. SNOOP DOGG
8. NAS
9. MF DOOM
10. CHUCK D
DOWN:
1. NOTORIOUS
2. LL COOL J
5. GHOSTFACE
6. RAKIM
7. ONE

7. COUNTRY FUNK
ACROSS:
2. JERRY
6. COOPER
7. BRIMSTONE
8. BOBBIE
10. FORD
DOWN:
1. FRANCISCO
3. JAKI
4. JOLENE
5. DENNIS
9. BYRDS

8. FOLK ROCK
ACROSS:
2. CLANNAD
4. DYLAN
5. TREES
6. SPAN
7. BUFFALO
9. BYRDS
10. ESPERS
DOWN:
1. CANDLE
3. PENTANGLE
8. FAIRPORT

9. FUSION FLINGS
ACROSS:
3. HANCOCK
4. MACHINE
6. REPORT
7. BILLY
8. VIBES
9. FRANK
DOWN:
1. ROCK
2. DAVIS
4. MAHAVISHNU
5. ENERGIT

10. GIRL GROUPS
ACROSS:
3. VOGUE
4. SUPREMES
6. ALOUD
7. TLC
9. SPICE
DOWN:
1. SHIRELLES
2. RONETTES
4. SHANGRI
5. MARVELETTES
8. CHILD

11. BOY BANDS
ACROSS:
5. BOYZONE
7. MONKEES
8. TAKE
10. EAST
DOWN:
1. JACKSON
2. DIRECTION
3. WESTLIFE
4. BLOCK
6. BACKSTREET
9. EDITION

12. POP PERFECTION
ACROSS:
3. BELIEVER
4. DAVID
7. HUMAN
8. BABY
9. BILLIE
DOWN:
1. SPEARS
2. ABBA
5. VIBRATIONS
6. LOVE
7. HEY

13. MUSICAL PERSONAE

ACROSS:
1. KISS
5. BAMBAATAA
6. MF DOOM
7. CLOWN
9. COOPER

DOWN:
2. STARDUST
3. SLIM
4. MADONNA
8. OSBOURNE
10. PEPPER

14. MUSICAL FAMILIES

ACROSS:
1. ISLEY
6. CARPENTERS
7. KINKS
9. BEACH
10. MARY CHAIN

DOWN:
2. SISTER SLEDGE
3. BEE GEES
4. OASIS
5. OSMONDS
8. JACKSON

15. ROCK-STAR CHILDREN

ACROSS:
3. KUTI
6. MARLEY
10. NORAH JONES

DOWN:
1. BUCKLEY
2. MILEY
4. GAINSBOURG
5. WAINWRIGHT
7. NANCY
8. CHERRY
9. LENNON

16. GREAT GIGS

ACROSS:
2. BEATLES
4. PULP
6. UNDERGROUND
7. ZIGGY STARDUST
10. SPIKE ISLAND

DOWN:
1. SEX PISTOLS
3. LIVE AID
5. NEWPORT
8. READING
9. JIMI

17. LIVE RECORDINGS

ACROSS:
3. FRANKLIN
4. THE WHO
5. DYLAN
6. PINK FLOYD
8. JAMES BROWN

DOWN:
1. FEMALE
2. FOLSOM
4. TALKING HEADS
7. JAMS
9. RUST

18. GIG VENUES

ACROSS:
1. CBGB
3. AMSTERDAM
7. ASTORIA
9. RED ROCKS
10. EINDHOVEN

DOWN:
2. BLACKPOOL
4. TROUBADOUR
5. ROUNDHOUSE
6. FILLMORE
8. BATACLAN

19. SONGS ABOUT SMOKING

ACROSS:
4. SPIRITUALIZED
5. ASHTRAY
7. BOGART
8. COFFEE
9. ARCTIC MONKEYS
10. FITZGERALD

DOWN:
1. OASIS
2. ANIMALS
3. CIGARETTE
6. GARFUNKEL

20. DRINKING SONGS

ACROSS:
5. BEASTIE BOYS
9. UNDERWORLD
10. TEQUILA

DOWN:
1. WHISKEY
2. BEER
3. FEELGOOD
4. HOUSEMARTINS
6. BOURBON
7. SUNDAY
8. JUICE

21. BLUES ROOTS

ACROSS:
2. HOOKER
3. LEADBELLY
4. ANGEL
6. ROSETTA
9. ROBERT JOHNSON
10. WILLIAMSON

DOWN:
1. SMOKESTACK
5. LEVEE
7. THRILL
8. BROONZY

22. BLUES AND BEYOND

ACROSS:
3. SALOME
5. WITCH
6. MELTING
7. BOND
8. ANIMALS
9. GROOVY

DOWN:
1. MOJO
2. ELEPHANT
4. BLUESBREAKERS
6. MANNISH

23. TRIPPY TROUBADOURS

ACROSS:
2. JONATHAN
4. MOON
6. BILL QUICK
7. LADY
8. ANNETTE
9. CHAINS

DOWN:
1. CROSBY
3. TIM BUCKLEY
5. RICHIE
6. BEARINGS

24. EASY LISTENING

ACROSS:
1. ODYSSEY
3. HAZLEHURST
4. MANSFIELD
6. BRASS
7. CONDOR
9. SUMMERTIME
10. JAMES LAST

DOWN:
2. SUPERSTITIOUS
5. DAYDREAM
8. VILLAGE

25. FOLK FINGERPICKERS

ACROSS:

2. WIZZ
5. GRAHAM
6. JACKSON
7. MARTYN
8. THOMPSON
9. BULL

DOWN:

1. NICK DRAKE
3. BERT JANSCH
4. JOHN
6. JOHN RENBOURN

26. SESSION MUSICIANS

ACROSS:

2. PRESTON
5. PURDIE
6. BOOKER T
8. MUSCLE
10. SULLIVAN

DOWN:

1. PARKER
3. BROTHERS
4. FLOWERS
7. WRECKING
9. KAYE

27. BRITISH JAZZ HEROES

ACROSS:

4. WINSTONE
7. COURTNEY
9. GARRICK
10. COLLIER

DOWN:

1. BASIL
2. WESTBROOK
3. IAN CARR
5. DANKWORTH
6. HAYES
8. BAKER

28. GRUNGE GREATS

ACROSS:

2. FLUID
4. MISSY
8. NIRVANA
9. WHIGS
10. MUDHONEY

DOWN:

1. GREEN RIVER
3. LEMONHEADS
5. SOUNDGARDEN
6. SCREAMING
7. ANACONDA

29. MOD MOVERS

ACROSS:

4. KINKS
5. WATER
6. CREATION
7. NICHOLAS
9. SMALL FACES

DOWN:

1. RUFUS THOMAS
2. SKATALITES
3. JACKIE
8. FLEUR DE LYS
10. ALIVE

30. GOTH GROOVES

ACROSS:

3. DANIELLE
4. STRENGTH
6. MARILYN
8. BAUHAUS
9. MERCY

DOWN:

1. KILLING JOKE
2. SANCTUARY
5. NINE INCH NAILS
6. MINISTRY
7. THE CURE

31. NEW ROMANTIC CLUB HITS

ACROSS:

2. JAPAN
3. VISAGE
5. SOFT CELL
6. ROXY
7. MINDS
8. DURAN DURAN
9. ULTRAVOX

DOWN:

1. DAVID BOWIE
4. ACTION
5. SPANDAU BALLET

32. SHOEGAZE SWAYERS

ACROSS:

3. CHAPTERHOUSE
5. PALE SAINTS
7. BREEZE
8. OBSOLETE
9. SOON
10. SCHNAUSS

DOWN:

1. VAPOUR
2. THOUGHTFORMS
4. EARLY YEARS
6. BELONG

33. CHILL-OUT TUNES

ACROSS:

1. LAMBCHOP
5. GLOBAL
7. APHEX TWIN
8. THE KLF
9. NOISE

DOWN:

2. CINEMATIC
3. SOLIDISSIMO
4. WESSELTOFT
6. SPACE
8. THE ORB

34. BRITPOP

ACROSS:

2. SUEDE
5. RETURN
6. BARNEY
7. WAKING UP
9. RADIOHEAD

DOWN:

1. BITTERSWEET
3. SUPERGRASS
4. COMMON PEOPLE
6. BLUR
8. OASIS

35. GREAT NIGHTS

ACROSS:

1. AC/DC
3. NIGHT FEVER
5. BENSON
7. ELTON JOHN
9. HEATWAVE
10. CRUISER

DOWN:

2. CONNECTION
4. ROLLING STONES
6. INDEEP
8. LIONEL

36. CLUBS

ACROSS:

4. BERGHAIN
6. MINISTRY
7. STUDIO
8. WAREHOUSE
10. AMNESIA

DOWN:

1. THE LOFT
2. SHOOM
3. WIGAN
5. PARADISE
9. HACIENDA

37. FUNK FLOOR-FILLERS

ACROSS:
2. RICK JAMES
5. FUNKADELIC
6. CURTIS
7. FUNK INC.
9. METERS
10. EDDIE BO

DOWN:
1. THANK YOU
3. SUPERSTITION
4. PANTS
8. ISLEY

38. DISCO DANCE-FLOOR BOMBS

ACROSS:
5. SUPERNATURE
8. DINOSAUR
10. ATMOSFEAR

DOWN:
1. MACHINE
2. HOLLOWAY
3. LOOSE JOINTS
4. I FEEL LOVE
6. CHIC
7. SALSOUL
9. DANCER

39. JAZZ FINDS THE FUNK

ACROSS:
2. CHAMELEON
3. INNER CITY
4. DONALD BYRD
6. ROY
8. HAMMOND
10. EXPANSIONS

DOWN:
1. PLACEBO
5. DARKNESS
7. GREEN
9. MULATU

40. THE PHILLY SOUND

ACROSS:
4. PEOPLE'S CHOICE
5. MONTANA
6. EAST
8. JACKSONS
10. BACK STABBERS

DOWN:
1. WHITEHEAD
2. LOVE
3. INSTANT FUNK
7. MFSB
9. O'JAYS

41. LESSER-KNOWN MOTOWN MOMENTS

ACROSS:
1. EDWIN STARR
3. MARVELETTES
6. MONITORS
7. PUNCH
9. COMMODORES

DOWN:
2. THE ELGINS
4. RANDOLPH
5. JOHNSON
7. POPCORN
8. LIVE

42. NORTHERN SOUL

ACROSS:
4. DR. LOVE
6. PATTI AUSTIN
8. BREAKAWAY
9. DOBIE GRAY
10. TAINTED LOVE

DOWN:
1. WILSON
2. SNAKE
3. PARISIANS
5. CLARKE
7. THE NIGHT

43. ELECTRONIC PIONEERS

ACROSS:
3. MORODER
7. TANGERINE
9. MORTON
10. DAPHNE

DOWN:
1. KRAFTWERK
2. BRIAN ENO
4. JARRE
5. PATRICK COWLEY
6. DERBYSHIRE
8. ROBOTNICK

44. ELECTRO

ACROSS:
2. JONZUN CREW
7. TYRONE
8. ROBOTS
9. HERBIE HANCOCK
10. HASHIM

DOWN:
1. TELEX
3. CYBOTRON
4. PLANET ROCK
5. MAN PARRISH
6. BREAK DANCE

45. HIP-HOP'S DEF JAMS

ACROSS:
5. SLICK RICK
6. EPMD
7. METHOD MAN
8. BROOKLYN
10. CHAMP

DOWN:
1. PUBLIC ENEMY
2. BASS
3. HIP-HOP
4. LL COOL J
9. REDMAN

46. FOUNDATIONS OF GOOD HOUSE

ACROSS:
2. XPRESS
4. STERLING VOID
6. DEEP BURNT
7. PRINCIPLE
8. MR. FINGERS
9. GLOVER
10. ON AND ON

DOWN:
1. MARSHALL
3. PHUTURE
5. UNDERGROUND

47. THE SYNTH-POP REVOLUTION

ACROSS:
3. ULTRAVOX
4. BLANCMANGE
7. DEPECHE
9. GARY NUMAN
10. SOFT CELL

DOWN:
1. NEW ORDER
2. HUMAN LEAGUE
5. EURYTHMICS
6. PET SHOP
8. HEAVEN

48. TOWERING TECHNO

ACROSS:
3. DRAGONS
6. UNDERWORLD
7. STRINGS
9. E DANCER
10. PAPERCLIP PEOPLE

DOWN:
1. AZTEC MYSTIC
2. UFO
4. ALLEYS
5. SHAREVARI
8. RON TRENT

49. POST-PUNK
ACROSS:
3. DEATH DISCO
6. PUNCHES
8. GANG OF FOUR
9. YELLO
10. PRESSURE
DOWN:
1. MAGAZINE
2. SHRIEKBACK
4. FOUNDATIONS
5. SEVERED HEADS
7. VOLTAIRE

50. INDIE DANCE
ACROSS:
2. BIG CITY
6. BLUR
7. MBV
9. ABANDON
10. FOOL'S GOLD
DOWN:
1. PRIMAL SCREAM
3. CHARLATANS
4. HAPPY MONDAYS
5. WEEKENDER
8. DAFFODILS

51. ROCK COMES TO THE DISCO
ACROSS:
3. CANNONBALL
7. JIVE TALKIN'
8. STREET PLAYER
9. HEART OF GLASS
10. MISS YOU
DOWN:
1. BRICK IN THE WALL
2. CASBAH
4. THIN ICE
5. CIRCUS
6. BITES THE DUST

52. SOUND SYSTEMS
ACROSS:
2. GIANT
5. JAH SHAKA
7. DOWNBEAT
8. TROJAN
9. SAXON
DOWN:
1. HOMETOWN
2. GREAT SEBASTIAN
3. BAMBAATAA
4. PEOPLE
6. HERCULORDS

53. SONGS FOR A WEDDING DANCE FLOOR
ACROSS:
2. THE FACES
4. SONICS
6. I FEEL FOR YOU
7. THOMPSON TWINS
8. JACKIE
10. HEARTS
DOWN:
1. BANBARRA
3. SISTER SLEDGE
5. YOUNG
9. CHIC

54. D.J.s
ACROSS:
3. ALFREDO
6. LARRY LEVAN
7. LEVINE
8. DAVID
9. FRANCIS
10. KNUCKLES
DOWN:
1. KOOL HERC
2. NORMAN JAY
4. HARVEY
5. GRANDMASTER

55. CITIES
ACROSS:
2. CALLING
4. VIVA LAS VEGAS
7. BERLIN
8. BOBBY WOMACK
9. CHICAGO
10. SINATRA
DOWN:
1. MACHO CITY
3. JOHANNESBURG
5. GREAT CITIES
6. LONDON

56. CARS
ACROSS:
3. VEHICLE
5. CORVETTE
6. CARS
8. PASSENGER
9. ON THE ROAD AGAIN
DOWN:
1. DRIVE MY CAR
2. MERCEDES
4. AUTOBAHN
7. FUN FUN FUN
8. PARTICULAR

57. YEAH YEAH TO YÉ-YÉ
ACROSS:
2. HARDY
6. ZOU BISOU BISOU
9. FILLES
10. LETTRE
DOWN:
1. CHRISTIE
3. MATIN
4. PETULA CLARK
5. ROLLERGIRL
7. FRANCE GALL
8. TIGRE

58. DUTCH BEAT GROUPS
ACROSS:
2. EARRING
4. OUTSIDERS
5. BINTANGS
7. SHOCKING BLUE
9. SIXTY-FIVE (65)
10. DE MASKERS
DOWN:
1. MOTIONS
3. DRAGONFLY
6. HUNTERS
8. ZIPPS

59. BALEARIC BEATS
ACROSS:
3. RAISE
5. BELOVED
9. BLOW MONKEYS
10. REY DE COPAS
DOWN:
1. STORIES
2. SIMPLE MINDS
4. ROOTS
6. PRIMAVERA
7. GOTTSCHING
8. TELLIER

60. PSYCHEDELIC SWEDEN
ACROSS:
1. MECKI MARK MEN
3. MIKAEL
6. BO HANSSON
7. KARLSSON
8. ROGEFELDT
10. PARSON
DOWN:
2. AMAZING
4. GRANDMOTHERS
5. GOAT
9. DUNGEN

61. EASTERN BLOC PARTY
ACROSS:
4. ALI BABKI
6. PUGACHEVA
8. TORPEDO
9. ILLES
10. BIG CHAIN
DOWN:
1. KOVACS
2. MONDIAL
3. MARTA
5. CZERWONE GITARY
7. LOCOMOTIV GT

62. KRAUTROCK
ACROSS:
2. TEMPEL
4. EMBRYO
5. KRAFTWERK
9. ZUCKERZEIT
DOWN:
1. NEU!
3. PHAEDRA
6. FAUST
7. HARMONIA
8. YETI
10. CAN

63. ITALO DISCO
ACROSS:
2. STEEL MIND
3. COMMUNICATE
6. TAKE A CHANCE
8. GAZNEVADA
9. PROBLEMS
10. WET
DOWN:
1. I NEED LOVE
4. HYPNOSIS
5. TRAIN
7. CHARLIE

64. GAINSBOURG'S GALLIC GREATS
ACROSS:
3. BONNIE
4. FORWARD
7. BRIGITTE BARDOT
10. NO, NO, YES, YES
DOWN:
1. ET CAETERA
2. CANNABIS
5. BB
6. NON PLUS
8. EN MELODY
9. LA HORSE

65. TRAINS
ACROSS:
5. MYSTERY
7. TRAIN IN VAIN
8. STEAM-POWERED
9. THE JAM
DOWN:
1. CLARKSVILLE
2. ATKINSON
3. PENTANGLE
4. TRANS-EUROPE
6. EXPRESS
9. TRAIN

66. DIGGING INDIA'S FUNKY SIDE
ACROSS:
1. ANANDA SHANKAR
4. JAGMOHAN
8. BURMAN
10. ANANDJI
DOWN:
2. DUM MARO DUM
3. ASHA BHONSLE
5. HEMANT
6. OBSESSION
7. CALCUTTA
9. ZINDAGI

67. SKA
ACROSS:
2. JUDGE NOT
4. DEKKER
5. LOLLIPOP
6. AITKEN
8. SIMMER DOWN
9. BE STILL
10. PATSY
DOWN:
1. ENJOY
3. THEY GOT TO COME
7. WASH WASH

68. REGGAE
ACROSS:
3. MELODIANS
6. THIEVES
7. BUNNY WAILER
8. CHERRY
9. ONE LOVE
DOWN:
1. BORING
2. JESTER
4. STARLIGHTS
5. DENNIS BROWN
6. TRIBAL WAR

69. SAILING
ACROSS:
2. SHIP SONG
4. LAND HO
8. A SAILOR'S LIFE
9. WOODEN SHIPS
10. SAILING
DOWN:
1. CAIRO
3. SHIPBUILDING
5. AHOY
6. MORSE MOOSE
7. SLOOP JOHN B

70. AFROBEAT
ACROSS:
2. TONY ALLEN
4. SOUL MAKOSSA
6. FEMI
8. ASSAGAI
9. FELA KUTI
10. SULLEY
DOWN:
1. HAASTRUP
3. ORLANDO JULIUS
5. ANTIBALAS
7. BIG THIEF

71. TROPICÁLIA
ACROSS:
2. TOM ZE·
4. VAMOS
5. BAT MACUMBA
7. TROPICÁLIA
8. JORGE BEN
9. ALGO MAIS
10. OS MUTANTES
DOWN:
1. RELANCE
3. GILBERTO GIL
6. GAL COSTA

72. FLYING
ACROSS:
1. BUFFALO
5. BIRD
6. SPARROW
8. FLY ME TO THE MOON
9. EIGHT MILES HIGH
10. SMOKIE
DOWN:
2. USSR
3. SILVER
4. EAGLE
7. FOO FIGHTERS

73. PRODUCERS

ACROSS:
5. BRIAN WILSON
6. QUINCY JONES
8. GEORGE MARTIN
10. NILE RODGERS

DOWN:
1. VISCONTI
2. BRIAN ENO
3. PERRY
4. PHIL SPECTOR
7. PREMIER
9. MEEK

74. DEBUTS

ACROSS:
3. BEASTIE BOYS
4. CLASH
7. RAMONES
8. ILLMATIC
9. NICO
10. JOY DIVISION

DOWN:
1. PLEASE PLEASE ME
2. DESTRUCTION
5. SEX PISTOLS
6. EXPERIENCED

75. "DIFFICULT" SECOND ALBUMS

ACROSS:
4. VAN MORRISON
5. NOWHERE
8. PUBLIC ENEMY
9. TAPESTRY
10. NEVERMIND

DOWN:
1. BENDS
2. PARANOID
3. JIMI HENDRIX
6. BOUTIQUE
7. FREEWHEELIN'

76. CONCEPT ALBUMS

ACROSS:
1. PRETTY THINGS
5. SMALL FACES
6. PINK FLOYD
7. BEATLES
10. VILLAGE GREEN

DOWN:
2. THE WALL
3. QUADROPHENIA
4. DAVID BOWIE
8. THE WHO
9. NELSON

77. ROCK & POP INSTRUMENTALS

ACROSS:
2. MOGWAI
3. EURYTHMICS
7. RUMBLE
9. JOHN BARRY
10. ECHOES

DOWN:
1. APACHE
4. COMMODORES
5. URIZEN
6. MELTING POT
8. TORNADOS

78. POST-BEATLES TUNES FROM THE FAB FOUR

ACROSS:
4. MACHINE
6. WAH WAH
8. INSTANT KARMA
10. SECRET FRIEND

DOWN:
1. GIMME SOME TRUTH
2. PAUL MCCARTNEY
3. WINGS
5. GEORGE HARRISON
7. AMAZED
9. HERO

79. ODD TIME SIGNATURES

ACROSS:
2. MANIC
7. TAKE FIVE
8. STRANGLERS
10. WARWICK

DOWN:
1. MONEY
3. CRUNGE
4. BEATLES
5. HEY YA
6. IMPOSSIBLE
9. RIVER MAN

80. COUPLES

ACROSS:
2. ABBA
4. CARTER
5. MEG
6. BEYONCÉ
9. TURNER
10. YOKO ONO

DOWN:
1. MARTYN
3. SPECTOR
7. CHER
8. STEVIE NICKS

81. TROUBLED SOULS

ACROSS:
2. KURT COBAIN
4. WINEHOUSE
6. MARVIN GAYE
8. NICK DRAKE
10. SMITH

DOWN:
1. WHITNEY
3. BRIAN WILSON
5. BARRETT
7. JOE
9. CURTIS

82. REVOLUTIONARIES

ACROSS:
3. GIL SCOTT HERON
5. BOB MARLEY
7. SUPER FURRY
9. FELA KUTI
10. SPACEMEN

DOWN:
1. THE CLASH
2. WOODY
4. THEE HYPNOTICS
6. T. REX
8. BEATLES

83. MUSICIANS-TURNED-FILM STARS

ACROSS:
2. WILL SMITH
4. KRISTOFFERSON
6. WAHLBERG
8. MADONNA
9. CHER
10. ELVIS

DOWN:
1. MOS DEF
3. JENNIFER HUDSON
5. SINATRA
7. BOWIE

84. FACTORY RECORDS' RELEASES

ACROSS:
1. HACIENDA
3. ATOM ROCK
4. COFFIN
7. SHE'S LOST CONTROL
9. HAPPY MONDAYS

DOWN:
1. HILLTOP
2. A CERTAIN RATIO
5. NEW ORDER
6. COLUMN
8. SAMPLE

85. MUSICIANS-CUM-ARTISTS
ACROSS:
1. MCCARTNEY
3. PATTI SMITH
5. BOB DYLAN
7. MILES
9. RONNIE WOOD
10. SQUIRE
DOWN:
2. CHILDISH
4. TONY BENNETT
6. JONI MITCHELL
8. GOLDIE

86. SONGS & ARTISTS INSPIRED BY ART
ACROSS:
4. JAY-Z
5. PABLO PICASSO
9. DAVE BRUBECK
10. ANDY WARHOL
DOWN:
1. INTERIORS
2. SHOCKING BLUE
3. STATUS QUO
6. DIAMONDS
7. TEENAGE
8. PRIDDY

87. SONGS & ARTISTS INSPIRED BY BOOKS
ACROSS:
2. KATE BUSH
4. POLICE
6. VENUS IN FURS
9. RADIOHEAD
10. DAVID BOWIE
DOWN:
1. THE CURE
3. SEEGER
5. CREAM
7. NIRVANA
8. WHIP IT

88. INFLUENTIAL RADIO D.J.s
ACROSS:
5. STONE
8. RODNEY
9. MIKEY
10. WOLFMAN JACK
DOWN:
1. WESTWOOD
2. EVERETT
3. JOHN PEEL
4. ALAN FREED
6. NIGHTINGALE
7. MARTIN BLOCK

89. GROUNDBREAKING VIDEOS
ACROSS:
1. DIRE STRAITS
6. SLEDGEHAMMER
8. SABOTAGE
9. WHITE STRIPES
DOWN:
2. AGAIN
3. TAKE ON ME
4. APHEX TWIN
5. PRAISE YOU
7. ROCKIT
10. THRILLER

90. SHOCKING VIDEOS
ACROSS:
5. CLOSER
6. STAN
9. LIKE A PRAYER
10. BORN FREE
DOWN:
1. LEMON
2. MICHAEL
3. TELEPHONE
4. THE PRODIGY
7. DURAN DURAN
8. HATE ME NOW

91. GOOD MORNINGS
ACROSS:
2. SUNRISE
5. MORNING
6. KANYE WEST
8. CHICAGO
9. VELVET
10. LATEEF
DOWN:
1. JONI MITCHELL
3. ARCADE FIRE
4. MORNING DEW
7. SPECIALS

92. DRESS TO IMPRESS
ACROSS:
3. ADIDAS
5. JEANS ON
6. BOOTS
7. PRINCE
8. KING'S LEAD HAT
9. PENTANGLE
DOWN:
1. SUNGLASSES
2. FASHION
4. SAMMY DAVIS
6. BLUE SUEDE

93. SONGS ABOUT FOOD
ACROSS:
3. LOBSTER
5. BROWN SUGAR
6. MOTHER
7. MILKSHAKE
9. LEMON SONG
10. PEACHES
DOWN:
1. STRAWBERRY
2. DR. JOHN
4. PASS THE PEAS
8. SQUEEZE

94. SONGS ABOUT LOVE
ACROSS:
2. AYERS
4. FUNNEL
8. NED DOHENEY
9. LULU
10. GENTRYS
DOWN:
1. TALKING HEADS
3. RIPPERTON
5. BEYONCÉ
6. QUEEN
7. JUSTIFY

95. HEARTBREAK SONGS
ACROSS:
2. WALK ON BY
3. JOE JACKSON
7. THE STREETS
10. JOY DIVISION
DOWN:
1. SOFT CELL
4. SURVIVE
5. RIVER
6. IT'S TOO LATE
8. RUFFIN
9. PHOENIX

96. CHRISTMAS SONGS
ACROSS:
2. NEW YORK
4. WONDERFUL
6. CRYSTALS
8. WHITE CHRISTMAS
9. JINGLE BELL
DOWN:
1. BRENDA LEE
3. DRUMMER
5. SANTA CLAUS
7. SLADE
8. WIZZARD

97. INSULTING SONGS

ACROSS:
2. CARLY SIMON
6. SEX PISTOLS
7. HIT 'EM UP
8. CAMBODIA
9. VACATION
10. CEE LO GREEN

DOWN:
1. STONE ROSES
3. IDIOT WIND
4. SLEEP
5. BILLY BRAGG

98. COVER VERSIONS

ACROSS:
3. TENDERNESS
6. SURFIN' USA
7. TIME
8. MOLLY'S LIPS
10. HURDY GURDY

DOWN:
1. LEMONHEADS
2. GET BACK
4. SPECIALS
5. WATCHTOWER
9. HURT

99. UNEXPECTED SURPRISES

ACROSS:
2. HOT CHOCOLATE
3. BEE GEES
5. BILL WYMAN
7. CLIFF RICHARD
9. MIRROR
10. GYPSY

DOWN:
1. ATTENTION
4. LAMPLIGHTER
6. THE OSMONDS
8. LUST

100. SONGS ABOUT YOUTH

ACROSS:
5. SONIC YOUTH
6. TEENAGE HEAD
9. THIRTEEN
10. NIRVANA

DOWN:
1. SCHOOL'S OUT
2. MY GENERATION
3. LOBOTOMY
4. UNDERTONES
7. ALRIGHT
8. TEENAGER

101. SONGS ABOUT ANIMALS

ACROSS:
5. AMERICA
7. ALBATROSS
9. CURE

DOWN:
1. PRINCE
2. THIN LIZZY
3. BLACK EYED DOG
4. WILD HORSES
5. ATOMIC
6. I AM THE WALRUS
8. MONKEY

102. DISNEY FAMILY FAVORITES

ACROSS:
3. FRIEND
4. PARADE
7. NECESSITIES
8. HAKUNA MATATA
10. UNDER THE SEA

DOWN:
1. I WANNA BE LIKE YOU
2. MARY POPPINS
5. MUPPET
6. CAT
9. TRAMP

103. MOVIE SOUNDTRACKS

ACROSS:
3. SPINAL
4. SUPER FLY
7. SATURDAY
8. THE BEATLES
9. PURPLE RAIN

DOWN:
1. PUTNEY
2. BLADE RUNNER
3. STRAIGHT
5. UGLY
6. HEAD

104. HALLOWEEN

ACROSS:
1. GOO GOO MUCK
5. DONOVAN
6. THE RATTLES
7. VAMPIRES
9. JAY HAWKINS

DOWN:
1. GHOST TOWN
2. OCTOBER
3. HUMAN FLY
4. MONSTER MASH
8. REDBONE

105. SPACE/SCIENCE FICTION

ACROSS:
3. RAMASES
5. REINCARNATION
6. I ROBOT
8. SPACE ODDITY
10. PLACE

DOWN:
1. SPIRITUALIZED
2. GALAXY
4. PINK FLOYD
7. ROCKET MAN
9. ODYSSEY

106. SONGS ABOUT SPORTS

ACROSS:
3. JORGE BEN
6. SURVIVOR
8. SERENA
10. THE RACE

DOWN:
1. TOUR DE FRANCE
2. NEW ORDER
4. BELFAST BOY
5. INSTANT FUNK
7. ROY HARPER
9. DREADLOCK

107. SONGS ABOUT TIME

ACROSS:
3. ORBITAL
5. TIME IS ON MY SIDE
7. MALLO CUP
9. BEASTIE BOYS

DOWN:
1. ZOMBIES
2. DOLLY PARTON
4. DEF CON ONE
6. BEAT THE CLOCK
8. SEVENTEEN
9. BILL HALEY

108. SONGS ABOUT DEATH

ACROSS:
3. FLAMING LIPS
4. REAPER
6. BOB DYLAN
7. MONTY PYTHON
8. BERT JANSCH
9. SHANGRI LAS

DOWN:
1. BILLIE JOE
2. WILD ROSES
5. ELLIOT SMITH
7. MY WAY

WORD SEARCH SOLUTIONS

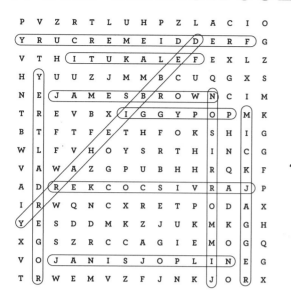

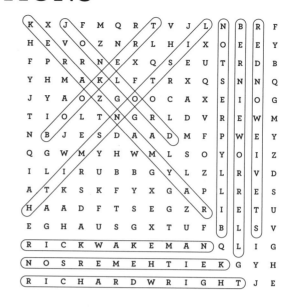

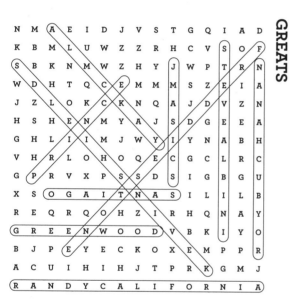

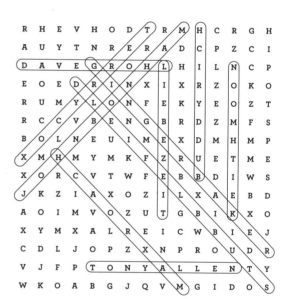

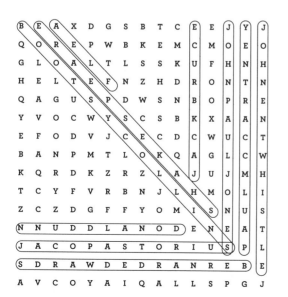

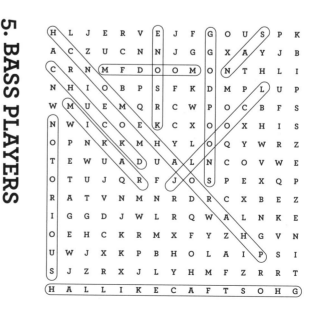

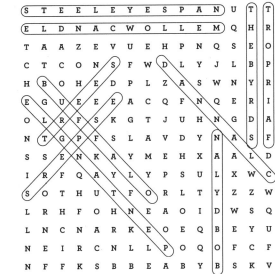

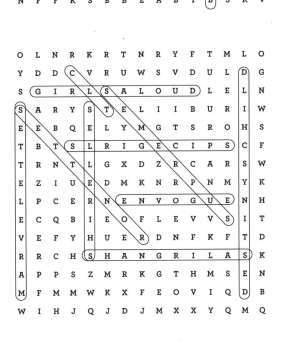

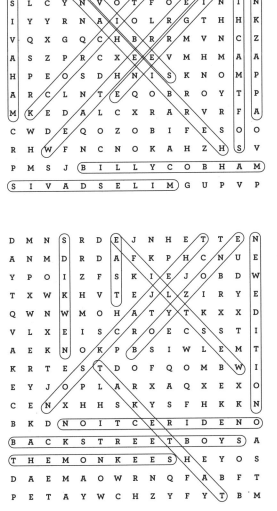

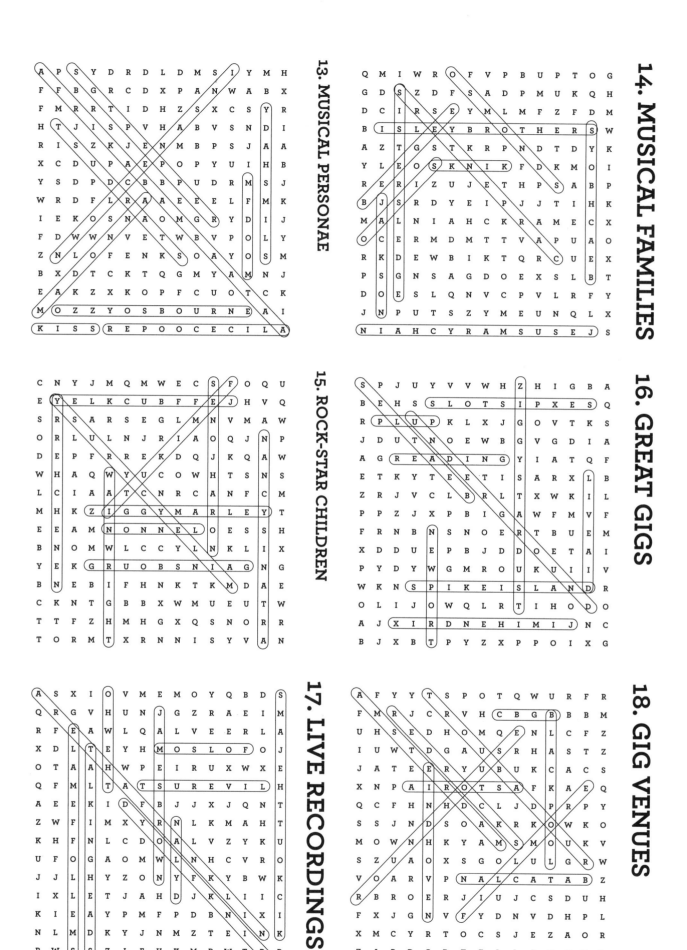

13. MUSICAL PERSONAE

14. MUSICAL FAMILIES

15. ROCK-STAR CHILDREN

16. GREAT GIGS

17. LIVE RECORDINGS

18. GIG VENUES

19. SONGS ABOUT SMOKING

20. DRINKING SONGS

21. BLUE ROOTS

22. BLUES AND BEYOND

23. TRIPPY TROUBADOURS

24. EASY LISTENING

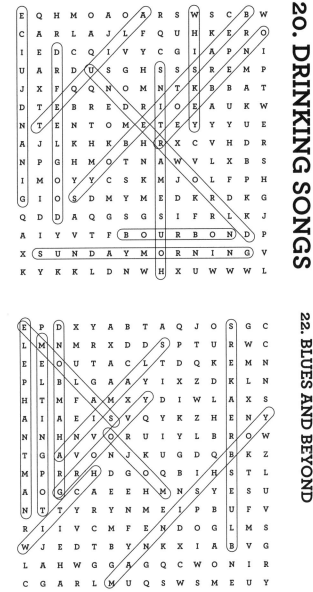

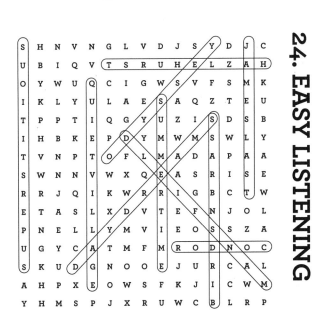

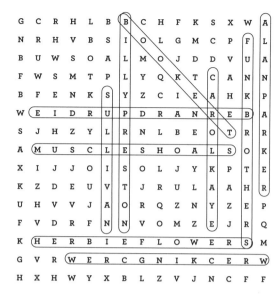

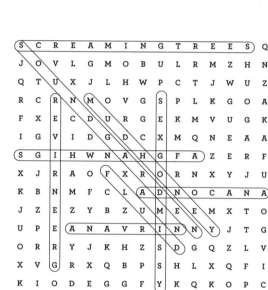

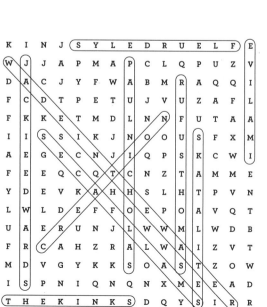

```
K M J Z I V T N F G L P K F U
X D A V I D B O W I E J M F O
X S P S N L Y I H Y C O A C O
L N A L P G H T U D C W D F S
L G N Y X A A C R L P F P W T
E R S P A N D A U B A L L E T
C D W J B O X E N T O Y E F P
T I A I L Q K V S C H O H K U
F E S V I U P O J X W J S V K
O C Z U D D N L M U D B S W S
S D N I M E L P M I S Y R X C
V Q E P S Y J R O R B K Q K O
N L C I F F X C X A S Q Z D
W X W J Z H X O V A R T L U H
S N A R U D N A R U D R D G Z
```

```
I X V A E N X E B S U N C V M
C F M C S W G C T F W K H P I
V V V I X D L P A E T E F A S G
H A P T J Q M B K U Z R L P E K T
V P O H P K T U K B E E T T B T O
F O U Q K A B P N S A E E A O R
I U R G O C D W I W O O T H B U
I T H G X P N F A O L L R M W G
X R A T W V T T B G V K E U H S
D A I O H S I O G B U S W S F N
Y I O S R A E Y Y L R A E P V
U L R I C H S C H N A U S S R
S R M E S A W E G I Q G O V Y
B U S W Y Y Y L W V W S E H M
```

```
N R U T E R T H G I L S D X G
Y C T D G M S I E X B E H Y B
D A E H O I D A R F I L J S U
R U K W S C T N B W Y P U Q J
S K Q A Z L M G A L A O T R J
B S O T R M E K K Y W E Z T U
T I A U P R I P M H E P P E I
J V E R P N S X O W C N I A I
R V E A G W D F S W H O R D L
I Y Y U J R G R J H I M V A E
R E P P F O E G H M N M I F B
O M K F S T Q P Y C O O A F P
Q H K B T O I H U H G C C A X
T J C I Q H J R P S K X L N M
E D B Z P J P O F N O Z J K M
```

```
G L O B A L N B N L C I K L V
Y A C E M F G I O C O T Y D D
U M H F L F W B I S N C C C E
F B V L P T R N S O T C U U J
Z C U K X O E Y E A E Q B L
I H O V E E M Y T M C W S U A I
Z Z O H H A I N Y P J A G X B L
S P T T S N Q T F A P K P B
A R I F T S Q G K R Z H S X X
K C P Y V I D N O L Q L A Y W
O O M F M D A J Z P Q J F I A
V I X C R I K P H Y O K Q N T
V Z T X N L J R E W C O O U E
M B R T F O T L E S S E W E I
P J Q X A S W K C M U O B G O
```

```
S S K I W Y O N W A W N L C U
E T M P J C I H A D J O O V S
D I U X E A Q S R N M K L M W
R A I D H C L F E N E Q O M J Z
D W P G I L L D H I R D O R G
G J R J A O R A O C E S U H A
W E B B C H M T U A D F M M S
B M S H Y S R S H A H V M N D F
Z P R R W V G E X R E Q P H
M I N I S T R Y O F S O U N D
Z E G A R A G E S I D A R A P
K C F F O E Z K A W W F C K K
W I G A N C A S I N O X N M R
T F O L E H T K X C K Y O D F
X L M M U W I J N K Y L O I L
```

```
O O N S P S W L N D P N E L T
Y J C E H H Y O I U I V H I C O
G O N N E Y E V G G A H U O N
X R W O X M R L H W I D T N N
Z S T T S C R T T U E G Z E E C
X N C S I N C A F O B I Y L T
E Z Q G Z R E W E G N H O R I
C Q S N U H V B V D J J P I T O
J L W I H A C F E Y T C O C I N
B D S L A M T E R G F C A H
Z E O L Z P H A H R T K I N
R W G O D Q J O X R U O T E Y
P N V R D A W Y K O P S E V J
C D C A D M Y S X L M V Z G X
J I H V C I S Q B B B Y A J P I
```

37. FUNK FLOOR-FILLERS

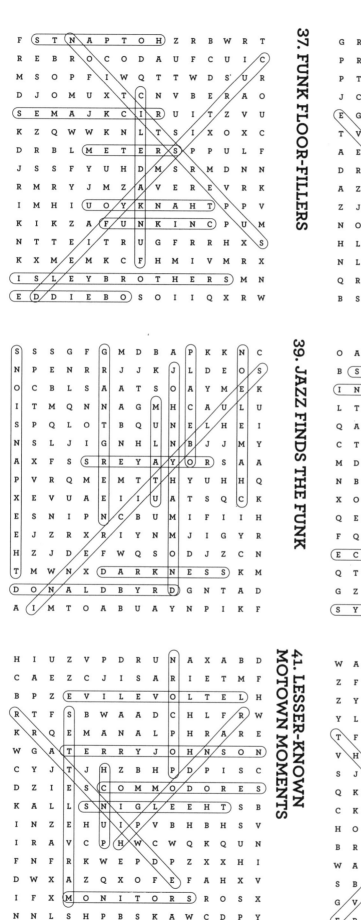

```
F S T N A P T O H Z R B W R T
R E B R O C O D A U F C U I C
M S O P F I W Q T T W D S U R
D J O M U X T C N V B E R A O
S E M A J K C I R U I T Z V U
K Z Q W K N L T S I X O X C
D R B L M E T E R S P P U L F
J S S F Y U H D M S R M D N N
R M R Y J M Z A V E R E V R K
I M H I U O Y K N A H T P P V
K I K Z A F U N K I N C P U M
N T T E I T R U G F R R H X S
K X M E M K C F H M I V M R X
I S L E Y B R O T H E R S M N
E D D I E B O S O I I Q X R W
```

38. DISCO DANCE-FLOOR BOMBS

```
G R S T U D A Y D A N C E R J
P R E B R C X S I H W N R G M
P T P R G S I P N W A L W G Z
J C K Q U S Z H O L L O W A Y
E G E Z A T M O S F E A R R W
T V V G G N A S A L S O U L C
A E O C H I C N U B R T F Q L
D R S L A O H E R A W Q J U H
A Z B U L J I R L E J S B Q I
Z J U A Y E N Q B Q P I D L Z
N O I P H S E D A K K U Q O O
H L U F I O S F B R F V S X R
N L J I L O X M I S D X X W
Q R J C I L C G U X S V L V W
B S C D K X Y H N O I A N I Z
```

39. JAZZ FINDS THE FUNK

```
S S S G F G M D B A P K K N C
N P E N R R J J K J L D E O S
O C B L S A A T S O H C M E K
I T M Q N N A G M U N E L U L
S P Q L O T B Q N H E L H E I
N S L J I G N H L N B J J M A
A X F S S R E Y A Y O R S A A
P V R Q M E M T T H Y U H B Q
X E V U A E I I U A T S Q C K
E S N I P N C B U M I F I I H
E J Z R X R I Y N M J I G Y R
H Z J D E F W Q S O D J Z C N
T M W N X D A R K N E S S K M
D O N A L D B Y R D G N T A D
A I M T O A B U A Y N P I K F
```

40. THE PHILLY SOUND

```
O A N T S O L I E V O L E H T
B S R E B B A T S K C A B S G
I N S T A N T F U N K U E N Z
L T G X Y S F F P Z V N F B L
Q A Y E J S T H O Y C S E S N
C T H S X H I I E D Z Y D W W
M D Q A V V M J S O M R H C K
N B J N K T U F J L B I X M B
X O H A D E N U F O T A K C T
Q E W T C S Y J Q E C P R X D
F Q K N E K D B H W V V V T O
E C I O H C S E L P O E P X
Q T L M S F A O V F P M U W T
G Z I A M D W D N C C Z N A I
S Y A J O E H T U S U H Z H Y
```

41. LESSER-KNOWN MOTOWN MOMENTS

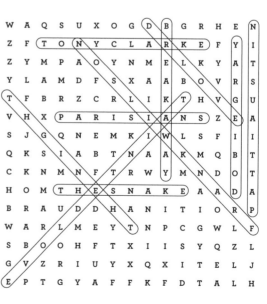

```
H I U Z V P D R U N A X A B D
C A E Z C J I S A R I E T M F
B P Z E V I L E V O L T E L H
R T F S B W A A D C H L F R H
K R Q E M A N A L P H R A R E
W G A T E R R Y J O H N S O N
C Y J T J H Z B H P D P I S C
D Z I E S C O M M O D O R E S
K A L L S S N I G L E E H T S B
I N Z E H U I P V B H B H S V
I R A V C P H W C W Q K Q U N
T N F E K W E P D Z Z X X H I
D W X A Z Q X O F E F A H X V
I F X M O N I T O R S R O S X
N N L S H P B B S K A W C D P Y
```

42. NORTHERN SOUL

```
W A Q S U X O G D B G R H E N
Z F T O N Y C L A R K E F Y I
Z Y M P A O Y N M E L K Y A T
Y L A M D F S X A A B O V S
T F B R Z C R L I K T H I U
V H X P A R I S I A N S Z E A
S J G Q N E M K I W L S F I T
Q K S I A B T N A A K M Q B O
C K N C M N F T R W Y M N D P
H O M T H E S N A K E A A
B R A U D D H A N I T I O R
W A R L M E Y T N P C G W L F
S B O O H F T X I I S Y Q Z L
G V Z R I U Y X Q X I T E L J
E P T G Y A F F K F D T A L H
```

43. ELECTRONIC PIONEERS

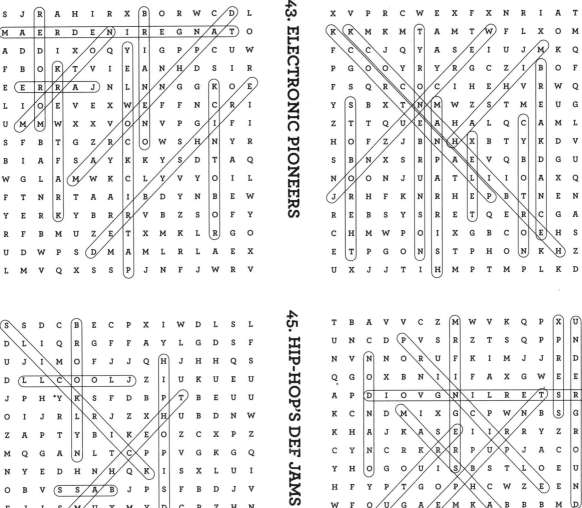

```
S J R A H I R X B O R W C D L
M A E R D E N I R E G N A T O
A D D I X O Q Y I G P P C W R
F B O K T V I E A N H D S I R
E E R R A J N L N N G G K O E
L I O E V E X W E F F N C R I
U M M W X X V O N V P G I F I
S F B T G Z R C O W S H N Y R
B I A F S A Y K K Y S D T A Q
W G L A M W K C L Y V Y O I L
F T N R T A A I B D Y N B E W
Y E R K Y B R R V B Z S O F Y
R F B M U Z E T X M K L R G O
U D W P S D M A M L R L A E X
L M V Q X S S P J N F J W R V
```

44. ELECTRO

```
X V P R C W E X F X N R I A T
K K M K M T A M T W F L X O M
F C C J Q Y A S E I U J M K Q
P G O O Y R Y R G C Z I B O F
F S Q R C O C I H E H V R W Q
Y S B X T N M W Z S T M E U G
Z T T Q U E A H A L Q C A M L
H O F Z J B N H X B T Y K D V
S B N X S R P A E V Q B G U
N O O N J U A T L I I O A X
J R H F K N H E P B T N E N
R E B S Y S R E T Q E R C G A
C H M W P O I X G B C O E H S
E T P G O N S T P H O N K H Z
U X J J T I H M P T M P L K D
```

45. HIP-HOP'S DEF JAMS

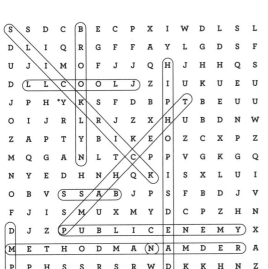

```
S S D C B E C P X I W D L S L
D L I Q R G F F A Y L G D S F
U J I M O F J J H J H H Q S
D L L C O O L J Z I U K U E U
J P H Y K S F D B P T B E U U
O I J R L R J Z X H U B D N W
Z A P T Y B I K E O Z C K P Z
M Q G A N L T C P P V G K G Q
N Y E D H N H Q K I S X L U I
O B V S S A B J P S F B D J V
F J I S M U X M Y D C P Z H N
D J Z P U B L I C E N E M Y X
M E T H O D M A N A M D E R A
P P H S S R S R W D K K H N Z
E J Z L Q U B L M R U E O V M
```

46. FOUNDATIONS OF GOOD HOUSE

```
T B A V V C Z M W V K Q P X U
U N C D P V S R Z T S Q P R N
N V N O R U F K I M J J R E D
Q G O X B N I I F A X G W E E
A P D I O V G N I L R E T S R
K C N D M I X G C P W N B S G
K H A J K A S E I I R R Y Z R
C Y N C R K R R P U P J A C O
Y H O G O U I S B S T L O E U
H F Y P T G O P H C W Z E E N
W F O U G A E M K A B B B M D
F T H K D E Q V J B L S Z M S
N P B K D K S S I W V L U I J
C R I S P I N J G L O V E R
L J H G M Z W O Y P J U K O Z
```

47. THE SYNTHPOP REVOLUTION

```
G S F G N S V X X H F Y Z G N
P W B Z E D O M E H C E P E D
B M G G V V Q S E G X I M H O
P E G N A M C N A L B W G X Q
V E I R E R E D R O W E N N F
Y F T S H M Y C H G E U J F J
I L F S C J P N C M T G S C J
U E L F H I E Y U P K A L G M
B W Y E S O M F L M P E M F N
Y I E Z C R P H I O A L C C H
U D F Z B T T B T M Q N A V T
C X C T Y K Y F R O Y M Z T C
X S E P S T R I S A S U P E W
U S J T X H U T J C B H E A C
```

48. TOWERING TECHNO

```
P R F E M U A S Z Q E C E M H
F O U S A O B S N E L M F K G
A N X B E Y T R R K P I I A I
Z T V W U N D E R W O R L D Y
T E C O M R X C T I E A F D O
E E T I A U M N U I P V E O T
C M N K G C L T A T Y P E S N
M Y N T O S G E L D F Z I R Y
Y N K U Z X I E K U L A N Y L
S Q S A F I Y R Y T C H I V L
T B X P S O U P Z S H S R Q D
I C E X I K S Q Y S E H T S N
C Y W H S B M L W H P S B Y
U H K G O L N G W Q A Z P B Y
Z G Y Z F J X W A G P V J N S
```

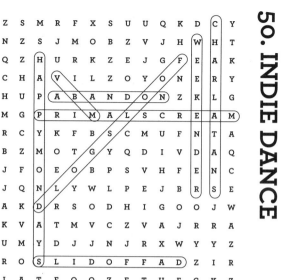

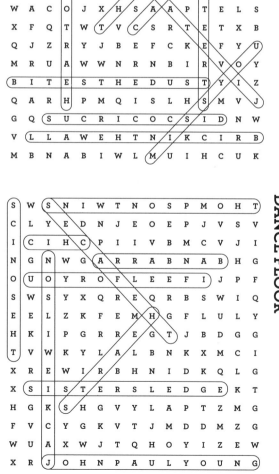

49. POST-PUNK

```
F U D U S R I E G O H E N X T
U O S K X N D Y D Z Y H I Z Q
N H C N A O W Z C F H S X J M
O D G A D E L E K Z I A Y P G
X X Z A B A H T A F G G Y H W
J M Q Z N K T D A X H H S M Q
H U A P L G E I E I P F I F Q
X H W G F B O I O R R S G K O
K L K C A N S F R N E E R B A
K Y X P V Z A T F H S V H W H
D E A T H D I S C O S C E G L
E L M A C A A N X G U S T S D
J L C Z X D U E E J R G J Y
G O Y J Q P W E D W E X U J S
```

50. INDIE DANCE

```
Y Z S M R F X S U U Q K D C Y
S N Z S J M O B Z V J H W H T
U Q Z H U R K Z E J G F E A K
D C H A V I L Z O Y O N E R Y
V H U P A B A N D O N Z K L G
R M G P R I M A L S C R E A M
U R C Y K F B S C M U F N T A
L B Z M O T G Y Q D I V D A Q
B J F O E O B P S V H F E B C
I J Q N L Y W L P E J B R S E
G A K D R S O D H I G O O J W
C K V A T M C Z V A J R R A
I U M Y D J J N Z R X W Y Y Z
T R O S L I D O F F A D Z I R
Y I A T F O O Z E T U F G K Z
```

51. ROCK COMES TO THE DISCO

```
T B C S H O L R G Y B R A O G
N E T S U X I K H X R E X H P
M L L A B N O N N A C Y H Q A
Z S N L S I I R E I W A R G A
M L U G U K D K N B L X U I
K L L F D N K I L S M P F K F
W A C O J X H S A A P T E L S
X F Q T W T V C S R T E T X B
Q J Z R Y J B E F C K E F Y U
M R U A W W N R N B I R V O Y
B I T E S T H E D U S T Y I Z
Q A R H P M Q I S L H S M V J
G Q S U C R I C O C S I D N W
V L L A W E H T N I K C I R B
M B N A B I W L M U I H C U K
```

52. SOUND SYSTEMS

```
N G N G B Y B B A T H M S Z V
A A T A A B M A B B O N D E T
Z S G N J X D N V S O O R N I
S E A V A O R W K X W S O C L
F H E I H R O Z N H U I U L O
I U L J S H G T B X U I U L
R N P Q H P Z E I V X V R F T
E E O E A C A M H X P R F Y
N J E X K T B O N T Y R E J
F L P I A I R H S A C T H K X
G R E A T S E B A S T I A N Y
K L H E Y X M Z I C E X R E O
J V T O T N Q V C F G K G J Q
J A R J N B Y C H M C V R G E
M F X F Y Q P J I P P A V O M
```

53. SONGS FOR A WEDDING DANCE FLOOR

```
S W S N I W T N O S P M O H T
C L Y E D N J E O E P J V S V
I C H C P I I V B M C V J I
N G N W G A R R A B N A B H G
O U O Y R O F L E E F I J P
S W S Y X Q R E S R N O S W I Q
E E L Z K F E M H G F L U L Y
H K I P G R R E G T J B D G D
T V W K Y L A L B N X M C I
X R E W I R B H N I D K Q L G
X S I S T E R S L E D G E K T
H G K S H G V Y L A B M Z M E
F V C Y G K Y T J M D M Z G
W U A X W J T Q H O Y I Z E W
X R J O H N P A U L Y O U N G
```

54. D.J.s

```
Y D F N B Z Z L F Q U O K G O
U E P O M W L Y K U O M I L P
D A V I D M A N C U S O D F R
V F F R Q E R G N C S I J U E
Y A J N A M R O N P A L K O T
A I D S J H Y F G N R I O E S
N Z W R T Q L L L N G N L E A
P E P G E I E E M A S K L M D
C Q D C Z T V A K R I K H N R
T G S V L I A X O S C I E N A
F R G P V Z N R P U N S C R G
I B Y E R F X Y N Y A Z C Y
D C C M U P R K F N R C S F G
Q B J H F Y S U F N S D
W M D X H D P G U R P P K L S
```

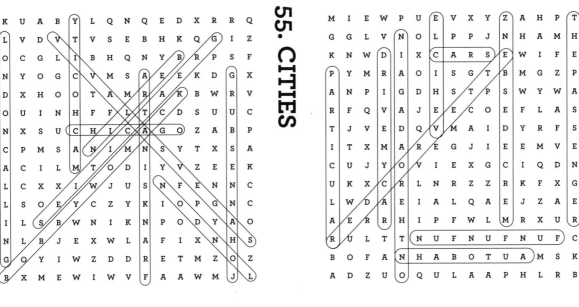

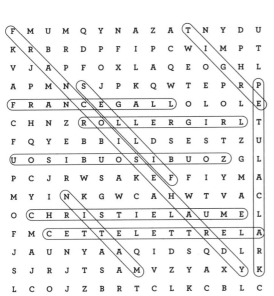

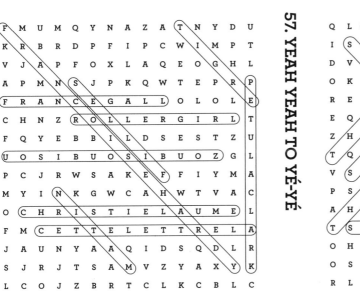

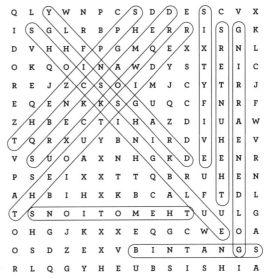

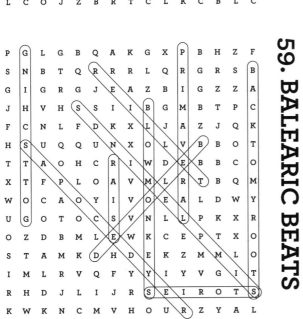

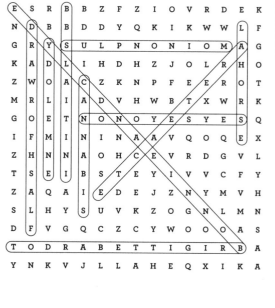

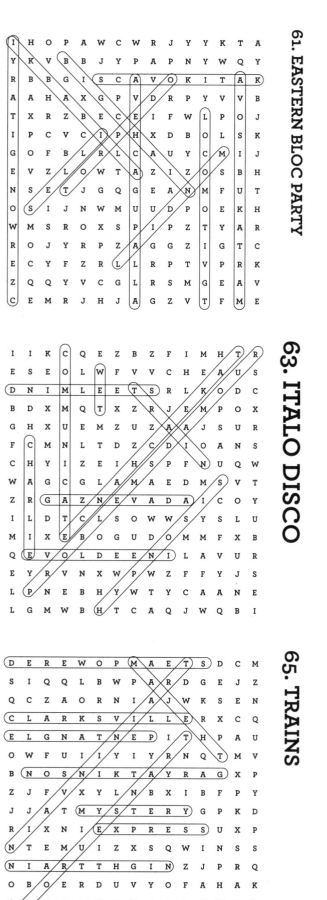

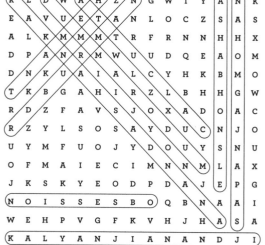

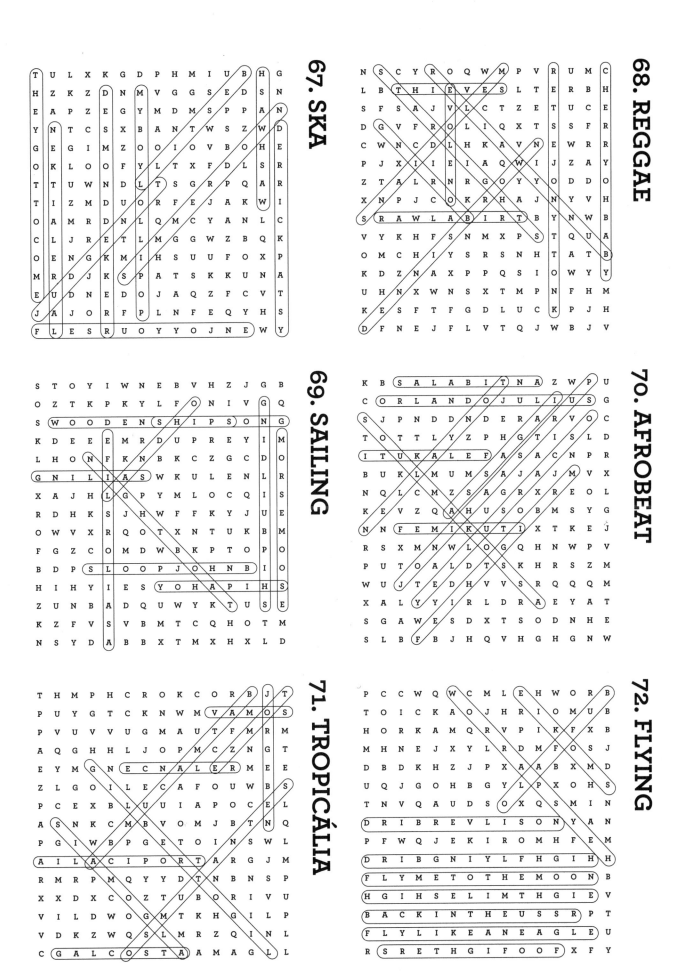

```
A N X L I M B K W T B N X J L
N I L E R O D G E R S A P A E
J T V L Q P I W I T Z S P E E
J R K M J M T A V X C G J J G
F A D Q U I N C Y J O N E S S
G M X A Z W O Q O C K J O O C
C E M J I I C I B H X Y Z H A
X G B L K B S Y S P P W C B T
Y R S R E I M E R P J D Z C T
X O E L I D V D O M Z S H F H
N E S W H A Y Q S K U K D L P
E G A B O T N L M U Q B X B E
A U G M F J O E M E E K E M R
Y B D E Q M T L N O P K P O R
P H I L S P E C T O R W R D Y
```

```
D B S S L O T S I P X E S R
E G Y W N J W X T N L L T I N
C A O X M C J H W O E Z W C S
N X B G Z Q E B N I A Q H J N
I R C E Z O C I N O T E E M O
R I T A K Q A A S U P S A S L
E R S C W M U G I R L S Q S A
P H A L E H B E V T N P D P M
X N E M P T E C I S A P I J W
E N B X O V P P S E Q E Y B
P S U M I N Z Q Y D E J E O D
F E J Z W S E T O Z M C E F T
X M N L Y T Q S J N E C Y I C
A M T M W F S E U E J K O S Q
```

```
U U N U P W M W M V J L W E D
W R O Q X N I C F T T B A U P
D O S N T P O M D C K M J Q F
U Y I Y F R E E W H E E L I N
A E R E H W O N S I S I H T D
P N R T H E B E N D S W U U X
Z E O N S H O C S S L J C O C
G Y M E N E C I L B U P A B T
S Y N V I R P E F O B A T S
R K A E M J A A I O F R Q L N
E T V R K B Y F T E C A E U D
U X L M U I A F N A O N P A U
J I M I H E N D R I X O M P D
K D T N Y F J G Q K I D X U
L L X D Q M O R H A L D N X
```

```
N P D L F L B D N X O I W C Z
F J A W S Q H M K L K U V K L
Z Y F P A R Q W F G P R Q L A
A D M U S I O R L E W S U L R
M Q N U E I W O B D I V A D H
S X C B H D I R A S R N D C P
S G N I H T Y T T E R P R C Y
O G T Y R O S O L C K U O G R
N X V P U W M X L A I P P F R
C O C M E M M L Y F G X H R Q
X P S W Y P A V H L L O H E D
P D G L G R W P C A L U N N G
J U N E E R G E G A L L I V N
M I Q H I N H K R M H J A P K
Q I T M J K A Z F S N A Q I I
```

```
Q U P O U X J P L V J X M B A
O T S H Z B Z S R N X H L Q C
S E N E V S M B C Y P K N M V
T P C I H D E H R P F P H E V
D E K Z R C X R H O F J C L R
D Z T O R N A D O S Z I U T O
Y B C E L B W P M D W P Z I B
R Y P C N R K Z A V O E T N I
A B M H W E B F B M S M O G M
Z P O O E M Z Y M Y H D M P R
G J G E D C U I Q V E F C O E
N G W S A N F V R A S A M T C
Q R A L L M L U C U S C C Y E
S C I M H T Y R U E L B M U R
D H I Y U W V C F U T D H U T
```

```
D K N M D Q V A D S G W Q V W
E A E R N Y I P A Q I O M N B
Z S P J R P N P T N M R S O P
A D A T D Y S X G F M K Y N I
M F U G D T T S E I E I E I R
A H L E M P A E Q B S N C R R
H U M L J M N H Z T O G I I E
I V C A D H T S S J M C S L W
E V C C T W K H N O E L T H U
B M A N N V A U N Q T A F I R
Y F R I S M R H K K R S I R I
A U T D A Y M B W U E H E O E
M L N Z U T A R E A T H E O
C H E C K M Y M A C H I N E L
A E Y M O O Z Z U V P Y D G V
```

80. COUPLES

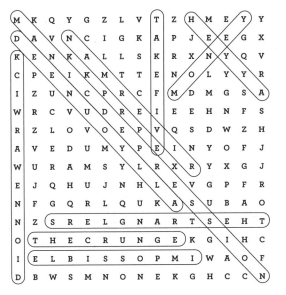

```
I I T I Y D K A G O X S A L J
T L N O N K J X O Q E I B I U
L Q I O H J W I P S M R B J N
B V M H V C L V V W J R A T E
A M I B P G Q M H B I C E L C
R H F V H D J R V K K B U G A
X V U O Y H N T E A T I N P R
B E Y O N C E A N D J A Y Z T
S Y O Z T Y N D E Z M X T Y E
B A K A J D M O Y I F W R R
G N O M T E R Q F Q N U A S
P D O I G G U W L M I N M C Y
S O N N Y A N D C H E R O C T
S A O J N D O X U X X A L R U
G D Z N S K C I N E I V E T S
```

79. ODD TIME SIGNATURES

```
M K Q Y G Z L V T Z H M E Y Y
D A V N C I G K A P J E E G X
K E N K A L L S K R X N Y Q V
C P E I K M T T E N O L Y Y R
I Z U N C P R C F M D M G S A
W R C V U D R E I E E H N F S
R Z L O V O E P V Q S D W Z H
A V E D U M Y P E I N Y O F J
W U R A M S Y L R X R Y X G J
E J Q H U J N H L E V G P F R
N F G Q R L Q U K A S U B A O
N Z S R E L G N A R T S E H T
O T H E C R U N G E K G H I C
I E L B I S S O P M I W A O F
D B W S M N O N E K G H C C N
```

82. REVOLUTIONARIES

```
H K C C T S U W U A V V X R Y
N S E S A B J O F S U S E N S
D J A W O O D Y G U T H R I E
T U H L B F N O U P F F T X L
G I L S C O T T H E R O N L
C T E W S E B D Z R I K Y T A
A U J L J Z H M U F D S P W E
A K D W N K T T A U G N Q C B
J A O I E Z Z R G R P E P F E
K L T S V L N T W R L M P Y H
C E S C I T O N P Y H E E H T
C F D M P G B Y L V C Y J M
M I F A W G Q O T I W A O Y O
F Y R G B F L H A F N P Y H P
P N H Q I L M P T I Q S T J Y
```

81. TROUBLED SOULS

```
U P Z Z U U T X U R W O J J O
Q Z E V V T T T G E H J D Z N
B K S C V O E X K L I R F Q K
R C U P P M R A W L T J L C W
I F O J X Q R U A I N L G R B
A P H G W D A E J O E M E E K
N V E V K I B Y K T Y H M W M
W G N C B A D A E S H H H V H
I Z I C Y H Y G T M O S Y D U
L N W Q I L S N Z I U H T F G
S J Y I B I X I Q T S M E J G
O W M Z G W K V Y H T Z I L M
N I A B O C T R U K O H X M J
S I T R U C N A I T N S J M U
E M K T N N N M L V B M J O Q
```

84. FACTORY RECORDS' RELEASES

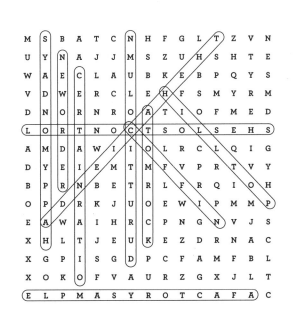

```
M S B A T C N H F G L T Z V N
U Y N A J J M S Z U H S H T E
W A E C L A U B K E B P Q Y S
V D W E R C L E H F S M Y R M
D N O R N R O A T I O F M E D
L O R T N O C T S O L S E H S
A M D A W I I O L R C L Q I G
D Y E I E M T M F V P R T V Y
B P R N B E T R L F R Q I O H
O P D R K J U O E W I P M M P
E A W A I H R C P N G N V J S
X H L T J E U K E Z D R N A C
X G P I S G D P C F A M F B L
X O K O F V A U R Z G X J L T
E L P M A S Y R O T C A F A C
```

83. MUSICIANS-TURNED-FILM STARS

```
L M P E L N K A V M C W D M P
A K A R T A N I S K N A R F P
M V B R O F X F Z B V Y O V I
G D E G K U N P F I N H B B H
L H F H O W X M D D T W F N C
C F Y T Z A A B R I D R W V M
D E L X X D O H M E U Y A O P
L R W B O W H S L F L G S J G
J C O N I A L V Q B E D A T N
D C N E E L I W E F E Z V M U
N A K R I S T O F F E R S O N
V L I W L F Y L B E Q G G B N
J E N N I F E R H U D S O N F
R U A H N G M H M B C A W I Y
G F F J K R R P X A H Z J V D
```

85. MUSICIANS-CUM-ARTISTS

```
D X T L B G D Z Q E R F H J U
A B J J F O O L C W Q J S H U
Z I O A O N O L S B F C I R J
W T N A N O D W Y D U M B D E R
H Z I Y N E V D I X U L S F
T X M B E W I W A E G I Q X
I V I E F O N V O R P V H I X
M S T M Y E N B H V A I C Y H
S I C T W T O Z N D K H Y O D
I G H E U R R H S L F W L N R
T Y E Q D Y Z E Q Y U A L M S
T S L Y O Q L G U L V U I Y R
A A L O P I T H I X B T B E Y
P A U L M C C A R T N E Y F W
N G X T T E N N E B Y N O T O
```

86. SONGS AND ARTISTS INSPIRED BY ART

```
M R F L C G V Z B O G P G M I
F L O H R A W Y D N A R A A Y
O L D A V E B R U B E C K T U
J V K I K V M F L M D U U C T
A I N T E R I O R S A X O H Z
Y Z N A N C Y P R I D D Y W S
F S F L C D J H M O A U K I J
M F V A X M L I N M R J H C V
H N S T Q W N C V A X A G K A
F S D Y Y W J V O I F L J M A
O G S M R T B K L D W W T E N
D R C L A P U W Z G W N I N
Z Y G K O M V C U W C L K E F
T E E N A G E F A N C L U B K
```

87. SONGS AND ARTISTS INSPIRED BY BOOKS

```
P E T E S E E G E R W W P X D
M Z J Q A C I R B F T W K O D
O M G S A L W W U Q E Q S G H
H B U C N I O S L C A V G H E
B D A E G M B S E Y G E P I M U
R L J N T V D C S L U H O X P
X I G T A R I L S T D T T Y Q
L C U L X N V K E Y M G L V M
H I I E S L A A S R I E U X B
E T K S Z T D C H X T W G O Y
C O G S E C I L O P E H T D S
K T B B I Y N M G B W I V Z G
S R U F N I S U N E V P Z C S
E S O Z Q V F M H U F I Q K S
H C M Q H W N S A F O T K P B
```

88. INFLUENTIAL RADIO D.J.s

```
U F Y T S L C P O H N W S X Z
Y U K K E G O Q G G T D W I E
W B C J T I M W E S T W O O D
S X O A J O H N P E E L A A E
T U L N R Q S K D U R P F I E
O N U N O B B E N I Q V V A K D
N Y I B B R Q M Y P E P N Q Y
E B G T W F Z T E T M Y O J X E
I Q R N J D S O W H N Y A W K
E L A G N I T H G I N F C R O M
D L M V B W F H N I E T K O Z
A J B D L V Z X C E K O Z Z S
A F C D N W B R S B M I V O W
U J Z O B U Z B Z J U J S N D
```

89. GROUNDBREAKING VIDEOS

```
D N F I U Y W K J Q D J V B K
N I U M W U O A C S I P D X F
V A R C X Y F Q A E X N K U H
E G E E F U A B T P H T T I J
I A M O S E O Z B I S H H S H
J S M Y I T M Y P R F T R H S
Y E A B A S R N E T T R I S V
N O H G K P A O S R A L S V
C G E K P H T Y I E I A L R Y
C T G N Z O T H D T K A E F D
L I D K S C U O I I S A R B D
I D E B T O L K D H V H T P B
W R L R E K C I L W O D N I W
M E S R A O J U S B E J L U S
W H I B R T L F X Z U T Q D T
```

90. SHOCKING VIDEOS

```
A F V N N F F F Y B M T G L Q
R L B N L D D A C L T W L H X
L E E E R F N R O B E E X H Q
N A P R E J T Y G S M G S Y C
J H M B Y L J Y P O S I U B A
J C W Q A K W G N Z B R W D W
M I X A R E O I O T D L K U G
N M C Z Y A N D T S G S M O N
P E C I A C E O U Y M O S C U
D G N L E V M P N A N A V X F
W R A S K A E P L F K E K
Q O T K I W T E H S E I Q W I
R E S O L C A H C A N L M C X
O G E N L L H T O E C M E R Y
B I J M L O K Z E E W R C T M
```

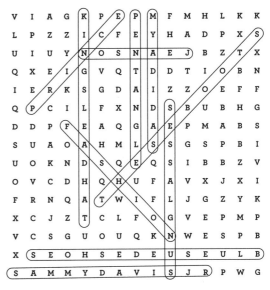

92. DRESS TO IMPRESS

91. GOOD MORNINGS

94. SONGS ABOUT LOVE

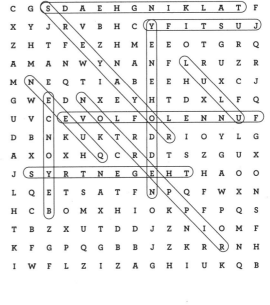

93. SONGS ABOUT FOOD

96. CHRISTMAS SONGS

95. HEARTBREAK SONGS

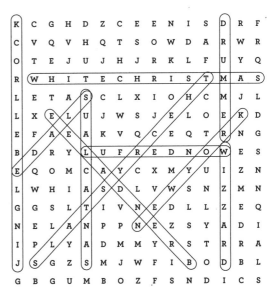

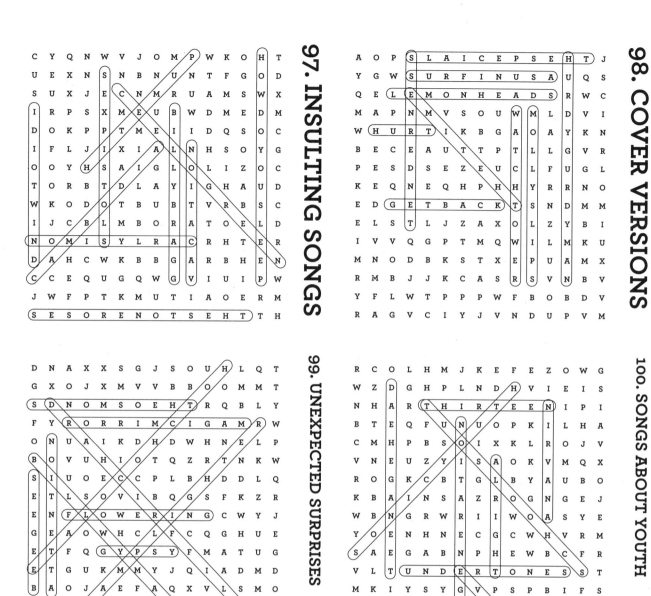